Register Now for Online Access to Your Book!

Your print purchase of *Nursing Deans on Leading* **includes online access to the contents of your book**—increasing accessibility, portability, and searchability!

Access today at:

http://connect.springerpub.com/content/book/978-0-8261-3484-4
or scan the QR code at the right with your smartphone
and enter the access code below.

0U5FFBU3

Scan here for quick access.

If you are experiencing problems accessing the digital component of this product, please contact our customer service department at cs@springerpub.com

The online access with your print purchase is available at the publisher's discretion and may be removed at any time without notice.

Publisher's Note: New and used products purchased from third-party sellers are not guaranteed for quality, authenticity, or access to any included digital components.

SPRINGER PUBLISHING COMPANY

View all our products at springerpub.com

Joanne P. Robinson, PhD, RN, CNE, FAAN, is a professor and associate dean for Research and Innovation at Thomas Jefferson University's College of Nursing in Philadelphia, Pennsylvania. From 2011 to 2017, she served as founding dean of the School of Nursing—Camden at Rutgers, The State University of New Jersey. There she led the growth and development of a small nursing department into a separate school with accomplished faculty and staff, pillar graduate and undergraduate programs, robust enrollment and revenue, transformative "learning abroad" courses, a scholar exchange program, a new Nursing and Science Building, and a visionary strategic plan. During her deanship, Dr. Robinson chaired New Jersey's Organization of Colleges of Nursing (2014–2016) and provided formal and informal mentorship to many new and aspiring academic nursing leaders.

As a scholar and educator, Dr. Robinson is known for her contributions to gerontological and urologic nursing. Her research on lower urinary tract symptoms in older adults has been supported by the National Institute of Nursing Research and recognized with six awards. Dr. Robinson is the (co)author of over 25 peer-reviewed publications, five book chapters, and two books. She is an experienced educator and holds certification in Nursing Education from the National League for Nursing. She currently chairs the Nursing Education Subcommittee of the International Continence Society and has been a fellow of the American Academy of Nursing since 2011.

Dr. Robinson received a BS in nursing from William Paterson University; MS in community health nursing from Rutgers, The State University of New Jersey, College of Nursing—Newark; MA in social gerontology; and PhD in nursing from the University of Pennsylvania.

Carole Kenner, PhD, RN, FAAN, FNAP, ANEF, is the Carol Kuser Loser Dean/Professor of the School of Nursing, Health, and Exercise Science at the College of New Jersey. Dr. Kenner received a BS in nursing from the University of Cincinnati and her MS and PhD in nursing from Indiana University. She specialized in neonatal/perinatal nursing for her master's and obtained a minor in higher education for her doctorate. She has authored more than 100 journal articles and 25 textbooks.

Her career is dedicated to nursing education and to the health of neonates and their families, as well as educational and professional development of healthcare practices in neonatology. Her dedication includes providing a healthcare standard for educating neonatal nurses nationally and internationally. Her passion led her to begin the journal *Newborn and Infant Nursing Reviews*, for which she served as an editor and then associate editor. She worked with the National

Coalition on Health Professions Education in Genetics (NCHPEG) and the American Nurses Association to develop genetic competencies. She helped develop the End-of-Life Nursing Education Consortium (ELNEC) Neonatal/Pediatric modules. She served as the co-chair of the Oklahoma Attorney General's Task Force on End-of-Life/Palliative care. She also helped development program recommendations for perinatal/neonatal palliative care as part of a family-centered/developmental care project sponsored by the National Perinatal Association. She serves on the Consensus Committee of Neonatal Intensive Care Design Standards, which sets recommendations for Neonatal Intensive Care Unit designs, and serves on the March of Dimes Nursing Advisory Committee. She is a fellow of the American Academy of Nursing (FAAN), a fellow in the National Academies of Practice, a fellow in the Academy of Nursing Education, past president of the National Association of Neonatal Nurses (NANN), and founding president of the Council of International Neonatal Nurses (COINN), the first international organization representing neonatal nursing in setting standards globally. She is the 2011 recipient of the Audrey Hepburn Award for Contributions to the Health and Welfare of Children internationally.

Jana L. Pressler, PhD, RN, is professor and assistant dean of the University of Nebraska Medical Center College of Nursing, Lincoln Division in Lincoln, Nebraska. Dr. Pressler received a BA in nursing from Bradley University, an MS and Pediatric Nurse Practitioner Certificate at the University of Iowa, a PhD in nursing from Case Western Reserve University, and a postdoctoral fellowship at the University of Rochester via the Robert Wood Johnson Foundation Clinical Scholars Program. She specialized in the nursing care of children for her master's and doctoral programs. She has worked in various nursing roles at children's hospitals located in seven states.

Dr. Pressler has been in higher education for over 30 years. She helped develop the neonatal nurse practitioner program at Vanderbilt University, the PhD programs at the Pennsylvania State University and the University of Oklahoma Health Science Center, and the DNP program at the University of Oklahoma Health Science Center. Her career is dedicated to neonatal nursing research and to the health of children and their families, with a focus on stabilization and resuscitation. She is presently working on research to test a dashboard for the crash cart to facilitate and support resuscitation.

NURSING DEANS ON LEADING

Lessons for Novice and Aspiring Deans and Directors

Joanne P. Robinson, PhD, RN, CNE, FAAN
Carole Kenner, PhD, RN, FAAN, FNAP, ANEF
Jana L. Pressler, PhD, RN

Copyright © 2020 Springer Publishing Company, LLC

All rights reserved.

No part of this publication may be reproduced, stored in a retrieval system, or transmitted in any form or by any means, electronic, mechanical, photocopying, recording, or otherwise, without the prior permission of Springer Publishing Company, LLC, or authorization through payment of the appropriate fees to the Copyright Clearance Center, Inc., 222 Rosewood Drive, Danvers, MA 01923, 978-750-8400, fax 978-646-8600, info@copyright.com or on the Web at www.copyright.com.

Springer Publishing Company, LLC
11 West 42nd Street
New York, NY 10036
www.springerpub.com
http://connect.springerpub.com

Acquisitions Editor: Joseph Morita
Compositor: Amnet Systems

ISBN: 978-0-8261-3472-1
ebook ISBN: 978-0-8261-3484-4
DOI: 10.1891/9780826134844

19 20 21 22 / 5 4 3 2 1

The author and the publisher of this Work have made every effort to use sources believed to be reliable to provide information that is accurate and compatible with the standards generally accepted at the time of publication. The author and publisher shall not be liable for any special, consequential, or exemplary damages resulting, in whole or in part, from the readers' use of, or reliance on, the information contained in this book. The publisher has no responsibility for the persistence or accuracy of URLs for external or third-party Internet websites referred to in this publication and does not guarantee that any content on such websites is, or will remain, accurate or appropriate.

Library of Congress Cataloging-in-Publication Data

Names: Robinson, Joanne P., author. | Kenner, Carole, author. | Pressler,
    Jana Lee, author.
Title: Nursing deans on leading : lessons for novice and aspiring deans and
    directors / Joanne P. Robinson, Carole Kenner, Jana L. Pressler,
    editors.
Description: New York : Springer Publishing Company, [2020] | Includes
    bibliographical references and index.
Identifiers: LCCN 2019028580 (print) | ISBN 9780826134721 (paperback) |
    ISBN 9780826134844 (ebook)
Subjects: MESH: Nurse Administrators | Leadership | Faculty,
    Nursing—organization & administration | Professional Competence
Classification: LCC RT89 (print) | LCC RT89 (ebook) | NLM WY 105 | DDC
    362.17/3068—dc23
LC record available at https://lccn.loc.gov/2019028580
LC ebook record available at https://lccn.loc.gov/2019028581

Contact us to receive discount rates on bulk purchases.
We can also customize our books to meet your needs.
For more information please contact: sales@springerpub.com

Joanne Robinson: https://orcid.org/0000-0003-1764-928X
Carole Kenner: https://orcid.org/0000-0002-1573-5240
Jana Pressler: https://orcid.org/0000-0001-8328-9441

Publisher's Note: New and used products purchased from third-party sellers are not guaranteed for quality, authenticity, or access to any included digital components.

Printed in the United States of America.

For Ron and Danny, who inspired, loved, and cared for me through the highs and lows of my "deaning" journey, and for Dr. Carol Germain, my "A+ deaning mentor," who always showed me the way.
—JR

For my many mentees who have taught me a lot about "deaning" through their questions and stories. To my faculty and administrators who shared the journey. Thank you, too, to my friend and colleague Marina Boykova who supported me in this writing.
—CK

To my mentors, Jean Johnson and Robert Herndon, and my colleagues, Donna McCarthy Beckett, Margaret Bull, Jo Ann Dalton, Susan Flagler, Lynda LaMontagne, Ruth McShane, Kathy Ross-Alaolmolki, and Sharon Wilkerson, from the Robert Wood Johnson Foundation Clinical Nurse Scholars at the University of Rochester School of Nursing.
—JP

Together we wish to thank Joe Morita and Hannah Hicks from Springer Publishing Company for their expert assistance in guiding this project from proposal to publication. A special thanks goes to our amazing contributors, whose wisdom, experience, generosity, and commitment to mentorship made this project possible. Finally, we thank our past, present, and future dean and director colleagues for stepping up to take nursing where it is today and will be tomorrow.

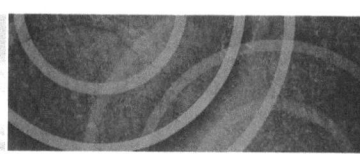

CONTENTS

Contributors   *xi*
Foreword   Terri E. Weaver, PhD, RN, FAAN, ATSF   *xiii*
Preface   *xv*

Section I Dimensions of the Nursing Dean/Director Role

1. Searching for a Dean/Director Position   3
   Carole Kenner and Jana L. Pressler

2. Stepping Into a Dean/Director Position   11
   Carole Kenner and Jana L. Pressler

3. Day-to-Day Deaning   23
   Jana L. Pressler and Carole Kenner

4. Deaning in a For-Profit Environment   33
   F. Patrick Robinson and Adele A. Webb

5. Interim Deaning   43
   Marie O'Toole

6. Stepping Up From Deaning/Directing   55
   Joanne P. Robinson

Section II General Responsibilities of Nursing Deans and Directors

7. Enrollment Management   73
   Linda D. Scott and Julie J. Zerwic

8. Student Success   83
   Jana L. Pressler and Carole Kenner

9. Recruitment and Retention of Qualified Faculty and Staff   91
   Carole Kenner and Jana L. Pressler

10. Academic Policies and Programs *Lynnette Leeseberg Stamler*	103
11. Fundraising: Mission Critical *Joanne P. Robinson*	113
12. Internal and External Stakeholder Engagement *Eileen M. Sullivan-Marx and Heather M. Young*	125
13. Perspectives on Financial Management for Deans of Nursing Programs: Culture, Policy, and Leadership *Gloria Ferraro Donnelly*	139
14. Strategic Thinking, Planning, and Doing *Karen J. Kelly Thomas*	159
15. Developing a Sustainable Nurse-Led Clinical Enterprise and Faculty Practice *Julie Cowan Novak*	177
16. Executive Leadership *Carole Kenner and Jana L. Pressler*	195

Section III Self-Care and Work–Life Integration for Nursing Deans and Directors

17. Challenges of Deaning and Directing in Nursing *Carole Kenner and Jana L. Pressler*	205
18. Finding the Joy and Satisfaction in Deaning and Directing *Theodora Sirota and Brenda Petersen*	211
19. Work–Life Integration and Self-Care Management *Janice Brewington*	225
Index	*239*

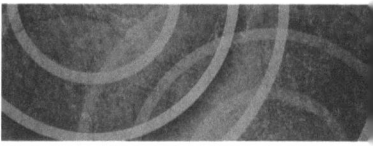

CONTRIBUTORS

Janice Brewington, PhD, RN, FAAN, Chief Program Officer and Director, National League for Nursing Center for Transformational Leadership, Washington, DC

Gloria Ferraro Donnelly, PhD, RN, FAAN, FCPP, Professor and Dean Emerita, College of Nursing and Health Professions, Drexel University, Philadelphia, Pennsylvania

Carole Kenner, PhD, RN, FAAN, FNAP, ANEF, Carol Kuser Loser Dean and Professor, School of Nursing, Health, and Exercise Science, The College of New Jersey Ewing, New Jersey

Julie Cowan Novak, DNSc, RN, MA, CPNP, FAANP, FAAN, Principal Investigator and Project Director, Hillman Innovations in Care, Neighborhood House Association Head Start; Professor Emerita, Purdue University, West Lafayette, Indiana; formerly, Nancy B. Willerson Distinguished Professor and Associate Dean, Practice and Engagement, UT Health, Houston, Texas

Marie O'Toole, EdD, RN, ANEF, FAAN, Senior Associate Dean and Professor, School of Nursing—Camden, Rutgers, The State University of New Jersey, Camden, New Jersey

Brenda Petersen, PhD, RN, APN-C, CPNP-PC, Associate Dean and Associate Professor, School of Nursing, University of Southern Maine, Portland, Maine

Jana L. Pressler, PhD, RN, Assistant Dean and Professor, College of Nursing—Lincoln Division, University of Nebraska Medical Center, Lincoln, Nebraska

F. Patrick Robinson, PhD, RN, ACRN, CNE, FAAN, Provost & Vice President for Academic Affairs, Arizona College, Chicago, IL

Joanne P. Robinson, PhD, RN, CNE, FAAN, Associate Dean for Research and Innovation; and Professor, College of Nursing, Thomas Jefferson University, Philadelphia, Pennsylvania

Linda D. Scott, PhD, RN, NEA-BC, FAAN, Dean and Professor, School of Nursing, University of Wisconsin–Madison, Madison, Wisconsin

Theodora Sirota, PhD, APRN, CNL, PMHCNS-BC, Professor, Department of Nursing, School of Interdisciplinary Health and Science, University of Saint Joseph, West Hartford, Connecticut; formerly, Director, Department of Nursing, Caldwell University, Caldwell, New Jersey

Lynnette Leeseberg Stamler, PhD, DLitt, RN, FAAN, Associate Dean for Academic Programs and Professor, College of Nursing, University of Nebraska Medical Center, Omaha, Nebraska

Eileen M. Sullivan-Marx, PhD, RN, FAAN, Dean and Erline Perkins McGriff Professor, Rory Meyers College of Nursing, New York University, New York, New York

Karen J. Kelly Thomas, PhD, RN, FAAN, CEO, Kelly Thomas Associates, Little Egg Harbor Township, New Jersey

Adele A. Webb, PhD, RN, FNAP, FAAN, Senior Academic Director of Workforce Development, Capella University, Wadsworth, Ohio

Heather M. Young, PhD, RN, FAAN, Professor & Founding Dean Emerita, Betty Irene Moore School of Nursing, University of California Davis, Sacramento, CA

Julie J. Zerwic, PhD, RN, FAHA, FAAN, Kelting Dean and Professor, College of Nursing, University of Iowa, Iowa City, Iowa

FOREWORD

Educational institutions require diversity of leadership to meet the challenges facing them today. Providing such leadership, current and future deans of nursing need a font of knowledge that is broad, yet essential to lead effectively. Indeed, on any given day, a dean handles a wide assortment of responsibilities ranging from addressing faculty and student issues, to finance and budget, human resources, facilities management, curriculum development, enrollment management, teaching excellence, interprofessional relationships, practice management, philanthropy, and legal and global affairs, in addition to knowing how and when to take risks. Indeed, the phrase "duties as assigned" is the everyday experience of a dean. Nevertheless, there are limited opportunities to gain the knowledge and insight needed. Fortunately, *Nursing Deans on Leading: Lessons for Novice and Aspiring Deans and Directors* covers the essential topics for understanding and executing the role of a dean.

Being highly dedicated to the role of dean, including mentoring the next generation, Joanne Robinson, Carole Kenner, and Jana Pressler have the commitment and experience to author such a "how-to" book on serving as a dean. They provide straightforward advice underscored with takeaway messages that will be revisited and reconsidered as one moves forward in their tenure as dean. Exhilarating, yet at times taxing, the role of dean requires high level problem-solving for a myriad of disparate challenges. The insights and shared experiences contained in this book will foster a perceptiveness that will be invaluable to novice and aspiring deans and perhaps offer some new understanding for deans with more experience. The combination of 17 different authors' thoughts and acumen on various activities and roles of deans in nursing ensures that this is worthwhile reading.

This book draws on the collective know-how of some of the most accomplished deans from different types of institutions and geographic locations to give a comprehensive examination of key topics. The value of this book is the lived experience of deans and those who are serving in similar roles. As a dean myself and having served on the board of directors of the American Association of Colleges of Nursing, I can attest that this book reflects my own experience and those of deans and directors of different types of institutions– public and private, large and small. For those aspiring to develop their leadership, leaning toward a career that involves higher education leadership, this book will be a required primer.

Terri E. Weaver, PhD, RN, FAAN, ATSF

PREFACE

Leading as a nursing dean or director is an honor and a privilege. No matter the setting, it is also an intense experience that demands full investment of your time, energy, wisdom, wit, and patience on a daily basis. In fact, evidence suggests that serving as the chief nursing officer in an academic setting can be an overwhelming, stressful, and lonely experience. On average, the tenure of nursing deans and directors is only about 5 years (Bouws, 2017). Role stress and strain are considered strong determinants of staying power. With this in mind, we offer this book as a primer and all-purpose guide for nurses who are either new to academic leadership or aspire to academic leadership roles. Our intent is to provide fundamental information in an engaging and conversational manner, with real-life examples that help the reader to understand and embrace the multifaceted opportunities and challenges of "deaning" and "directing."

Our target audience is novice academic nursing leaders: deans, associate deans, assistant deans, chairs, and directors of nursing programs, departments, and schools. We believe that nursing faculty and students who aspire to academic leadership positions will also find it useful, as will professional organizations that offer academic leadership development programs for nurses. In addition, academic search firms can use the book to groom prospects for nursing dean and director positions, as well as to groom faculty search committees charged with screening and selecting candidates for deanships. Finally, scholars and students who study academic nursing leadership can use scenarios presented in the book to inform their work.

The book features contributions by 17 different academic nursing leaders from across the United States. Most are presiding or recent past nursing deans or directors from schools that offer baccalaureate and higher degree nursing education programs. The book's 19 chapters are divided into three sections: Dimensions of the Nursing Dean/Director Role (Section I); General Responsibilities of Nursing Deans and Directors (Section II); and Self-Care and Work–Life Integration for Nursing Deans and Directors (Section III).

Section I introduces readers to selected aspects of the nursing dean/director role, including the searching and stepping-in processes; day-to-day, for-profit, and interim deaning scenarios; and, finally, the process of stepping up from a dean or director position. Section II covers general responsibilities of nursing deans and directors, including enrollment management, student success, recruitment and retention, academic policies and programs, fundraising, stakeholder engagement, budgeting, strategic planning, clinical enterprises and faculty practice, and executive leadership. The book concludes with Section III that "puts it all together," with chapters on common challenges faced by nursing deans and directors, job satisfaction and joys of the role, and self-care. Each chapter includes a situation or case to engage the reader and contextualize the material, followed by discussion of pertinent information and principles, challenges and opportunities, and best practices. Additional resources, references, or both are listed in each chapter.

As editors, preparation of this book represented a way to live up to our expectations relative to leadership and scholarly productivity. We believe that writing and record-keeping are hallmarks of civilized societies. Neglecting to leave a paper trail deprives future generations of valuable lessons learned and accumulated wisdom. As executive leaders in nursing education, we realize that we have enormous opportunities to influence nursing and healthcare for generations to come. We have all learned a great deal during our tenures as nursing deans, and this book represents our commitment to finding time for scholarly reflection and writing in the interest of "succession-planning-at-large" for future nursing deans. The book aligns with initiatives by the nursing profession to prepare the next generation of academic nursing leaders, and we hope that our current and future colleagues will find it useful.

Joanne P. Robinson
Carole Kenner
Jana L. Pressler

REFERENCE

Bouws, M. (2017). The nursing dean role: An integrative review. *Nursing Education Perspectives, 39*(2), 80–84. doi:10.1097/01.NEP.0000000000000277

ACKNOWLEDGMENTS

The idea for this book originated at a meeting of the American Association of Colleges of Nursing early in my academic leadership journey. There, experienced dean Dr. Susan Gennaro made time to talk with me about the practice of daily reflection and its contribution to her own personal and professional growth. She also reminded me of our obligation "as members of a civilized society" to find a formal way to share lessons learned with those who follow us. Later in my career, I had the privilege of participating in the National League for Nursing (NLN) program, Executive Leadership in Nursing Education and Practice. There, I was exposed to the brilliant vision and nurturing leadership of Dr. Janice Brewington, director of NLN's Center for Transformational Leadership, who provided the structure and encouragement to launch this project and see it to fruition. Finally, finding my co-editors, Drs. Carole Kenner and Jana L. Pressler, and their past "Rx for Deans" column in *Nurse Educator* was like striking gold. The wealth of knowledge and experience they provided in both "deaning" and producing a book was extraordinary. I am extremely grateful to all!

Joanne P. Robinson

DIMENSIONS OF THE NURSING DEAN/DIRECTOR ROLE

SEARCHING FOR A DEAN/DIRECTOR POSITION

CAROLE KENNER | JANA L. PRESSLER

INTRODUCTION

You have decided that you want to be a dean/director or pursue a new deanship/directorship. Where do you start? This chapter discusses how to go about deciding that you want to be a dean/director, make an employment change, complete preliminary work, and actually search for a perfect position.

DEAN/DIRECTOR OR NOT? CHANGE OR NOT?

You must first think about why you want to be a dean/director. The decision to seek a deanship/directorship is life-changing, so it is critical that you recognize why you want to serve in that type of role. Do you think that you are in a rut in your current position? Maybe you have served as an associate/assistant dean or as an interim dean, and you like the challenges and opportunities of this type of position. You might already be serving in a deanship but think that you need to change locations or environments but not the position per se. All of these are good reasons to consider becoming or serving as a dean/director.

SEARCHING FOR A DEAN/DIRECTOR POSITION

When searching for a deanship/directorship position, there are many places where one can gather information about potential jobs. If you are initiating a job search, look online at places such as Academic Keys, American Association of Colleges of Nursing (AACN) Career Center, American Academy of Nursing, the Chronicle of Higher Education, Indeed.com, Careerbuilder.com, Monster.com, Hotjobs.com, Job.com, Simplyhired.com (part of Indeed.com), USA.gov, or the university's website if you know of an institution that you are particularly interested in joining. LinkedIn is another resource that is used by some recruiters for posting dean/director job opportunities. Sign up for email alerts to be notified of executive positions as they become open. Word-of-mouth through colleagues is another resource.

If you have been an assistant/associate dean/director, recruiters or headhunters might contact you directly about openings. Headhunters will send a general job description and ask that you follow up with questions. If you are serious about a position being managed by a headhunter, set up a telephone appointment to gather information beyond what the position description has stated in writing. You might ask about the upper administration, the structure of the institution, and how long the immediate supervisor and president have been in their positions. If you are considering a specific position and cannot find information on the web that will help you to decide whether you want to apply, ask the recruiter for this information. If you know someone in the institution of interest, you might contact her or him for more insights concerning the institution's culture.

It can help your job search if you let your colleagues know that you are searching for a dean/director position. Your colleagues can let you know when they are aware of an opening. Realize that once you start talking to others, the word will be out to your current institution that you are looking for another job. Decide how you want to tell your institution about your interest. If you are just exploring dean/director jobs and you have a good relationship with your current dean/director, talk to her or him about your goal to become a dean/director.

WHAT DO YOU WANT IN A DEAN/ DIRECTOR POSITION?

Before you enter into the search process, determine what you want or need in your next position. Know your moral compass and outline where you "draw your line in the sand" in terms of business practices, ethics, and the amount of work that you can take on yourself. This may sound odd, but in today's competitive world, it is important that you are honest with yourself about what you will and will not do for an organization. For example, if you are faced with a mandate to increase enrollments quickly but are uncertain about the availability of sufficient resources, you might not want to enter into a situation that you perceive is doomed for one reason or another. If you are one who is very concerned about building relationships and you find that you are not permitted to be transparent with faculty and staff, this institution might not be a good job fit for you.

Job location can be a very important factor in selecting a position. Other characteristics to consider are whether the institution is public, private, faith-based, or for-profit. Institutional size stands out as a major factor in determining the expanse of job responsibility. There will be different expectations for a dean/director relative to whether the job is located at an institution that is a small liberal arts college, a community college, an academic health center, or a research-intensive university. Other factors to consider are whether the institution is primarily focused on undergraduate or graduate education or delivers a mix of undergraduate through graduate programs, including doctoral studies. All of these factors comprise decision-making criteria that should be considered when looking at job opportunities. If your ideal institution is not available at the time you are searching, you might have to decide how many of these factors would be deal-breakers for you. For example, you might ask yourself if you are willing to oversee a nursing program that is housed in a faith-based university.

INTERIM DEAN

Due to the myriad of unfilled dean and director positions in nursing, there is a growing market for interim deans. There are search firms that place a person in an interim position while a search moves forward. These interim positions may evolve into a regular formal position as a dean/director. For deans/directors who have retired or stepped out of an executive position, this might be a good intermediate step. Interim positions can be difficult as faculty and staff members know that the interim person is not the permanent unit head. On the other hand, an interim person can sometimes avoid some of the politics associated with the actual position because the interim person is viewed as a temporary appointee.

NEXT STEPS

Preparing Your Application

You think that you have found a dean/director position that you believe is a good fit for you. Make sure that you brag about your accomplishments in your cover letter. Use the position description to guide your cover letter of interest. Use selected buzzwords from the institution's mission/vision/core values in your writing. Using this type of verbiage lets the institution know that you have done your homework exploring the job and that you have determined that you are a good fit. If fundraising is a job expectation, state how you have been involved in that endeavor, even if it was only on a community level. Curriculum development and personnel experiences that stand out to you are important to include. If you have designed new programs, be sure to include that in your letter of interest. If you have held state or national leadership positions in professional organizations, include that information. Your cover letter is not a time to be shy or timid about your accomplishments. Stress why you believe that you are the best person for the job. This cover letter is your own best marketing tool for a position. The letter should not stress areas in which you lack experience. You should be honest in your interview, knowing that no one ever possesses all qualities that an institution aspires to find in a single individual. Make sure your curriculum vitae is up-to-date and submit it as an attachment to your cover letter.

Interviewing

Once your application is sent, your next experience is "the waiting game." If the job search is being managed by a search firm, the head of the search firm may contact you for more information; otherwise, the head of the search committee may be the contact person. At this stage in your job search, either you are invited for an off-site interview or you learn that you have been eliminated from consideration. Occasionally a headhunter will give you some hints about the reasons why you were turned down. For example, the search committee might not have been able to see in your application any evidence of your experience with managing budgets. Usually, however, headhunters offer only general feedback, such as telling you that your application lacked details that the search committee considered important.

The onsite interview, or first-level interview, is generally with the search committee, but you also may see the provost or to whomever you will directly report. At the on-site interview, interviewers will want to see how you think on your feet and will ask you to elaborate on your work experience. If a search firm is involved, the head of the search may prepare you for what to expect in the interview. For example, the headhunter might mention what to expect during the interview process, who will be present, what might be asked, and how long the interview will last. Knowing the names and titles of members serving on the search committee can be very helpful. Finding out as much as possible about these people, their interests, and their areas of expertise prior to the on-site interview can be useful as well.

Make sure you review the institution's programs, anything outstanding about the organization, and their mission/vision/core values/strategic plan. During the interview, ask questions about the organizational chart, in particular, to whom the dean/director position reports, and how the dean/director interfaces with the president or chancellor. This interview will be the intermediate step before coming to campus. The candidates' names might or might not be released to the campus or posted on the website. Releasing candidates' names for a dean/director position depends on the institutional policy as well as state requirements if the institution is funded by the state. Be sure to ask about the parameters of confidentiality pertaining to the search process. If your candidacy is posted on the institution's website, it could be found easily on an Internet search, and your home institution could find out that you are interviewing for a different job. Be prepared for this situation and how you want to respond if it becomes common knowledge that you are seeking another position.

During the on-site interview, the applicant needs to watch her or his body language as people ask questions. In addition, watch how people interact with each other. Ask yourself whether or not the interviewers make direct eye contact with you and others. The job applicant needs to ask his or her questions and, at the same time, try to get a feel for the institution, the hierarchy, the faculty involvement in decision-making, and the institution's culture. It is very important that the applicant ask the search committee what they are looking for in their next leader.

For those applicants who are successful with the on-site interview, the on-campus interview is the next step. This means that you have made the second cut if you are invited for an on-campus interview. Now the pressure is on to receive a job offer. This is the time to really think about whether or not this institution appears to be a good fit for you and your aspirations. If it is not, the applicant should pull out now and decline the next interview. If this is your first time to campus, go the day before and wander around. See what you see when no one is taking you from place to place. Talk to students about how they like the institution. Ask faculty and staff the same question as you walk the campus. Before your interview, review your schedule, and make sure you know with whom you are meeting. If you cannot find anything out about the interviewers, ask the search firm for information, or at least see if you can find out how long the interviewers have been in their positions. Try to determine if most people are graduates of this institution or whether the other deans/directors and faculty are from other institutions. If you are asked to give a lecture on your views of teaching or area of scholarship/research, try to align your talk with the institution's strategic plan. This is also another good time to ask any additional questions that you might have.

Negotiating

Once you receive a job offer, it is time to decide what you will and will not accept. If the salary is lower than you anticipated, ask for more money. You have probably already done your homework and know what other deans are making in the area, or you have used comparison data from organizations such as the AACN. It may be possible that you negotiate some start-up funds—more than your discretionary funds. If you lack a crucial position, like a development or advancement officer, now is the time to try and get that position. Sometimes a dean/director may have someone she or he wants to bring with her or him. Ask if this is possible. If you do not ask, you will never know the answer. This is the time to be really honest with yourself. What is your bottom line? What is more important to you—the culture as you see it or other aspects of the job, such as support staff, control over your school/college, salary, or other perks? Only you can answer the question about what and when to accept. With the current dean/director shortages in nursing, it is highly possible that you can gain a more robust package for yourself and your unit. Once you have the offer you want, accept it and celebrate! Congratulations on a successful journey. If you decide to walk away, there will be another job, and just think how much you have learned in the process.

CONCLUSION

The search for a dean/director position can be stressful. The search can also be exciting. By going through the interview process, dean/director job applicants usually learn about alternate ways of addressing situations that are currently happening in their home institutions. Knowing the audience during interviews cannot be emphasized enough. Being prepared for the application and interview process is pivotal. Once the work of preparation is behind you, consider your interviewing and negotiating encounters with members of the target institution as a learning adventure to be enjoyed.

RESOURCES

American Association of Colleges of Nursing Career Center: https://www.aacnnursing.org/Career-Center/Faculty-Vacancies

AcademicKeys: https://www.academickeys.com/

American Academy of Nursing: http://www.aannet.org/resources/job-postings

ChronicleVitae: https://chroniclevitae.com/job_search?job_search%5Bposition_type%5D=131

HigherEdJobs: https://www.higheredjobs.com/executive/search.cfm?JobCat=165

Indeed: https://www.indeed.com/q-Dean-of-Nursing-jobs.html

LinkedIn: https://www.linkedin.com/

SimplyHired: https://www.simplyhired.com/search?q=dean+of+nursing&job=KWhT0JPxxZv96z3Pov_nkZ9ipE4Hqih4CgJ-QwuHI4_vzywJtJryUg

Vaillancourt, A. M. (2013). What search committees wish you knew. *The Chronicle of Higher Education.* https://www.chronicle.com/article/What-Search-Committees-Wish/136399

STEPPING INTO A DEAN/ DIRECTOR POSITION

CAROLE KENNER | JANA L. PRESSLER

INTRODUCTION

Whether or not this is your first dean/director position, each time you step into a leadership position, you begin again. You would not have been hired into this leadership role if you did not bring a wealth of needed skills, experience, and expertise to the position. But you must read the academic culture, determine the highest priorities, and verify these priorities with your upper administration. The first 90 days are critical for a dean/director, as they set the tone for your tenure as an academic leader. How will you survive, grow, and thrive in this role transition? This chapter explores the transition involved in becoming a dean/director for the first time or in a new setting. Selected lived experiences of stepping into a deanship are shared by the first author (CK).

BACKGROUND

The journey starts as soon as you accept a dean/director position, before you are even formally employed. In my own experience, once my appointment was announced, even though the start date was still several months away, faculty and administrators began reaching out to me. Because I was moving from another state, meetings were set and planned with stakeholders when I came to look for housing. These "informal" meetings were an introduction to the culture and a forecast of several ongoing issues. I liken these early and informal meetings somewhat to speed dating—as you move from group to group, each person is trying to size up your management style. The new dean/director is precisely attempting to do the same thing: Size up what the environment is really like and find out whether or not there any surprises coming her or his way.

The new dean/director in waiting must be aware that her or his first interactions set the stage for the first phase of the dean/director journey. For me, the early informal meetings were always a great time to observe subtle interactions among stakeholders. After the meetings were finished, I thought about who had attended and who had not. I wondered whether there was any hidden message embedded in attendance; for example, was it scheduling that prevented certain individuals from attending, or were there other reasons for not being present? The informal meetings gave me a chance to ask what were the first things that stakeholders would like to see happen when I started the position. Insights into their real concerns emerged as the transition to my new leadership role took place.

If you are assuming a dean/director position within your current organization, you will quickly find that your former faculty peers will seek you out to genuinely welcome you to your new role. At the same time, they will also be evaluating how you respond to them now that you are their official leader. Never underestimate the importance of these informal meetings: They are encounters that you and your former peers need to have to understand how your relationship with them will change with your new role. If you have served as an interim dean/director, you may have more insight as to what to expect as you assume the official title of dean/director. You will definitely be viewed differently given that you are no longer a possible candidate for the role but actually are the chosen dean/director. It is critical to note that, as the official leader, you must realize that your "hallway" conversations or chance meetings are no longer casual. Hallway conversations and the like will influence your initial reception as the school, college, or program dean/director.

ARRIVAL PHASE

You arrive! The day has finally come! You are brand new to the dean/director role in the institution. Whether you are a first-time dean/director or seasoned to the role, your arrival is very exciting as well as a little scary. Each time that I have assumed a new deanship, I have seen my arrival as a time of great opportunity attached to a fast learning curve. At some institutions, there will be official welcomes for new deans/directors. But for the most part, arrival is just a time when people drop by your office to greet you. Of course, there are the mundane tasks of getting an official identification badge, a parking decal, and an email account that remind you of your new surroundings. Even these tasks help you to meet key people across the institution who will be important for you to know.

I am always curious to see who will drop by my office during the first few days on the job, as well as which individuals want to make sure that they rapidly get to know the new dean for a variety of reasons. I use the first day in the role to work with my assistant to determine the normal workflow of the office. As the new dean/director, you might desire to change the normal workflow. Yet, in the first days in the role, you will want to see how things have been accomplished in the recent past before you institute any changes.

I use the first week on the job to meet with my leadership team and "get a feel" for their jobs. I ask the leadership team about their roles—not just their job descriptions but what their role is in nursing, what they like about their positions, and what they would like to change. The information that you, as the new dean/director, glean in these first few days can be invaluable as you learn the institutional culture and determine how there might have been task drift over the years. Acknowledging early that the current staff will have input into their jobs as they go forward seems to ease the staff's transition anxiety to some extent while also helping the new leader see which staff members want to move forward in the organization.

HONEYMOON PHASE

The honeymoon phase of any relationship is when everything is exciting, with both the new leader and the other stakeholders in the organization only seeing possibilities and not limitations. The first 90 days were critical for me when I accepted my first deanship because this was the time when I set the vision and course for the school. The first 90 days is sometimes the time when there is a sort of "honeymoon" phase and neither the dean/director nor the faculty nor the staff are "in the wrong." While faculty and staff generally tend to express excitement about having a new dean/director and a new direction, realize that some are not enthusiastic about either scenario. However, most faculty and staff want to embrace the new leader and help make everything highly successful.

There is also the need for faculty and staff to "please" the new dean/director. However, having started over as a dean several times, my own assessment is that the honeymoon phase is often almost or completely nonexistent due to external pressures to move the school/college/program forward. This early time in the dean/director role offers tremendous opportunities for building people's trust and for building a team. I use this time to test the water regarding new ideas and to find out where the barriers or resistance might be with respect to changing a curriculum, adding a new program, or making a significant change on a fast timeline.

The honeymoon phase also applies to working with upper administration and trying to figure out the style in which upper administration wants information delivered to them, when they want to be notified, and under what circumstances they want to be notified. A new dean/director can also try out ideas to gain perspective on what is an acceptable idea and what ideas will need to gain traction over time. For me, being engaged in these first meetings sometimes meant asking a series of questions of the provost to make sure that I was clear about the expectations of me in the role of dean as well as expectations for my school or college. I went into these early meetings with an agenda but also asked what agenda the provost had for me. It was a great time to build rapport with upper administration and, in turn, build relationships with faculty and staff.

Meeting with key campus leaders is important too. I made rounds to meet people such as the registrar, as well as the staff in charge of institutional data, alumni affairs, and development. In one institution, I had my own development officer, while in another, I was assigned a shared person. In each case, I met with the development officer to determine what goals were already set for the school or college and then began to shape my own development priorities and style of interaction with stakeholders. I met with alumni groups to engage them in a shared vision and to gain insights from them about where they wanted to see the school or college headed in the future. The honeymoon period is exciting as well as critical for solidifying the organizational place of the new leader.

LAUNCH PHASE

The launch phase of your dean/director journey occurs when the honeymoon period ends. The honeymoon period does not have a specific time boundary, like 90 days, for example, but instead typically ends when the dean/director has to make a hard decision that is not completely supported or is perceived to be moving the organization in a different direction than past administrators have gone. This is also the time that organizational challenges as well as opportunities are identified. In most organizations, this is the time when discussions begin to resemble a grant-writing exercise such that when a question is articulated, a needs assessment is performed, and an intervention/program is developed with a timeline. More often than not, external forces accelerate an action plan for addressing some organizational challenge that was put on hold until the new leader was in place. This is also the time when the "dance" starts between you and administration and you and faculty, as the timeline for change on both sides is generally not the same. Guess what? You are right in the middle! Take advantage of the goodwill built during the honeymoon phase and be clear with administration about what you view as feasible and where you need support to move the organization forward.

My best example of the launch phase was when I was charged with starting two new programs as soon as possible. One was fairly easy as it was my area of expertise—a master's program that was focused on a neonatal nurse practitioner track. The other one was more challenging, as it was to start the first PhD nursing program in the state. There was one major stumbling block to developing a PhD program: The school had no externally funded research. I also knew that we did not have enough full-time faculty lines and were dependent on the state to secure these. About 92% of our funding depended on state resources. This situation did not give me a lot of flexibility. I had to brainstorm possible solutions for questions such as the following:

- How could I get resources for these new programs without straining our state support?
- How could I start the first neonatal nurse practitioner program (NNP), which was much needed in the state, without hurting potentially larger program tracks and without looking like I was just giving into my passion for neonatal nursing?

I thought I could quickly achieve the neonatal program and buy time to start the doctoral program. I gathered community and faculty leaders together. Over the course of several months, we developed a plan to start the new neonatal NNP through a partnership with another university across state lines. I also had faculty from my institution begin to talk to faculty from other NNP programs. We signed a contract to join two NNP student groups together via Internet protocol (IP) video, and each university was approved to grant the NNP degree to its students. In other words, rather than argue about tuition and fees for an NNP program, we paid a fee to have its faculty teach our students online, but our faculty would co-teach to get mentored in the content in case we had to assume teaching the courses ourselves in the future. If a student matriculated with us, it was our degree and our degree requirements for the core. My clinical partners were hired as adjunct faculty, which cut my start-up costs and provided coverage for clinical courses. However, these clinical partners also needed to go through the program, which increased our revenue with little increase in costs. When needed, I co-taught theory courses as the program expanded. The students and faculty loved the program and had good outcomes on certification exams. Administration was extremely happy with the NNP program because revenue increased. And faculty understood that I meant what I said about resources and enrollments—they had to grow concurrently. We worked as a team to create and implement the program. This experience built trust.

We used the same launching model to start the PhD program. We partnered with two other universities and shared resources until we could hire faculty with extramural research grant funding. I also brought in a nationally recognized nurse researcher as a consultant to work with administration and faculty to formulate a plan to build credible research. With help from the consultant, I worked out a plan for a very gradual build-up of our program. Faculty were involved in each phase of program development and were given opportunities to seek funding to build their programs of research. Even today, many years later, this PhD program is very successful. I gained credibility with the state, legislators, and most importantly administration, faculty, staff, and students. At the same time that I was gaining these successes, I also had many challenges.

CHALLENGES/OPPORTUNITIES

Challenges as well as opportunities often reveal themselves during the job interview. These are the things I tried to follow up on during my individual meetings with faculty and staff as I began a new deanship. For example, I would ask, "What did you mean by your comment…?" Questions like this would provide context for their concerns and/or ideas about the school's future. Most of the conversations centered around three areas: personnel, accreditation, and finances.

Personnel

I have found during my listening tours that one or two names will pop up as "difficult faculty" or "bad actors." I take this with a grain of salt, as I want to go in with an open mind and maybe some wishful thinking that the behavior might change under new leadership. I try to give the person(s) the benefit of the doubt without dismissing the comments of coworkers. As I have grown wiser, I am less likely to listen to comments and more likely to trust my instincts. For example, I found that one person who periodically caused a stir with coworkers and faculty was very intelligent, held high standards for the profession, and felt underappreciated. I worked hard to acknowledge strengths, gain trust, and then work on communication. Over the course of my tenure with this person, we had some disagreements, but we had mutual respect for each other and worked through issues. This approach will not always work, but many people just want attention and to be acknowledged for their work. If this can be done without damage to the morale of the unit and achieved in an honest manner, some positive forward movement can occur.

If there is a difficult personnel situation that threatens the unit's work climate, then it must be addressed head-on. I find that each institution has a different approach about when to get human resources involved. As a new dean/director, it is important that you find out how and when the human resource department wants to be involved. My approach is to use direct confrontation—I do not mean in a spiteful or mean way, but it simply means to address the issues head-on. Early in my first deanship, one faculty member told me that she did not want to confront her coworker with a behavior issue because confronting the person might make the person angry. My assessment was that both parties were already angry, so either bringing them together or addressing the issue individually in a direct manner was not going to make the coworker with the problem angrier. This is definitely not a comfortable situation, but, in general, direct confrontation helps you to establish that you will address issues and will not let them simmer until the situation is out of control.

I have mentored many new deans. Along the way, I have discovered that the area of personnel is the most prevalent area of concern. I always suggest that new deans/directors find out how and when the provost or their immediate supervisor wants to be informed of a situation and how that person wants to be involved. I advise new deans to always use their resources. For me, it is often a dean colleague, not necessarily in nursing, who is my biggest resource and advocate. Your willingness to take risks to tackle the difficult problems is what Alessio (2017) calls being an intentional dean.

Accreditation

Accreditation issues or accreditation opportunities are other areas that come up early in a new dean/director position. Even when the next scheduled accreditation visit is not due for several years, faculty will begin to talk about changes as if accreditation is looming. Faculty will report that changes cannot be made until after the site visit. Issues of low NCLEX-RN® pass rates or deficient areas that require interim reports from the board of nursing are often a root cause of leadership changes. If you come into one of these situations, try to gather as much information about the accreditation concern as soon as possible, ideally while you are still in the honeymoon phase. Use your professional network for consultation, and determine if upper administration will support a consultant to help you develop an action plan and a feasible timeline for correction. If this is not done right away, a new dean/director can be doomed in the leadership position because upper administration wants the problems fixed immediately and you recognize that that is not feasible.

Collaborating with an accreditation consultant, upper administration, and recognized faculty leaders will enable the dean/director to gain the trust of all involved. These steps will help solidify the dean/director's ability to assess and create an action plan. This process might be slower than some would like to see, but a process that is accepted by faculty and upper administration is most helpful in the long run. Coercion by upper administration to move too quickly and/or exclude the faculty will most certainly set up resistance to change. I have used accreditation as a mechanism to encourage, for example, changes in data collection and outcome analysis, and curricular changes to reflect new standards and as a way for faculty to take pride in their program. While I try to be the guide on the side, I am also clear that I will steer the direction of any programmatic changes. Faculty might state that they did well last time, that they have good outcomes, and that they do not need to change. As dean/director, you must find your faculty champions who recognize that change is needed, especially when trends are different and standards have changed. With your backing as dean/director, these faculty champions will move the program changes forward. I also look at accreditation as an opportunity for new faculty to gain insight into curriculum design, systematic evaluations, and many aspects of the educational process that might not have been covered in their graduate education.

Finances

Finances and the budgeting process are other areas of challenge and opportunity. If you work in a state institution, the budget from the state generally gets reduced or tightened each year. If you work in a private institution, the budget may be dependent on diversified revenue streams. Unfortunately, it is not until you step into your dean/director position that you really find out how solvent your school/college/program is. At the onset of your dean/director appointment, the budget process, and even your control of the budget, might not be transparent. During the honeymoon phase, it is best to try to find out as much as you can about your budget, what and how budget requests are made, what accounts are eliminated at the end of each fiscal year, and how much control you have over your budget. Some new deans/directors will find that they have little input into the budgeting process and that the process for reallocating funds is complex. When I had a budget officer or business manager in my school or college, I met with that official weekly at first to get a feel for the budget and points of tension in the budget. I always asked to review the last 3 years of the budget to see the trends. If I did not have a budget officer or business manager, I asked the provost and treasurer for relevant information concerning the budget.

Where possible, I have also been transparent with the faculty and staff about the budget to squelch any rumors floating in the hallway about how school or college monies are allocated, how monies are spent, and how such decisions are made. I do not reveal personnel salaries but do discuss operating budgets. Personnel costs are the biggest part of the operating budget. One time, we were faced with a significant budget cut, so I went to faculty and outlined what we were facing. I told them that, if possible, I did not want to lose positions, so I asked them to look at the expenses we had and to make some suggestions about how we might cut costs without losing positions. I received excellent suggestions from the faculty, and within 3 weeks, we cut expenses by 30% and were able to save all full-time positions. I could not have come up with such creative solutions on my own accord. At least once each year, I now share our budget with faculty and staff, including discretionary funds. Each dean/director has to judge whether or not this is a good idea for her or his school/college/program.

In my current situation, I do not have a lot of extra funds and want faculty and staff to know that. I have been at institutions where I might be more cautious about revealing the total amount of discretionary funds but instead might reveal the percentage of increase or decrease in these funds annually and what initiatives the funds supported. Budget discussions can lead to many creative, innovative ideas. Of course, there will be some skeptics and naysayers; however, they are usually not the majority of faculty and staff.

MANAGING EXPECTATIONS

Managing expectations is extremely important for your well-being as well as for the well-being of your school/college/program. Your first task is to manage your own expectations. Ask, for example:

- What do you want to accomplish in the first 90 days?
- What do you want to accomplish in the first year?

Be realistic and set personal goals. Make sure to review these goals periodically (e.g., quarterly or every 6 months) so that you can see which goals you are meeting, exceeding, and failing to meet. Falling behind might not be your fault. It could be that unexpected factors or events are interfering with your progress. If that is true, simply do a course correction. Do not worry about falling behind unless upper administration is concerned.

Managing the expectations of upper administration is important. In some institutions I had regular monthly meetings to review issues and points of progress and determine expectations. Many times I found that even when I was not satisfied with my progress toward goals, upper administration believed that I was doing fine. Such meetings with upper administration help me to know if I am on the right course. If I learn that I am not on the right course, I need upper administration to be clear about what I need to accomplish and the time frame. I try to point out impediments that I am facing and to discover if there is an area in which upper administration wants me to move more quickly than I am able to do. I have asked for help in these areas in the form of suggestions for strategies to address the pressing issues. These discussions help to build trust so that when things do go off course, I can call upper administration and look for solutions as a team.

Faculty, staff, students, and the community also have expectations of the dean/director. Some of these stakeholders will have high expectations for what they want you to accomplish. They may look to you to change some aspect of the academic culture and/or change the direction of the school/college/program. The community might want you to be more visible externally or to quickly create new partnerships. Manage these community expectations by listening to their wants and needs and then setting priorities that are feasible. Once you are clear on how you want to proceed as dean/director, communicate your plans to your stakeholders. Make sure they know that you as dean/director value their input and ideas and encourage them to keep these coming to you. At the same time, you must convey to community partners what you can realistically be expected to accomplish, what support you must gain from others to move forward, and those things that just simply cannot be addressed, at least at the present time. The community partners will respect you for being forthright and also for not promising everything they request or setting unrealistic timelines for achievement of goals. If you fail to achieve your goals, you risk losing the trust of your community partners.

WORK-LIFE BALANCE, OR NOT?

The notion of balance and a dean/director position is always difficult. There are times when there appears to be no downtime, such as at the beginning or end of a school year or when a crisis has occurred. As the dean/director, you must decide early on how you are going to manage your personal time (Danielsen & Wilson, 2018). Some deans/directors find it best to indicate that they are not available after 5 p.m., except for emergencies. These deans/directors do not answer emails or phone calls after hours. Some deans/directors will accept texting with faculty and staff after hours if one or more problems arise. As the dean/director, you must decide what works best for your personal lifestyle. I sometimes answer emails very late at night or early in the morning but have learned that I must acknowledge that I do not expect faculty and staff to be on call 24-7. In some systems, I can delay sending messages by saving them as drafts and then sending them during working hours or on a Monday versus a Saturday or Sunday. Again, as dean/director, you must decide what feels best. I tend to answer calls and emails after work hours and on weekends, but that is my own personal communication style. No dean/director should feel that she or he must be on call 24-7. It will not be effective or efficient in the long run. If you are going to be unavailable for several hours, you can let your assistant or someone who works closely with you know; if a problem arises, the assistant then knows approximately when you can be reached. I conduct a lot of international travel and many times cannot be reached for 15 to 20 hours at a stretch. Thus, when I engage in international travel, I make sure that my department chairs and/or assistant know when I will be available again to respond to concerns.

CRISIS MANAGEMENT

Managing crises requires planning. Does that seem odd or sound funny? What I mean is this: Think ahead about what you will do if and when a crisis occurs.

- How would you be able to communicate?
- How do you want to respond?

For example, I have been in two delicate situations where all cell towers were jammed and I needed to reach faculty and students. We had an emergency telephone tree to triage communication at the school. I found that I could send text messages and then ask whom I had reached and for that person to send a text message to the next person. That was the only way of communicating in that instance for about 12 hours—until it was known whether or not everyone was safe. For the next 3 days, the cell tower was always active, and I answered around the clock. The moral of this story is to determine what, how, and with whom you need to communicate in case of an emergency—a natural disaster, a shooting, or other event. Conserve your energy in times of crisis as you are the leader and must be able to take the lead in responding. It is important to rest when you can, as some of these situations can linger for several days.

SELF-CARE

Self-care is important for a leader. You cannot support your faculty, staff, and students if you are depleted. You must find some "me time." You must determine what makes you relaxed. I know that I have a tendency to go too long before taking a break. I also know that if I get good rest, I can solve problems, think critically, and generally be a better leader. Some deans/directors find that relaxation techniques, mindfulness exercises, physical exercise, reading, needlepoint, painting, massage, petting furry "children," and other such diversions are helpful. I have learned to make appointments with myself. I block some time during the week to work on my scholarship, go for a walk, or engage in another enjoyable activity. Placing these times on the calendar reminds me they are just as important as one of our school/college/program meetings.

Deans/directors cannot book every minute of their days exclusively with work activities and maintain productivity in the long run. I worked with a personal coach for a while who suggested that I take off at least one weekend day and not work. I found that I could not always do that, so I tried to take off 4-hour time blocks instead. Four-hour blocks of time away from work have proven to be helpful to me overall.

CONCLUSION

Stepping into a dean/director position is very exciting. It also takes considerable courage. Enjoy the dean/director adventure, but take care of yourself so that you are best able to handle whatever opportunities and challenges come your way.

RESOURCES

American Association of Colleges of Nursing. *New Dean Resources*. Retrieved from https://www.aacnnursing.org/Deans/New-Dean-Resources

Coll, K., Niles, S. G., Coll, K. F., Ruch, K. F., Charles, P., & Stewart, R.A. (2018). Education Deans: Challenges and Stress. *Journal of Organizational and Educational Leadership, 4*(1). Retrieved from https://eric.ed.gov/?id=EJ1196329

REFERENCES

Alessio, J. C. (2017). *The intentional dean: A guide to the academic deanship*. New York: Routledge and Taylor & Francis Group.

Danielsen, R., & Wilson, C. (2018). Balancing act. *Clinical Reviews Career Center: The Work/Life Blog of the Clinical Reviews Career Center*. Retrieved from http://www.clinicianreviews.directory/misc-category/balancing-act/

DAY-TO-DAY DEANING

JANA L. PRESSLER | CAROLE KENNER

INTRODUCTION

Some might think that a dean/director's job in nursing administration consists of almost the same activities from day to day. Initially the job of the dean/director might seem relatively predictable. It is true that there are some tasks that a dean/director completes nearly every day; however, even over a short period of time in the position, day-to-day activities begin to vary considerably. In fact, responding to emergent needs, issues, and opportunities is an integral part of the dean/director's job and demands a high level of organization and flexibility. What follows is a general rather than exhaustive guide to day-to-day deaning/directing as well as some key considerations and tips as you take on the role.

ORGANIZATION OF DEAN/DIRECTOR ACTIVITIES

There are a multitude of required activities that a dean/director of nursing must not overlook or forget to address. Upon starting a position, it is a good idea to keep an Excel spreadsheet of these activities, which typically fall into four categories: regular meetings, events, assessments, and professional development. A spreadsheet can be edited and updated as needed, as well as shared with others when there is a need for them to know when the dean/director is working on a specific task. Another alternative is to use an electronic task or "to-do list" with a timeline for completion. Typical items that should be incorporated in a spreadsheet or task list are listed in Table 3.1.

In addition to these routine activities, the dean/director must also allow for time to meet with students, parents, faculty, and staff about academic progression issues, personnel issues, and a myriad of other concerns. The list also does not include responding to the massive amounts of email that a dean/director

24 I Dimensions of the Nursing Dean/Director Role

TABLE 3.1 Routine Activities of Nursing Deans/Directors

Regular meetings	■ Your supervisor (i.e., the chancellor/provost or equivalent) ■ Your administrative assistant ■ Your unit's leadership team: associate/assistant deans; directors (e.g., academic programs, student services, continuing education, faculty development); department chairs; budget officer; development or advancement officer ■ Faculty ■ Staff ■ Student groups (e.g., student nurses organization, student advisory group) ■ Peer leaders/leadership team in your institution (e.g., peer deans/directors of other units, associate/assistant provosts) ■ Local nursing and healthcare leaders (e.g., chief nursing officers of hospitals/clinical agencies; leaders of other disciplines in hospitals/clinical agencies as appropriate) ■ Community partners and stakeholders (e.g., clinical advisory board, corporate advisory board, donors, alumni) ■ Professional meetings (e.g., national dean meetings, state-wide dean/director meetings)
Events (attendance and preparation of remarks)	■ Orientation for new faculty and students ■ Fall semester welcome/"call back" ■ State of the college/school/department ■ Convocation ■ Commencement
Assessments	■ Performance appraisals (e.g., direct reports, promotion, and tenure reviews) ■ Program evaluation (i.e., systematic evaluation plan, strategic plan, accreditation standards, best practices, performance of peer and aspirant institutions) ■ Annual review of physical plant (e.g., structures, maintenance needs, space requirements)
Professional development	■ Scholarly activities (e.g., publication, presentations, grants) ■ Leadership (e.g., professional organizations, boards) ■ Continuing education

receives. If it seems that all of this would likely result in "death-by-meetings," it can if it is not managed properly.

THE DEAN/DIRECTOR'S CALENDAR

The administrative assistant reporting directly to the dean/director keeps the dean/director's calendar. It is critical that the calendar be carefully maintained so that the dean/director knows where she or he needs to be when and what activities need to be addressed at what time and place. Because of high demand for the dean/director's time, it is easy for her or his schedule to become very tight and even overbooked. The dean/director needs to let the administrative assistant overseeing her or his calendar know how to budget time so that there are ample amounts allotted for important dialogue, yet not so little unscheduled time that the dean/director cannot take any breaks throughout the day. It is a good idea to have some dedicated blocks throughout the week for "thinking and processing time." It is not uncommon for a new dean/director to forget to schedule time for lunch except if there is lunch associated with a meeting. Sharing the dean/director's calendar with an assistant is a survival strategy that will lessen the burden on the dean/director.

Many deans/directors have open door policies for faculty, staff, and students. An open-door policy still requires time management in terms of limiting the time that "drop-in" individuals spend with you, particularly if you already have a tight schedule.

CHANGING PRIORITIES

Nearly every day, a new event arises or a challenging problem becomes manifest that creates a need for a schedule change. The dean/director has to be able to cope with such unexpected demands and not become flustered. Having the attitude that "something positive can be worked out with the schedule" is advisable because it can be upsetting to faculty and staff to see the dean/director either at a complete standstill or at the height of frustration or irritation due to frequent schedule changes. Therefore, keeping a positive outlook and being happy to be serving as the dean/director are essential mind-sets for the leader.

As registered nurses, we are used to changes in the clinical schedule or changes in a patient's condition that dictate a schedule change. Yet as we move from a clinical setting to academia, nurses seem to lose the ability to reframe days that seem out of our control. Our advice is to try to remember that academia is not a clinical situation and that we rarely have "a life hanging in the balance." Keeping these two realities in mind should improve your ability to take a schedule change in stride and maintain a positive outlook.

Change is never something that occurs without a few glitches or mishaps. Having a smorgasbord of options for dealing with concerns, issues, and problems can prove beneficial. It is always good to remind others that there is typically more than "one right answer" or solution to a problem. Knowing that there can be multiple "right" or appropriate answers can alleviate worry in those who believe that there is only "one right answer" and multiple "wrong" answers. Seeking advice from others, including faculty and staff, is helpful with not only sharing the burden but also empowering them to express their opinions. At the end of the day, the dean/director is still the one who must decide the course of action.

CHECKING IN WITH THE BUDGET OFFICER

It is important to determine where the school/college/department stands with the assigned budget on a quarterly (12 week) basis. It is essential to have someone, namely a budget officer, who the dean/director can trust to keep the budget balanced. It is perfectly acceptable for the faculty and staff to think that the primary budget officer of the school/college/department either is stereotypically "tight" and proceeding as if every payment is coming out of her or his own pocket, or is a "pennypincher" or even a "low baller." If the budget officer was the opposite, either a "spendthrift" or "waster," the school/college/department could find itself in significant debt very rapidly.

If there is no budget officer in your school/college/department, find a person upon whom you can rely to go over the budget and help you determine how to "move money" around. This person might be a staff person with budget and finance experience. If there is no one in your unit, then seek advice from the treasurer's office or even an external ally who can give you guidance while not seeing the actual budget, which is typically confidential and not able to be shared. Deans/directors of nursing, in particular, experience noteworthy challenges with exceedingly tight budgets and oftentimes have less revenue and resources than the medical dean or dean of the academic health center (Bouws, 2018). Therefore, it is imperative that the dean/director spends time creating innovative ways to increase budget resources.

It is extremely helpful to have a discretionary fund that can be used by the dean/director to pay for expenditures that do not fit within the formal budget. This is not always possible. However, sometimes when a dean/director is hired, a start-up fund is given to her or him to meet those sorts of needs. For example, having funds to pay for refreshments for special meetings, take important contacts out for lunch, and pay for parking meters can be quite helpful. Using funds to support emergencies, such as a student who suddenly faces extreme financial hardship or a staff person who has been diagnosed with a devastating illness, helps maintain the morale of the organization. Such emergencies are usually not able to be funded through normal budgetary means. These discretionary funds are typically not swept at the end of a fiscal year so they can build over time for use by the dean/director.

EMAIL

Because email messages and communication can be misconstrued or not fully understood within a given context, it is best that the dean/director keep email responses short and to the point. Rather than sending a lengthy email, it is safer and better received to respond to complicated questions posed in email with short answers, such as "Let's talk about this further," "Please give me a call so that we can talk about this matter in more detail over the phone," and/or "Please make an appointment with my administrative assistant to see me in person." Your approach will come across as more friendly if communication is completed orally before any decision is placed into writing. In addition, if a disagreement concerning a major problem ever arises at a later point in time, email scan be subpoenaed through the discovery process and used as evidence in court.

TEACHING

The faculty know that the dean/director has teaching expertise, which eliminates the need for her or him to showcase this formally in courses. Going back to the topic of time management, preparing to teach and teaching can be very time-consuming activities. If the dean/director has free time in her or his schedule, she or he occasionally might decide to present a guest lecture or oversee a seminar or class. Generally speaking, deans/directors do not need the responsibility of teaching added to their numerous administrative duties and tasks. Intermittently assisting with capstone projects or dissertations can be a possibility for deans/directors. These teaching activities should only be done when deemed necessary or desired rather than on a regular basis.

HIRING NEW FACULTY

A large portion of the process of hiring new faculty can be delegated to a faculty search committee or task force. Faculty applicants can be screened, selected for interviews, and interviewed by selected school/college/department faculty. The dean/director will be interested in attending applicants' scholarly presentations and meeting with the applicants. Typically, the faculty search committee or task force discusses the various applicants and makes a recommendation for which person(s) they would like to nominate for the position. That group also can solicit professional references, compile the findings from the professional references, and submit a recommendation with rationale for selecting one or more of the applicants. The assistant dean or department chair can then submit a formal request to the dean/director using the findings of the search committee or task force so that an offer(s) can be made.

The assistant dean or department chair might actually be the point person for making the job offer and negotiate salary and resources with direction and approval from the dean/director. Before a contract is presented, the human resource department typically completes a criminal background check. The budget officer or appropriate staff member in the dean/director's administration, or in human resources, can oversee other necessary paperwork, including getting a contract signed. Obtaining copies of a new faculty member's nursing license, passport or driver's license, verification of required immunizations, and CPR certification can be delegated to appropriate staff members. It is important for the dean/director to know when and what parts of the hiring process to delegate. Each institution is a bit different in what a dean/director must do versus what can be done by others.

FIRING FACULTY AND STAFF

Letting someone go from a position is never easy. Some institutions insist that the immediate supervisor—the assistant dean, department chair, or person who completes the individual's evaluation—conduct the firing. Other institutions require the dean/director take on this responsibility. Someone is fired only after the appropriate process/procedure is followed. In most cases, this process comes from human resources and, if totally contentious, with input from the legal department. Written warnings are given that indicate what must be done to improve performance and include a time frame for the performance change. Once it is clear that insufficient or no progress has been made, the firing should be done swiftly, respectfully, and in a manner that preserves the person's dignity.

Bring the person who is being fired into your office. Be clear that the person's performance has not improved and that their services are no longer required as of a specific date. In some institutions, the dean/director can let the person go immediately and offer pay until the end of the pay period if there are only a couple of days left. In other institutions, the person to be fired has to remain until the end of the pay period. This is not a time to say what the person did well or prolong a discussion about job performance as anything said could be used in a legal action that might ensue. It is wise to have any written documents that you are going to give to the person reviewed by legal counsel and human resources. The dean/director should plan to keep these final firing meetings brief and to the point. Should the dean/director have any concerns about her or his safety during such a meeting, security should be called ahead of time and arranged to be in the vicinity. If the person being fired asks the dean/director what options they have, depending on the institution and state's policies, the dean/director can refer the person to human resources or give them a copy of the firing policy.

If the person being fired is a tenured faculty member, the dean/director must make sure that she or he knows the formal procedure for handling the personnel issue. In some institutions, there are post-tenure reviews that are clear about performance expectations. If there are no post-tenure reviews, there are generally very narrow categories of faculty actions that would result in a tenured faculty member's dismissal. In these cases, the provost or equivalent and the university president are usually involved, and there also might be a peer review committee. If faculty are unionized, a union representative must be involved, too.

Although firing someone is not pleasant, it is part of the dean/director's job. It is also necessary to support positive morale since people who do not perform well place heavy burdens on the rest of the faculty/staff.

STUDENT SERVICES

The office of student services offers many supports for students throughout their recruitment, admission, and academic life. This office often organizes the student orientation, transfer student welcome, open houses for recruitment, convocation to welcome incoming students, and graduation activities. The office also houses support services such as disability services to help students obtain special accommodations, financial aid, writing assistance, academic coaching, and career services. Psychological and counseling services are also typically offered through either student services or the university's health center. Title IX coordinators offer support for students who experience sexual assault. Getting to know the personnel in the student services division and university's health/counseling center can help a dean/director guide students to obtain academic and psychosocial support. Psychological services are extremely important for today's students who might be exhibiting extreme anxiety or expressing suicidal thoughts.

Deans/directors handle student complaints. These complaints range from relatively minor issues involving class times or open lab hours to concerns around discrimination, grading of assignments, course grade appeals, or probation and dismissal notices. The timing of the issues is cyclic. Most complaints occur at the beginning and end of a semester or quarter. Policies guide the dean/director as to how student complaints are handled and what role the dean/director plays in the process. Responding to complaints will take precedence over many of the day-to-day tasks of the dean/director because the process is usually time sensitive.

Today, many institutions have a diversity officer, such as a "director of inclusion," who works with campus police to address hate crimes or related problems. The dean/director must get to know the diversity leader and use her or his expertise with students as well as with faculty and staff. It is up to the dean/director to create a civil environment and to denounce incivility (Clark, 2017).

The registrar's office works closely with student services to ensure that all students receive credit for courses taken and complete the type and number of courses required for degree completion/graduation. Meeting with the registrar a few times each year can help a leader with the following tasks: ensuring proper coding of students; getting new courses or programs into the system; developing transfer credit processes; and creating articulation agreements with other institutions, including a process for getting course credits from other institutions to appear on your students' transcripts. It is important to get to know the leaders in student services before you really need them. Building these relationships before an inevitable crisis is especially helpful when the time comes to work through hard issues.

DELEGATION: WHO, WHAT, WHEN

Just as we teach nursing students about how, when, and to whom they can delegate tasks, we as leaders must do the same. Who, what, and when can a task be delegated in your institution? Assistant deans can be the first line of support when it comes to getting students enrolled in classes, changing majors, advising about transfer credits, guiding faculty with advisement questions, meeting with students and parents seeking academic progression advice, and handling transfer receptions and student orientations. The dean/director will participate in open houses and meet and greet new students. However, the assistant dean can actually be responsible for planning these events. The dean/director can provide guidelines for department chairs or faculty who want to develop new courses or programs.

Preparation of substantive change or new program reports required by accrediting bodies or state review committees can be delegated with oversight by the dean/director. Other faculty members might be the ones doing the actual writing of these reports. Accreditation reports should be guided by the dean/director but can be written by an outside consultant, a faculty member overseeing evaluation for the school/college/department, or a faculty member who is willing to take the lead. Accreditation always involves faculty and is faculty led. Faculty assigned to working on accreditation reports typically welcome help with the writing.

The dean and alumni leaders should do the vast majority of the work on development or fundraising. If available to your school/college/department, the development officer can assist in the planning of these events. Including the assistant dean and department chairs in these events helps to spread responsibilities and provides professional development to those who assist.

Grant-writing can be delegated to others with oversight by the dean/director. At times, the dean/director may choose to lead grant-writing activities or direct the development of key elements; other times, adding to a grant as it develops can be the best approach. By serving in both capacities, the dean/director sends the message that she or he is willing to contribute to or take the lead on a grant activity. Working side-by-side with faculty can help the dean/director to be seen as a partner and mentor. It also provides an opportunity to learn a lot about faculty.

Delegation must be done with considerable thought. It must not be seen as a shirking of dean/director responsibilities but rather as a lightening of the load. Delegation sends a message of trust to the individual(s) who are assuming these additional responsibilities.

RECOGNITION AND AWARDS

Efforts by a dean/director to showcase faculty and staff go a long way to develop and cement relationships. It is important to send congratulatory messages to all members of the school/college/department when a faculty or staff member receives an award, secures a grant, or produces a publication. Nominating faculty and staff for internal and external awards is another important role for the dean/director. These actions empower faculty and staff, plus show them that you, as dean/director, are aware and appreciative of their strong performance. Soon other members of the faculty and staff will send opportunities your way for team members to be recognized at local, state, regional, national, and international levels.

CONCLUSION

As a dean/director, it is easy to fall prey to an impossible schedule. Reliance on others is a necessary part of the job. If you are feeling as if you cannot breathe and you have no thinking time, then take control of your schedule. Only you can change the situation and change expectations. Only you can be responsible for remaining positive on the job.

RESOURCES

5 Duties of a College Dean: https://www.top10onlinecolleges.org/list/5-duties-of-a-college-dean/

So You Want to Be a Dean?: https://www.chronicle.com/article/So-You-Want-to-Be-a-Dean-/234900

REFERENCES

Bouws, M. (2018). The nursing dean role: An integrative review. *Nursing Education Perspectives, 39*(2), 80–84. doi:10.1097/01.NEP.0000000000000277

Clark, C. (2017). *Creating and sustaining civility in nursing education.* Indianapolis, IN: Sigma Theta Tau International.

DEANING IN A FOR-PROFIT ENVIRONMENT

F. PATRICK ROBINSON | ADELE A. WEBB

INTRODUCTION

You are being recruited for a nursing deanship in a for-profit university with a good reputation. Degree programs are innovative, enrollment and graduation rates are robust, and the salary is attractive. Yet, concerns about the quality, cost, and mission of for-profit higher education make you hesitate. This chapter covers the evolution of higher education in the U.S. for-profit sector, similarities and differences between for-profit and nonprofit schools, and essentials for successful deaning in the for-profit environment.

THE FOR-PROFIT SECTOR

For-profit education has long been embedded in American culture. As far back as colonial times, people flocked to clergy, who offered classes in their homes and churches in order to supplement their income (Ruch, 2003). This model of education persisted throughout the development and refinement of education in the United States. Over time, for-profit schools grew exponentially due to demand. By the time Dr. John Sperling started the University of Phoenix in 1976, for-profit education was enrolling about 0.2% of all students seeking degrees in higher education (University of Phoenix, n.d.).

According to Arbeit and Horn (2017), the percentage of undergraduates attending for-profit schools more than doubled between 1996 and 2012. In fact, in 4-year institutions, the percentage increased from 1% to 17%. Mirroring a drop in decreased enrollment in postsecondary institutions overall, for-profit school enrollment decreased by 6.8% in 2018 (National Student Clearinghouse Research Center, 2018).

For-profit schools have experienced significant challenges over the past several years. Reports of questionable recruitment practices, high amounts of student debt, inflated statistics on job placements, and false graduation rates led to increased scrutiny and contraction of the sector. An example of a high-profile failure is Corinthian College. Over a 20-year period, Corinthian College dramatically increased its student enrollment. At the time of its collapse, Corinthian boasted over 110,000 students and 100 campuses (Beaver, 2017). Plagued by evidence of questionable practices in recruitment, job placements, and so on, Corinthian's stock dropped from $33 dollars to $.02 in the summer of 2014. The Department of Education suspended the college from the federal student financial aid program. Without this revenue, the college closed shortly after. ITT Technical Institute soon followed, closing its doors in September of 2016 (Beaver, 2017). These high-profile closures have led to increased oversight and regulation of for-profit programs.

In addition to low graduation rates, students attending for-profit schools accumulate high levels of debt (Deming, Goldin, & Katz, 2012). Studies found that students at for-profit schools borrowed at higher rates than students at public and nonprofit schools and defaulted on the loans at a higher rate (Belfield, 2013).

Political opposition to for-profit schools increased during the administration of President Barack Obama. Concerned with complaints of for-profit schools enrolling students with false promises that lead to high amounts of debt and little opportunity for employment, the "gainful employment" rule went into effect in 2015 (Grasgreen, 2015). This rule requires schools to track their graduates' ability to obtain employment in their field and could cut off federal financial aid funding to programs if benchmarks are not met (Grasgreen, 2015). While the gainful employment rule applied to a few programs at nonprofit and public universities, for-profit schools were its target.

Despite the overall challenges in the for-profit sector, for-profit nursing programs are on the rise due in part to the current and predicted nursing shortage. In the report *The Future of Nursing: Focus on Education* (Institute of Medicine, 2010), there is support for a variety of educational models to improve the education system and achieve a more educated workforce. Part of the recommendations include further development of for-profit schools.

LOOK-ALIKES, ACT-ALIKES

There are distinct models of doing business that are more likely found in for-profit schools. Much of the success of for-profit schools is attributable to their ability to serve the working adult market seeking online education. Nonprofit and public schools are increasingly capturing measurable shares of this market. Southern New Hampshire University and Arizona State are two examples of public universities that have scaled their online offerings to impressive levels. Western Governors University is a nonprofit school that was founded as an online university to help satisfy the demands for a college-educated workforce not being met through traditional schools. Purdue University Global and Grand Canyon University are examples of former for-profits that have transitioned to nonprofit status but run at the scale and efficiencies of their for-profit competitors.

Nonprofit and public schools also adopt business models most commonly found in the for-profit sector through the use of online program management (OPM) companies (Hill, 2018). OPMs most commonly provide a bundle of services at little, if any, upfront cost in exchange for long-term contracts where the OPM takes the majority of tuition revenue from the programs they manage. The most common services include marketing, enrollment management, instructional design and technology, and faculty recruitment and salary support. Universities that engage OPMs are able to reach the scale and efficiencies of their for-profit competitors. Two major players in the nursing education space, for example, are Academic Partnerships, Dallas, Texas, and Orbis Education, Carmel, Indiana.

These innovative and disruptive players in higher education provide ample leadership opportunities for senior-level nursing education administrators. If one is intrigued by deaning in the for-profit space, these look-alike, act-alike players should also be considered.

WHAT'S THE SAME?

While there are multiple distinctions between for-profit and nonprofit schools, there are also many similarities. First of all, students are students. Students come to each type of school with the hope of either entering the nursing workforce or advancing their nursing career. The diversity of the overall population of nursing students in terms of gender, race, and age is on the rise at both nonprofit and for-profit schools.

The great equalizers for all types of nursing programs are accreditation and regulatory standards. There are no differences in standards for nonprofit and for-profit programs among the three major nursing programmatic accreditors; they are the Commission on Collegiate Nursing Education (CCNE) associated with the American Association of Colleges of Nursing, the Accreditation Commission for Education in Nursing (ACEN), and the Commission for Nursing Education Accreditation (CNEA), both associated with the National League for

Nursing (NLN). Similarly, state boards of nursing apply the same requirements to all types of nursing education programs in terms of program approval, ability to operate, and criteria for graduates to sit for licensure through the authorization to test.

TRAITS FOR SUCCESSFUL DEANING IN THE FOR-PROFIT SECTOR

Arguably, there is significant duplication in what drives success for deans regardless of the sector of their schools. Business acumen is important for all deans. However, since for-profit schools are often located within large, complex, corporate structures where financial performance is closely monitored and scrutinized, financial business skills are critical for success in the sector. Essential is the desire to manage profit and loss to ensure a net operating profit. Such desire should be accompanied by a tolerance for the pressure that comes with such management.

The for-profit school sector is generally fast-moving with nimble governance structures, so successfully deaning means willingness to change with speed. Due to the competitive nature of the sector and the desire to capture increasing market share, differentiation of programs is essential. Thus, deans should be innovators and internal entrepreneurs (Foley, 2007), highly focused on the student experience and interested in bringing new programs and products to market.

GROWTH AND SCALING

From an operational perspective, programs in the for-profit sector are intended to grow capacity to meet enrollment demand. This differs significantly from many traditional schools that are selective in their enrollment. Many for-profit institutions are termed *open enrollment*, that is, completion of high school or general equivalency diploma (GED) is sufficient for admission. However, this level of open enrollment is rarely found in for-profit nursing schools; rather, a standard is set that may include a particular grade point average (GPA) and a standardized test score. Still, for the most part, the objective would be to enroll all those who meet the minimum standard. For example, a for-profit school would seek to enroll all 100 qualified applicants who applied, whereas a traditional school would more likely have a set capacity and enroll the top 20 most highly qualified applicants.

Part of the dean's challenge is not only to grow his or her programs, which includes adding additional resources to accommodate growth, but also to figure out ways to scale—that is, to add revenue exponentially while only adding incremental resources (Startups.com, 2014). Such a model works well with a post–registered nurse (RN) licensure degree (RN-to-BSN) or with graduate degrees that do not require advanced practice nurse preceptors and clinical sites, which is why these types of programs are common in the for-profit sector. For-profit deans face the same challenges as other deans in securing clinical sites and attracting qualified faculty for classroom and clinical instruction. The pressure for growth can intensify these challenges.

UNDERSTANDING COMPENSATION

Compensation models in the for-profit school sector can differ significantly from traditional academic models. The main difference is that, in all likelihood, a portion of a dean's salary will be *at risk*. That is, there will be a baseline guaranteed salary and then a bonus structure based on individual and/or company performance. Common performance metrics by which bonuses are awarded include a measure of profit, enrollment, persistence, student satisfaction, and licensure/certification exam pass rates.

Depending on the type of for-profit structure, the bonus may contain various components. A direct monetary bonus is most common; usually, this is in the form of a percentage of base salary and maximum allowable that often exceeds the percentage. For example, a monetary bonus may be 20% of base salary and 200% maximum. So, for a base salary of $200,000, a dean may have an additional money bonus of 20% ($40,000) with a maximum of 200%, which is an additional $40,000. Thus, the total monetary salary would be a possible $280,000 with $80,000 of that at risk.

Other financial compensation may come in the form of stock for publicly traded companies or ownership shares for those privately held. These come in multiple forms. While there are differences between stock and private ownership shares, the term *stock* will be used for simplicity. However, note that ownership shares in a private company cannot be sold on the stock market, so they will not be of value unless the company is sold or goes public. Commonly, deans are offered stock options as part of their bonus structure. An option is a stock award that is granted where the awardee has the option of purchasing it at an agreed-upon price (called a strike price), which is below market value (Investopedia.com, n.d.-b). Thus, the awardee can sell the stock at market value prior to its expiration date. These may be on a vesting schedule, as subsequently described.

Increasingly, restricted stock units (RSUs) are offered as additional compensation at publicly traded companies. As the name implies, these stock shares are granted to deans, usually based on performance, and are subject to a vesting schedule (Investopedia.com, n.d.-a). For example, a dean may be given an additional $20,000 in RSUs; however, they cannot be sold until vested. Vesting schedules can vary widely depending on the school. If the $20,000 worth of stock vests equally each year over 4 years, then one quarter of the stock can be sold annually. It is the percentage of stock that vests, so depending on the market performance of the company, that stock may be worth more or less than $5,000 each of those years. If the dean is awarded the same $20,000 in RSUs each year, then incrementally more stock will be available each year to sell. As such, RSUs can provide a powerful incentive to stay with the company.

MEASURES OF SUCCESS

Similar to nonprofits, for-profit school success is measured by persistence, graduation rates, NCLEX® pass rates, and employment. While there is concern for student satisfaction at all types of schools, it is a major focus for schools in the for-profit sector. In the typical for-profit school, the student is explicitly viewed as a customer (Bennett, Lucchesi, & Vedder, 2010). For-profit schools rely almost entirely on student tuition and fees for revenue, and a high level of student satisfaction is thought to result in current students and alumni recommending the school to others (Reichheld & Markey, 2011).

Since enrollment directly drives revenue, volume of students is a significant success measure in the for-profit sector. Historically, the Safe Harbor Act allowed for incentives to recruiters based on the success of securing student enrollment. In October of 2010, as part of a broad set of rules enacted by the U.S. Department of Education, the Safe Harbor Act provisions were removed, prohibiting schools from compensating admissions recruiters for student enrollment numbers (Hamilton, 2010).

MANAGING UP AND TO THE SIDE

For-profit schools come in all sizes, but since a growth mind-set is common in the sector, it is likely that most nursing deans therein will find themselves in large complex organizations. It is common for such complexity to be managed via a matrixed leadership team composed of functional experts in multiple areas, such as admissions, student services, and regulatory and accreditation affairs (Reh, 2018). Deans are often considered one of the functional leaders within a for-profit school with their function being academics. This is in contrast to deans in the traditional sector whose accountabilities may be more comprehensive. The strength of such an approach is that highly skilled leaders are narrowly focused on their areas of expertise. While all functional leaders have the same goal, student success, their focus and priorities are going to differ. A dean must learn to be a leader within an interprofessional team of leaders. This is team-based leadership. To successfully manage, the dean has to be willing and able to influence from the side and to fill gaps in understanding related to nursing and higher education. Conversely, the dean has to be open to the expertise of other leaders and be willing to learn from them.

Similarly, it is common for deans in the for-profit sector to report to a non-academic business leader, with perhaps a dotted line to someone who holds the role of chief academic officer. This can be a strong model but may have challenges if implemented poorly or if either leader is unprepared for such a reporting structure. The key to success is the development of a collaborative partnership. Both the leader and the dean have different perspectives and expertise. For example, a business leader may come out of the manufacturing or hospitality industries, so they will need support in understanding the complexities of a highly regulated industry like higher education. Academic leaders can learn much by looking at nursing education through the lens of these other industries in terms of customer service and user experience. Conversely, deans will likely need assistance in navigating the norms of a corporate environment. The key to managing up is realizing that there will be differences in perceptions, language, and focus. Neither set is right nor wrong. In fact, the combination can be leveraged well to run a highly successful business. It is important to develop a transparent interaccountability for outcomes. It is also important to clarify what accountability the dean has from a regulatory and accreditation perspective so there is no confusion on the part of the business leader. Also, deans need to check their ego if such a reporting structure causes concern, as there is nothing inappropriate or problematic with regard to reporting to someone without an academic background or a doctoral degree.

COMPLIANCE AND SCRUTINY

Higher education is exceedingly regulated at the federal level by both statutes and rules of the U.S. Department of Education, especially in terms of eligibility for federal financial aid. Likewise, each state has complex sets of regulations and rules that govern the conduct of higher education, including the ability to operate within the state. When you add the myriad rules and standards of regional, national, and programmatic accreditors, compliance is one of the most important and complex tasks for deans. While this is true for all deans, internal and external scrutiny of compliance is heightened in the for-profit sector due to widely publicized failures and abuses therein (Cao & Habash, 2018).

It is not uncommon in the for-profit sector to require multiple levels of approval for all manners of public- and student-facing materials, especially those related to recruitment. Such approval safeguards are hallmarks of for-profit schools that operate with integrity. This level of oversight will be unfamiliar to many in nursing academia who may be more accustomed to having a generally looser rein when it comes to word choice, making claims, and the manner in which academic programs are profiled. However, it is important to bear in mind that the purpose of such rigorous oversight is for the protection of students and school reputation.

CONCLUSION

Deaning in the for-profit sector is an exciting career option for academic nursing leaders. A key takeaway for those considering this unique type of deanship is to understand that the dean works at the intersection of two worlds that are inhabited by individuals with different backgrounds, ways of operating, and who use different languages. Deans must navigate both worlds successfully in order to achieve desired outcomes. Achieving such biculturalism is a positive and gratifying aspect of the professional development that comes from this unique type of deaning and can be leveraged for future career growth in nontraditional settings.

REFERENCES

Arbeit, C. A., & Horn, L. (2017). *A profile of the enrollment patterns and demographic characteristics of undergraduates at for-profit institutions. Stats in Brief.* Washington, DC: United States Department of Education.

Beaver, W. (2017). The rise and fall of for-profit higher education. *American Association of University Professors*. Retrieved from https://www.aaup.org/article/rise-and-fall-profit-higher-education#.W6u3b5KWyUk/

Belfield, C. R. (2013). Student loans and repayment rates: The role of for-profit colleges. *Research in Higher Education, 54*(1), 1–29. doi:10.1007/s11162-012-9268-1

Bennett, D. L., Lucchesi, A. R., & Vedder, R. K. (2010). *For-profit higher education: Growth, innovation and regulation.* Washington, DC: Center for College Affordability and Productivity.

Cao, Y., & Habash, T. (2018). *College fraud up 29 percent since August 2017.* Retrieved from https://tcf.org/content/commentary/college-fraud-claims-29-percent-since-august-2017/?agreed=1

Deming, D. J., Goldin, C., & Katz, L. F. (2012). The for-profit postsecondary school sector: Nimble critters or agile predators? *Journal of Economic Perspectives, 26*(1), 139–164. doi:10.1257/jep.26.1.139

Foley, S. (2007). *Entrepreneurs inside: Accelerating business growth with corporate entrepreneurs.* Bloomington, IN: Xlibris.

Grasgreen, A. (2015, July 1). *Obama pushes for-profit colleges to the brink.* Retrieved from https://www.politico.com/story/2015/07/barack-obama-pushes-for-profit-colleges-to-the-brink-119613/

Hamilton, J. (2010, October 28). *Department of Education establishes new student aid rules to protect borrowers and taxpayers.* Retrieved from https://www.ed.gov/news/press-releases/department-education-establsihes-new-student-aid-rules-protect-borrowers-and-tax/

Hill, P. (2018). *Online program management: Spring 2018 view of the market landscape.* Retrieved from https://mfeldstein.com/online-program-management-market-landscape-s2018/

Institute of Medicine. (2010). *The future of nursing: Focus on education.* Retrieved from http://www.nationalacademies.org/hmd/Reports/2010/The-Future-of-Nursing-Leading-Change-Advancing-Health/Report-Brief-Education.aspx/

Investopedia.com. (n.d.-a). *Restricted stock unit - RSU.* Retrieved from https://www.investopedia.com/terms/r/restricted-stock-unit.asp

Investopedia.com. (n.d.-b). *Stock options.* Retrieved from https://www.investopedia.com/terms/s/stockoption.asp

National Student Clearinghouse Research Center. (2018). *Term enrollment estimates.* Retrieved from https://nscresearchcenter.org/wp-content/uploads/CurrentTermEnrollment-Spring2018.pdf/

Reh, F. J. (2018). *Challenges and benefits of matrix management in the workplace.* Retrieved from https://www.thebalancecareers.com/matrix-management-2276122

Reichheld, F., & Markey, R. (2011). *The ultimate question 2.0: How net promoter companies thrive in a customer-driven world.* Boston, MA: Harvard Business Review Press.

Ruch, R. S. (2003). *The rise of the for-profit university.* Baltimore, MD: Johns Hopkins University Press.

Startups.com. (2014). *Growth vs. scaling.* Retrieved from https://www.fundable.com/blog/post/growth-vs-scaling

University of Phoenix. (n.d.). *About University of Phoenix.* Retrieved from https://www.phoenix.edu/about_us/about_university_of_phoenix.html/

INTERIM DEANING

MARIE O'TOOLE

INTRODUCTION

The terms *interim* and *acting dean* both imply a temporary state of leadership. Regardless of the prefix, the most important characteristic for an interim or acting dean is continued leadership during a time that will be characterized by uncertainty. It is a wonderful opportunity to make an important contribution to a school when leadership is critical. Although an interim position is temporary, individuals who have held this position caution colleagues to remember that they are the leader when assuming the interim role. The interim dean of a law school provided this sage advice:

> *It is important to be mindful of the temporary nature of the position, but it is also inevitable, and, I believe valuable and important for both the institution and you, to inhabit the transitory space as though it were permanent, and to find a way to make the deanship your own. (Crocker, 2013)*

This chapter reviews strategies to assist individuals considering the role of interim dean to make good decisions for themselves and their school. The chapter also provides suggestions for those who have accepted the role.

IN THE BEGINNING...

In this era of emails, one with the header "Important Announcement re: Dean" from the president or chancellor often catches faculty and staff by surprise. Regardless of the circumstance—a planned retirement, a return to the faculty, promotion to another position, illness, or the desire for a change in administrative direction—the departure of a dean leaves a void. Successfully stepping into an interim role allows individuals invested in the success of a school to support faculty, students, staff, and alumni to adjust to the inevitable change that accompanies the departure of the dean. Boyle, Chesnut, Hogue, and Zgarrick

(2016) note that there is no such thing as an interim dean. The commitment on behalf of the institution requires the leadership expected of a dean regardless of the length of the appointment. Although the titles of interim or acting dean certainly exist, the obligation to lead as the chief nursing officer is critical.

The circumstances of stepping into the interim or acting role often play a major role in the type of leadership necessary. A planned retirement gives a school the opportunity to search for a replacement, a process that often takes 6 months to a year. Although there will probably be a sense of loss as a former leader transitions to retirement, there is also an opportunity to celebrate the accomplishments of the former dean as they move, often joyfully, to the next phase of their lives. The interim dean in this situation has the opportunity to use the outgoing dean as a resource and mentor. If the interim dean is a candidate for the dean position, the interim position provides the opportunity to explore the role and examine the goodness of fit for the dean position. Prioritizing the needs of faculty, students, and staff and encouraging collective decision-making works well for the short-term interim dean following the retirement of the dean. Often, the effective retiring dean has a succession plan in place, and the interim dean has been prepared for leading the academic unit. If not a candidate for dean, it is an opportunity to appreciate the demands of the role of dean and return to a previous role with a new understanding of a deanship. Many colleagues who have served as interim deans discover they have a talent for the role and go on to deanships at their own or other institutions.

When a dean is returning to the faculty, it can be prompted by either the dean or the individual to whom the dean reports. When the decision to leave the deanship is made by the outgoing dean, the interim dean is usually prepared and the transition requires an orientation to dates, events, and responsibilities. When the individual to whom the dean reports makes the decision, there may be an abrupt departure of the outgoing dean with an "on-the-job" orientation to dates, events, responsibilities, and the addition of crisis management. Providing a steady sense of direction and purpose is always important, but never more so when there is an undercurrent of insecurity. Simmons (2017a, 2017b) describes the temptation to keep a low profile to avoid the perception of exceeding your authority but warns of not neglecting the important leadership and ceremonial responsibilities associated with a dean's role. Interim deans need to recognize that they are the leaders of an academic unit, not simply a caretaker. However, prudent care is crucial. The reputation of a school influences potential applicants, students, alumni, and faculty. It can also be a major factor in the recruitment of the next dean for the school. Quelling destructive rumors and constructively working with the public relations department to reassure communities of interest that the school is moving forward in a productive fashion can yield long-lasting benefits.

The interim dean who is replacing a dean who is dealing with illness or family emergencies faces a unique situation. The beginning of the interim term is known but often sudden, and the outcome and duration of the term is unknown. The vision and direction for the school has been established, and there is an expectation that it will not change, but a care transition is occurring. The interim dean is caring for the legacy of the dean who is on a temporary leave, whereas the dean on leave is attending to care necessary for an appropriate work–life balance. Hopefully, the illness is short term and self-limiting. In some situations, an associate dean will temporarily assume responsibilities for the dean on leave. In fact, many job descriptions for the associate dean include the phrase "acts on behalf of the dean in the dean's absence" or "provides continuity in the absence of the dean." However, not all systems have assistant or associate deans whose role is to act on behalf of the dean. In this case, the void may have to be filled by a faculty member.

When the period of absence by the dean is lengthy, it is unreasonable to expect that an associate dean or other designee can effectively carry out the role of the dean while simultaneously enacting their own role. Bunton, Sass, Sloane, and Grigsby (2018) highlight the importance of succession planning as vital in avoiding a decline in institutional performance in times of transition. The wisdom of having an emergency succession plan in place minimizes challenges for both the interim dean and the dean on leave. In addition, knowing that one's legacy will not be abandoned is undoubtedly a source of comfort to a dean on leave during an already stressful time.

LEADING IN A TIME OF CHANGE

Likewise, a change in administrative direction mandated by the individual to whom the dean reports presents another unique challenge to the interim dean. In this case, succession planning by the outgoing dean may be counterproductive to the administration's desired direction. Assuming the interim role in this situation requires careful examination of one's ability to lead during a period so disruptive to the status quo. Administration, chairs, and faculty within the school of the departing dean may be taken by surprise and experience a profound sense of loss, potentially accompanied by uncertainty as to their own future. Even with a suspicion that "all is not well" between the dean and her or his immediate superior, the departure may be abrupt and the timing a challenge. At times, an ineffective dean vacating the deanship brings a sense of relief. Regardless of the reason for an abrupt change in direction, assuming the role of interim dean in this circumstance requires objective analysis of the situation and acting in the best interest of the school. Without a doubt, the interim dean is leading in this time of change.

More often than not, the abrupt firing or resignation under pressure by a dean results in a sabbatical to re-establish the research and scholarship of the departing dean while a search for a new dean begins. The interim dean is charged with establishing forward momentum for the school. Minimizing negativity is important to avoid speculation and rumors about the future of both the departing dean and the school (Mundt, 2004). At times, the story plays out in the local or school press. In that situation, it is critical to coordinate statements with the public relations department. More often than not, it occurs in the halls of academe, and it is imperative for the interim dean to convey a sense of purpose. The purpose of the best interim dean is to act in the best interest of the school.

CONSIDERING THE FIRST STEP

If you are in the position of being an internal candidate for the position of interim dean, consider yourself fortunate if you are working with a well-established dean who is transitioning to a carefully planned retirement. You will have time to consider your options. You should ponder how the assumption of an interim position would affect your long-term personal goals. You will have the luxury of exploring working conditions to ensure that you are not adding high-profile administrative responsibilities while still maintaining current responsibilities. In short, you have the time to carefully explore an important career opportunity.

However, very often, the appointment to the position of interim dean must be made quickly because of the dean's departure circumstances. The internal candidate will still need to consider options, foremost among which is whether you would like to be considered for the position of dean on a permanent basis. In some schools, assuming the interim dean role eliminates you from consideration in the search for a new dean. In other situations, an interim dean who was closely aligned with the outgoing dean has the opportunity to demonstrate her or his capacity for independence. The person considering the interim role must also keep in mind that making unpopular, though necessary, decisions may undermine the likelihood of selection by the school faculty on the search committee. An internal candidate for interim dean should be familiar with the culture of the school and her or his own long-term goals. Interim deans often go on to permanent deanships at other institutions. They find that the dean role suits them and are uncomfortable with the prospect of returning to a previous position with the new skill set developed as interim dean. Moreover, the experience as an interim dean can make a candidate very appealing to search firms.

On the other hand, Vaillancourt (2018) notes that an interim assignment has the potential to derail a career. If you are not successful in an interim role—even if the circumstances are beyond your control—doubts are raised about your abilities in any leadership position on the campus. Establishing a mutual understanding of responsibilities with the administrators to whom you report is critical to avoid errors and unrealistic expectations that undermine credibility. Consultation with mentors familiar with your career aspirations can be invaluable in avoiding an administrative detour as interim dean that interferes with long-term personal goals.

An interim dean may be an emeritus faculty member asked to step out of retirement. This situation may be appealing to the retired faculty member who still would like to contribute and more firmly establish a personal legacy within the school. Helping a school in a time of need is a powerful motivator for retired faculty. Individuals who have retired must consider Social Security, Medicare, and other retirement benefits, as returning to employment may impact these.

The external interim leader is also an option in education and other nonprofit institutions. It provides an experienced leader as well as consultative expertise that the institution might not otherwise be able to afford (Vincent, 2014). External candidates may also be appealing when change or reorganization is viewed as necessary by the administration or board to whom the interim dean will report. There are a number of firms that provide interim placements for senior administrative positions, including deans. These firms prescreen experienced executives who lead in the interim and may also provide consultative services for the incoming dean when that individual is announced.

Regardless of internal, emeritus, or external status, compensation for the role of interim dean is a factor to consider. Nurse leaders must learn to negotiate a fair and equitable rate of pay for the work they do. An administrative supplement to current salary is a frequent mechanism for internal candidates assuming an interim position. The American Association of Colleges of Nursing (AACN) can provide a customized report with aggregate salary information to inform discussions. Additionally, compensation should not be limited to monetary issues. A consideration of the resources necessary to lead the school efficiently during the interim period should be negotiated before accepting the position. An internal candidate should also consider how existing responsibilities will be managed during the interim period. It is never a good idea to accept two full-time positions and then manage both poorly.

An interim dean assumes a temporary position of leadership. Personal scholarly activities will not be a focus when leading as an interim dean. Before accepting an interim deanship, the candidate should think about her or his own career trajectory when the permanent dean is appointed. A sabbatical or reduced teaching load at the conclusion of the appointment is often a consideration for internal candidates.

A clear understanding of any leadership position is important to ensure harmonious expectations for both the leader and the individuals to whom the leader reports; thus, expectations of the administrative team for the interim dean should also be explored in depth. Deans are the academic leaders of a school, a representative of the school to both internal and external bodies, and a steward of resources. An assessment of one's own strengths, identification of areas where assistance will be needed, and clear communication of expectations during the interim period set the stage for a productive interim assignment.

One interim dean shared this advice: "Establish a concrete timeline for the position and the metrics expected during the interim period" (A. Phalen, personal communication, November 26, 2018), noting a tendency for administrators to become comfortable with an individual who is effective in the role of interim dean. This comfort can delay the hiring of a search firm and/or the permanent appointment of a dean. An interim dean may serve for months or years, but lingering in a temporary position for too long is in the best interest of neither the interim dean nor the institution.

THE FIRST STEP

You decide to accept the position of interim dean and the role of chief nursing officer transfers to you. Some schools differentiate between an interim and acting dean. In a forum hosted by the Chronicle of Higher Education (2014), respondents noted that *acting* is a term used while filling in for the permanent dean for a limited amount of time, while *interim* is the term used for the individual holding the position until a permanent replacement is identified. This is the tradition in many schools, but not all.

Additionally, the individual who is responsible for a nursing program is not always called a dean. It may be a chair, director, or associate dean. Likewise, in some schools, acting or interim deans may not be required to hold academic rank or tenure. However titled, the individual responsible for a nursing unit MUST be a registered nurse with the appropriate academic credentials. The AACN, the National League for Nursing (NLN), and State Boards of Nursing have minimum requirements and different terminology for the leader of a nursing school. For example, the Commission on Collegiate Nursing Education (CCNE) specifies "chief nursing administrator," the Accreditation

Commission for Education in Nursing (ACEN) and the NLN Commission for Nursing Education Accreditation (CNEA) both specify "chief academic nurse administrator," and State Boards of Nursing vary in nomenclature. Regardless of title, one of the first actions of the interim dean must be to notify accrediting agencies of a change in leadership. This notification is known as a *"substantive change"* and alerts accrediting agencies of the individual who should be notified of required administrative actions and meetings designed to support deans. Notification of the communities of interest is also a critical step. Faculty will want to be reassured, students may be concerned about graduation ceremonies and other events, and community partners will want to know that projects will not falter and stop. Individuals who have served as interim deans often note the importance of the avoidance of perception as a caretaker until a permanent dean is appointed. Visibility is important during this period. A posting should be made on the school's website to announce the appointment of the interim dean as soon as possible. The website should be carefully reviewed to ensure that email and phone communications are routed to the interim dean rather than the former dean. Calls to supporters and donors should also be a part of the transition plan. These calls may fall into the realm of responsibility of the University's Office of External Affairs or the Development Office. It is critical to determine who will make these contacts so that individuals who are invested in the school continue to feel valued and appreciated. In-person meetings should be scheduled with faculty and students. This is a time for careful and thoughtful communication. These activities not only ensure good communication in the interim period but also lay the groundwork for the next transition when a new dean is appointed.

    The interim dean should also balance the temporary and the permanent, determining if pending decisions should be deferred until the new dean is appointed. This is particularly difficult if the search for a new dean is not progressing rapidly or the search fails. Some decisions can wait; for example, reviewing and updating the school's mission and vision statements is not the best use of time. On the other hand, faculty reappointments and promotions cannot be deferred. Budgets must be submitted on a timely basis. The interim dean must have the capacity to manage change and determine the nature of decisions as well as manage the timeline for the decisions.

    Unanticipated needs will emerge, partly as a result of the normal day-to-day activities in a school of nursing and partly due to the transition itself. Accountability for decisions related to the accomplishment of the school's established mission and goals is an expectation for any leader. The internal interim dean usually has the knowledge necessary to create a calendar for decision points throughout the year. A transition team or group of trusted advisors from the faculty and administrative staff can also assist in the anticipation of actions needed throughout the year.

In a school where faculty governance is effective, the partnership of the interim dean with the faculty can be exceptionally helpful and lead to meaningful shared decisions. If the departure of the permanent dean created chaos and distrust among the faculty, it is obvious that the interim dean will need to carefully and diplomatically navigate faculty factions. In terms of leadership, a combination of servant leadership, ensuring that the highest priorities of stakeholders are met, and steward leadership, focusing on the management of people and resources available for growth, can be effective (Wilson, 2016). The interim dean fills a void but does not automatically eliminate concerns of faculty regarding change and how change will affect them on a personal level. Recognizing these concerns and proceeding in partnership with faculty is critical to the success of the interim dean.

Experienced colleagues, both within the school and external to it, are sources the interim dean can turn to for assistance as needed. Many states have leadership forums for the chief academic officers of nursing schools to meet and share challenges and their resolutions. The AACN has meetings throughout the year that are of enormous assistance to an interim dean. These meetings provide an opportunity to network with established deans and other individuals in the role of interim dean. A mentor who is an experienced dean is an invaluable asset to the interim dean.

Despite a paucity of research related to the role of interim dean, advice abounds. A consistent theme of this advice is momentum. Do not be a placeholder: Have the energy and commitment to move things forward. Taking the long view in a temporary position mandates moving forward without radical change, but this can be tricky, as avoiding stagnation often requires change. In an academic institution, shared governance with faculty allows for making necessary changes without disrupting forward momentum, and while faculty may challenge your legitimacy for a wide variety of reasons, working with other talented leaders to whom you need to prove your worth will make you a better leader. Remember that although at times you might feel like an imposter, you are the leadership for the school, and despite the temporary nature of the appointment, the interim dean will have a long-term impact. Once you accept the position, own it with pride and enthusiasm.

Keep in mind, however, that unlike a new permanent dean, an interim dean does not get a "honeymoon" period. Thus, although the interim dean is expected to be a decision maker, some decisions are best left to the newly appointed dean who will enjoy a period of time where new directions and administrative structures can be established. The sobriquet "First among equals" carries with it an appropriate reminder of the responsibility of an academic administrator who will facilitate short-term gains with long-term impact and minimize radical disruptions.

THE PHILANTHROPIC CHALLENGE

Faculty and other senior administrators are usually familiar with the internal day-to-day operations of the deans' office, even if they have not been mastered. The biggest challenge for most interim deans is mastery of the philanthropic responsibilities of the dean. Fundraising is an increasingly important role for deans, and this work is often not obvious to others. The interim dean should work closely with the development officers to craft or continue the message that is shared with donors. Donors expect that their investments will have impact. A donor who has established a close personal relationship with the previous dean will need to be reassured that her or his contributions will continue to have impact. Alumni considering a gift will need to be reassured that the interim nature of an appointment is indicative of the stability of a school. It has been noted that outside of academia, the dean is the dean regardless of the interim prefix. It is critically important to maintain personal relationships with donors and alumni as well as to nurture new relationships during the interim period. It is also important to acknowledge donors and appropriately express appreciation for gifts. The role of a dean is to ensure the quality of programs, and this cannot be accomplished in the absence of adequate funding. There can be no period of time where the role of fundraising is neglected. A gap in attention to philanthropy can have a long-term deleterious impact on the fundraising ability of a school.

NEW STEPS ON THE HORIZON

Throughout the period of an interim deanship, it is important to plan for a smooth transition for a newly appointed dean. Maintaining records, establishing a calendar of events, and noting recurring deadlines are all important. Depending on the type of departure by the previous dean, the interim dean may be in a position of creating these documents throughout the year. Consultation with deans internal to the institution can provide a mechanism to anticipate local reports and events; consultation with deans in other schools of nursing can provide a mechanism to anticipate reports required by accrediting agencies and the State Board of Nursing.

MAINTAINING PERSONAL CAREER BALANCE

A former interim dean noted:

> *I accept the notion that being an interim dean is much like being John the Baptist; you prepare the way for the one to come. I just hope that the ultimate fate of the interim dean is not that of John the Baptist. (Boschmann, 2012)*

This quote highlights the importance of planning a smooth transition for one's self. A newly appointed dean may want to reorganize the administrative structure of a school, and that may mean that the position that the interim dean once held will no longer exist. There is no doubt that you will have gained insight into both your own strengths and the role of the dean in an academic institution. This is a time to celebrate your accomplishments and achievements and reflect on your next career steps. There is no reason to anticipate a grisly outcome like that of John the Baptist. An effective interim dean will have many career options.

THE LAST STEP: STEPPING IN A NEW WAY ON THE STAIRCASE

It can be exhilarating to serve as an interim dean. Once you have settled into the role, it may be time to relinquish it to the permanent dean. There is often a sense of relief that this transitional period in your career is over. Academia is structured in a hierarchical fashion, and the leadership associated with the interim role will be relinquished. It is the time to make the next transition as easy as possible for the permanent dean. If the interim dean becomes the permanent dean, there is still a transition.

Although the admonition throughout this chapter has been to avoid being tentative, the temporary nature of the interim deanship is always a factor. If the interim dean is selected as the permanent dean, she or he will have in-depth knowledge of the opportunities for the school and can quickly seize those opportunities. If you are appointed as the new dean, waste no time in establishing priorities for the school and reflect on the lessons learned in the interim role. Ensure that your appointment is announced and shared in all the appropriate venues. Do not simply slip into the role of dean; jump into it with the confidence that you have no doubt developed in your time as interim dean.

The interim dean returning to a previous role will have a deep appreciation of the challenges of the dean's role. The unique insights gleaned during an interim period should be shared with the incoming leader and reflected upon by you. Sharing the workflow with the permanent dean is a mechanism for the interim dean to recognize accomplishments, relinquish tasks with grace, and experience a sense of relief. It is helpful to provide official reports and communications for reference, but do not have the expectation that they will be reviewed in detail.

For the internal interim dean, your role in the new administration may be different than the role you had prior to assuming the interim deanship. Your role will be vastly different from the role of interim dean. Remain an involved and committed colleague. Recognize that the new leader should have the opportunity to lead in the way that is most comfortable for her or him and beneficial to the school. Be available to provide information and/or council as requested—without interference—and move to the background. Your relationships with senior administrators will change, and your daily agenda will no longer be populated with meetings. At times, your relationship with fellow faculty members will change now that you are no longer the interim dean. You have an opportunity to refresh your professional identity and move to the next phase of your career. This is an appropriate time to carefully consider your own career timeline. Using the analogy of steps, you are now coming down the staircase that you carefully considered climbing. However, it is best to think of each stage in your career as a launchpad. As you have stepped up to the responsibilities associated with the role of interim dean, you now step up to other opportunities.

If you are interested in becoming a dean on a permanent basis, register with search firms specializing in higher education and upload your curriculum vitae to their websites. Your curriculum vitae should highlight your new skills in strategic leadership, philanthropic expertise, and academic leadership. Network with new colleagues in the dean's group who will be aware of upcoming retirements and vacancies.

During your period as interim dean, other senior administrators have had the opportunity to observe your leadership. These individuals can be enormously helpful as you plan the next steps in your career. Letters of reference from those with first-hand knowledge of your skills will be of enormous value as you explore other leadership opportunities both in and outside of your current school.

The interim dean coerced out of retirement will return to retirement. Like the internal interim dean, this individual can serve as an invaluable resource to the incoming dean. Some schools offer office space to emeritus faculty, a privilege that would be appropriate for someone who served in an interim dean role. The bylaws of an institution are usually very specific about the roles and privileges permitted for faculty who have retired.

The external interim dean may go on to another institution to fill the critical role of interim dean. Some firms placing interim administrators encourage the incoming dean to rely on the interim dean for consultation.

CONCLUSION

Without exception, individuals who have assumed the role of interim dean share that it is an amazing opportunity to learn, explore a role critical to the success of a nursing school, and experience personal transformation. Although there are many nuances associated with the role of interim dean, learning or refining leadership skills associated with maintaining stability while moving will be useful in any position.

REFERENCES

Boschmann, E. (2012, March 01). Rent-a-Dean. Retrieved from https://www.chronicle.com/article/Rent-a-Dean/130957

Boyle, C. J., Chesnut, R., Hogue, M. D., & Zgarrick, D. P. (2016). The influence of interim deans: More than keeping the ship afloat and warming the captain's seat. *American Journal of Pharmaceutical Education, 80*(7), 112. doi:10.5688/ajpe807112

Bunton, S. A., Sass, P., Sloane, R.A., &Grigsby, R.K. (2018). Characteristics of interim deans at U.S. medical schools: Implications for institutions and individuals. *Academic Medicine, 93*(2), 241–245. doi:10.1097/ACM.0000000000001920. PubMed PMID: 28906262.

Chronicle Forum. (2014, April). Interim vs. acting [web forum comment]. Retrieved from https://www.chronicle.com/forums/index.php?topic=161859.0;imode

Crocker, P. L. (2013). The paradox of being an interim dean: The permanent nature of a transitory position. *University of Toledo Law Review, 43*(2), 319–326.

Mundt, M. H. (2004). Leading in a time of change: Assuming interim academic administrator positions. *Journal of Nursing Education, 43*(11), 496–501.

Simmons, E. (2017a). Ad interim: Practice. *Inside Higher Ed*. Retrieved from https://www.insidehighered.com/advice/2017/08/31/how-be-effective-acting-director-chair-or-dean-part-i-essay

Simmons, E. (2017b). Ad interim: Performance. *Inside Higher Ed*. Retrieved from https://www.insidehighered.com/advice/2017/09/07/how-be-effective-acting-director-chair-or-dean-part-ii-essay

Vaillancourt, A. M. (2018). Are you sure you want that interim job? *The Chronicle of Higher Education*. Retrieved fromhttps://www.chronicle.com/article/Are-You-Sure-You-Want-That/243408

Vincent, M. (2014). 4 levels of transitional leadership. *The Organizational Development Muse*. Retrieved from https://www.designgroupinternational.com/theorganizationaldevelopmentmuse/4-levels-of-transitional-leadership

Wilson, K. R. (2016). *Steward leadership in the non-profit organization*. Downers Grove, IL: IVP Academic.

STEPPING UP FROM DEANING/DIRECTING

JOANNE P. ROBINSON

INTRODUCTION

You are the new dean of a well-established school of nursing at a leading university, and it is your dream come true! It is a busy and exhilarating time, and you are enjoying the honeymoon period that is typically bestowed on newly appointed deans. Although it is probably the furthest thing from your mind, it is not too early to begin thinking about the when, why, and how you plan to step up from the deanship into the next phase of your career journey.

This chapter first covers the uniqueness of the nursing dean/director role, what it takes to succeed, and hazards to side step as your leadership journey unfolds. Frameworks for understanding and navigating normative and cataclysmic role transitions are presented next. The chapter concludes with a section on best practices for transitioning out of the nursing dean/director role in both normative and cataclysmic contexts.

UNIQUENESS OF THE NURSING DEAN/DIRECTOR ROLE

Nursing deans and directors are a unique breed of academic leaders. Fundamental expectations include excellent command of the complex systems of higher education and healthcare, as well as political savvy, connections, and exquisite interpersonal skills for building relationships with a wide variety of external stakeholders (Bouws, 2017). Creativity and fortitude are also essential for navigating today's nursing education challenges, including nationwide shortages of nurses and nursing faculty; funding cutbacks; ongoing tension between nursing education and practice; and finally, demands for new ways of teaching, greater use of educational technology, and better integration of information science into nursing curricula (Adams & O'Neil, 2008; Bouws, 2017).

For many nursing deans and directors, the singular lure of the role is the opportunity to advance the discipline and influence professional nursing practice (Bouws, 2017; Giddens & Morton, 2018). Yet the average tenure of nursing deans and directors is 5 to 7 years, and high vacancy rates prevail. Poor preparation for the responsibilities associated with the dean/director position is thought to account for early burnout, lack of job satisfaction, role ambiguity, and role stress (Bouws, 2017). In addition, evidence suggests that organizational culture exerts a strong influence on job satisfaction and intent to stay among nursing deans and directors. Specifically, personal and family policies and workplace collegiality affect job satisfaction, whereas institutional leadership, approach to governance, and departmental engagement affect both job satisfaction and intent to stay (Emory, Lee, Miller, Kippenbrock, & Rosen, 2017). It should be noted that all of these factors are modifiable in the interest of smoother transitions to the role of nursing dean/director and longer terms of office.

WHAT IT TAKES TO SUCCEED

It is clear that the nursing dean/director role is not for the faint of heart. In fact, courage in all of its forms—physical, moral, and personal—is at the heart of what it takes to succeed as a nursing dean/director. Schwartz (2013) defines courage as "a willingness to pursue a noble goal or purpose despite risk, danger, or fear" (p. 8). For the nursing dean/director, the noble goal is advancement of the profession. High stakes decisions, such as admission criteria, student dismissal, program closure, budget cuts, promotion, and tenure, require physical courage to either charge ahead or endure; moral courage to either take a stand or let it go and forgive; and personal courage to either be true to yourself or submit to change (Schwartz, 2013). Hannah et al. would argue that a "courageous mindset" evolves over time in nursing deans and directors with positive dispositions (i.e., upbeat, resilient, confident) in the context of positive social forces (e.g., mentorship, training) and repeated exposure to situations that trigger courageous action (Hannah, Sweeney, & Lester, 2007).

Beyond a courageous mind-set, experts suggest that nursing leaders in all settings, including higher education, should be equipped with core competencies in four interrelated dimensions of leadership: *purpose*, the vision to lead; *people*, the passion to work with and through others; *process*, the skill to manage change; and *personal*, the self-knowledge to thrive (Adams, 2008). Similar to courage and clinical practice, core competencies in each of these areas are honed over time in the context of mentorship, continued professional development, and experience in the role.

HAZARDS OF LEADERSHIP IN HIGHER EDUCATION

Higher education is a strange beast. Although industry leaders always have their eyes on the future, they run institutions that are steeped in tradition. Most are passionate about innovation, free expression, collaboration, diversity, and inclusion, but they nurture cultures in which formality and hierarchy are de rigueur, credentials are prized, asking for help is a sign of weakness, and risk-taking is dangerous (Sanaghan & Lohndorf, 2018). Appointment or promotion to a leadership position in higher education is often based more on intellect rather than evidence of emotional intelligence, which sets the stage for four toxic leadership dynamics that prevail in higher education: *derailment*, *seduction of the leader*, *arrogant leadership*, and *micromanagement* (Sanaghan, Mrig, & Fusch, 2018). Hallmarks of each are described in Table 6.1.

These self-destructive behavior patterns are fodder for reflection and correction in your own leadership. If observed in others, especially your supervisors, be aware that these behaviors can jeopardize your effectiveness, tenure, and legacy as a nursing dean or director.

Higher education is also a slow-moving beast that clings to time-honored traditions and protocols. As a rule, change is a deliberative process that is

TABLE 6.1 Hallmarks of Toxic Leadership

Derailment	Overreliance on a sponsor or mentor; arrogant; lacks integrity; overuses strengths; poor team building; fails to meet long-term goals
Seduction of the leader	Poor accessibility; allows sycophants, gatekeepers, great expectations, ego, or a combination of these to block information, honest feedback, and ideas for change
Arrogant leadership	Late for meetings; does not ask questions; uses condescending gestures; interrupts others; talks too much and listens too little; does not apologize for inappropriate behaviors
Micromanagement	Reliance on operational versus executive skill set; fears negative outcomes and being uninformed; uses "my way or the highway" approach; distrusts judgment of others; thrives on a sense of urgency

SOURCE: Sanaghan, P., & Lohndorf, J. (2018). *How higher-ed leaders derail: A survival guide for leaders*. Denver, CO: Academic Impressions.

undertaken with a healthy measure of caution and planning. Borwick (2013) distinguishes between evolutionary and revolutionary change. Evolutionary change is a team sport that involves conversation, multiple iterations, broad participation, and ultimate persuasion. In contrast, revolutionary change involves "a high-pressure mandate from above" (p. 1). Although evolutionary change is the usual modus operandi in higher education, Borwick (2013) notes that revolutionary change is fairly common in response to a change in leadership or a crisis. As a nursing dean or director, you are an executive leader and officer of your institution. At the same time, you are most likely an "at will" employee, who serves at the pleasure—and disposal—of your immediate supervisor. Be aware that few protections exist for even high-performing nursing deans and directors who are removed without warning by a new supervisor with "a different vision," dismissed suddenly by a desperate sitting supervisor in the face of an actual or perceived crisis, or ousted by any number of other unsavory or unwarranted circumstances.

PROFESSIONAL ROLE TRANSITIONS: NORMATIVE AND CATACLYSMIC

Most leaders have a fairly well-developed exit strategy when they first assume a leadership role, or at least start to think about their exit at the point of entry. Even so, if and when to move on from a leadership role has been described as every leader's most difficult decision (Martin, 2005b). The decision to move on triggers a role transition that is lengthy for most leaders, including nursing deans and directors. Meleis (2016) suggests that the process of "undeaning" is typically long, with a course that is influenced by the circumstances prompting the change in role. Whatever the circumstances, Meleis (2016) proposes that the "undeaning" process always entails "stepping up" (vs. "stepping down" or "stepping aside") on the career ladder "to a higher place in our lives, taking with us what we learned in the previous ladder rung" (p. 187). Like all role transitions, the undeaning process ends for the exiting nursing dean/director when the following benchmarks are achieved: (a) emergence and adoption of new roles and sets of interactions; (b) achievement of a sense of stability; and (c) easy movement between pre- and posttransition roles and actions (Meleis, 2016).

Donnelly (2017) distinguishes between normative and cataclysmic professional role transitions. Normative transitions are voluntary, planned role changes such as the pursuit of retirement, promotion, relocation, or reassignment. In contrast, cataclysmic transitions are involuntary and unplanned and arise from disruptive situations such as unresolved conflict, unexpected illness, sudden dismissal, or organizational shutdown. In her memoir, Donnelly (2017) describes cataclysmic role transitions in her own professional life that "shook to the core my beliefs about career, people, organizations, and the nursing profession" but "also strengthened my resolve, honed my skills, and provided new insights and learnings" (p. 223).

Regardless of the circumstances, a healthy, productive professional role transition is always the ultimate goal (Meleis, 2016). In the case of a normative transition from a nursing dean/director role, the goal is a graceful exit that focuses on maintaining the school's momentum; participating in celebrations of the accomplishments of the exiting dean/director and leadership team; orienting the incoming dean so that she or he can hit the ground running; and preparing external constituents for the change in leadership (Meleis, 2016). In contrast, a cataclysmic transition from a nursing dean/director role demands an immediate shift in focus from caring for the organization to caring for self. The primary goal for the exiting dean/director must be to detach and either rebuild or retire in the interest of posttraumatic growth (Justice, 2018). Posttraumatic growth or *benefit-finding* refers to positive psychological change that occurs in response to adversity and triggers progression to a higher level of functioning (i.e., thriving) rather than merely a return to baseline (i.e., resilience) ("Posttraumatic Growth," 2018).

In the context of a cataclysmic transition from a nursing dean/director role, Martin (2005a) suggests that posttraumatic growth is realized when the individual finds another "psychological success job" that stretches competence, yields career satisfaction, sustains career involvement, and leads to the conclusion that the benefits of the role transition exceed the losses. In some cases, the "psychological success job" may consist of retirement from the workforce to pursue opportunities and roles that have been postponed for a lifetime.

BEST PRACTICES FOR STEPPING UP FROM DEANING/DIRECTING

Best practices for stepping up from a nursing dean/director role differ relative to the context of the transition. In normative contexts, Meleis (2016) describes five nonlinear, overlapping phases of the undeaning process: the decision to step up; the search for a new dean; the naming of the new dean; the exit; and reclaiming professional voice. Leadership and tangible contributions from the exiting dean are expected during each phase. In cataclysmic contexts, the exiting dean is typically excluded from any involvement in the undeaning process described by Meleis (2016); even the exit scenario and parameters for reclaiming professional voice within the organization are often dictated. Instead, the undeaning process in cataclysmic contexts has been likened to Kubler-Ross's Stages of Death and Dying (Justice, 2018; Martin, 2005a). Best practices for stepping up from a nursing dean/director role in both normative and cataclysmic contexts are discussed in the next sections.

Best Practices in Normative Professional Role Transitions

Each phase of normative "undeaning" entails best practices that have been articulated by Meleis (2016). In addition, several former nursing deans/directors have proposed best practices in the specific normative "undeaning" contexts of retirement (Hart, 2005), relocation (Clarke, 2005), promotion (Anderson, 2005), and pursuit of unfulfilled aspirations in teaching and/or scholarship (Edwardson, 2005). All of these perspectives are reflected in the following discussion of best practices for nursing deans/directors as they navigate each phase of Meleis's undeaning process.

Phase 1: Deciding to Step Up

In all normative contexts, the decision to step up involves substantial personal reflection, assessment of organizational readiness for change, and strategic communication of the decision. Best practices for personal reflection include stepping into a dean/director role with a tentative plan for stepping up; considering your needs and aspirations for personal growth and nursing leadership, whether there is organizational support for these, and whether you are able to express your vision in your current role and/or organization; recognizing internal signals of your readiness for change; listing pros and cons of stepping up; involving family and significant others in decision-making; and remaining open and flexible within defined parameters to options for life after deaning/directing but preparing a response to the question that will be asked by everyone: What is next for you? (Clarke, 2005; Edwardson, 2005; Hart, 2005; Meleis, 2016). Additional reflection in the context of stepping up to a promotion should focus on your success as a dean/director; the attractiveness of higher level positions; your desired destination; and necessary preparation for your targeted role(s) (e.g., requesting broader assignments; professional development programs such as those sponsored by the American Council on Education, the American Association of Colleges of Nursing, and the National League for Nursing) (Anderson, 2005).

Best practices for assessing organizational readiness for change essentially involve analyzing the status of your organization's strategic plan and deciding whether you have accomplished all that you can in the organization, that is, whether continuing to lead would be a productive versus head-banging experience (Edwardson, 2005; Hart, 2005; Meleis, 2016).

Strategic communication of the decision to step up requires careful planning and execution (Meleis, 2016). Institutional norms for stepping up should first be clarified, followed by confidential conversations with your supervisor and other organization officials as appropriate to discuss the decision and negotiate terms (e.g., effective date, new role, salary, perks). Confidential conversations with your leadership team should occur next, always in the context of a confident and optimistic view concerning organizational changes that lie ahead. The decision phase culminates with the official announcement of your plan to step up, which should be subject to your input and authorization in terms of its content, mode, timing, and flow (Meleis, 2016). For example, the experience of some former nursing deans/directors suggests that the official announcement of a dean's or director's decision to step up is best made at the end of the academic year so that faculty members have the time and space to process the decision, its impact, and their personal response (Hart, 2005).

Phase 2: Searching for a New Dean

In most schools of nursing, the search for a new dean/director does not involve the exiting dean. However, Meleis (2016) identifies a number of general best practices for exiting deans/directors during the search phase of the undeaning process. These include transparent and timely communication; designating an administrative point person to support the search process; encouraging and providing time and space for reflection and dialogue among faculty and staff; maintaining organizational momentum with a focus on completing unfinished business; preparing an exit/welcome letter for the new dean/director that outlines the state of the school; and ongoing efforts to mitigate stressors imposed on faculty and staff by imminent organizational change.

Phase 3: Naming of a New Dean

Likewise, the naming of a new dean/director is typically a hands-off activity for the exiting leader. However, Meleis (2016) again identifies general best practices for exiting deans/directors as the organizational transition to new leadership unfolds. These include celebrating the choice; allaying the anxiety of faculty and staff concerning leadership changes; beginning to orient the new dean/director; establishing a clear framework for decision-making (i.e., exiting dean/director vs. new dean/director vs. both) during the transition period; recruiting a transition team; and facilitating transparent interaction by faculty and staff with the new dean/director.

Phase 4: Exiting

During the exit phase, the long-awaited change in leadership becomes real and should be guided by a structured action plan that is developed and executed jointly by the exiting and entering dean/director (Meleis, 2016). The plan should have clear timelines and cover all aspects of onboarding, including designation and preparation of office space and other amenities (e.g., parking) for both parties; organization of records and files; computer and software setup; selection and appointment of administrative support personnel; and transfer of calendar and budgetary information and responsibilities (Hart, 2005; Meleis, 2016). Joint decision-making and regular interaction between the exiting and entering dean/director should be established, and boundaries should be negotiated for the duration of the transition and thereafter. The welcome letter prepared earlier by the exiting dean/director should be sent, and celebrations to honor the exiting dean/director and welcome the new leader should not be missed (Meleis, 2016).

In the case of retirement, the exiting nursing dean/director should be aware that she or he is most likely stepping up from a high profile, extremely demanding, and intense executive leadership position. To ease the sudden transition to a "free" schedule, a well-developed retirement plan is encouraged that incorporates both personal and professional goals and activities, including some that begin immediately following the exit phase (Hart, 2005; Meleis, 2016). Savoring connections with family and friends, cultivating new connections and opportunities, and the newfound freedoms associated with "having your life back" eventually become replacements for the power, prestige, and day-to-day collegial relationships that were once enjoyed as a nursing dean/director (Hart, 2005).

Phase 5: Reclaiming Professional Voice

This final phase of the undeaning process necessitates constructing an integrated identity that incorporates the experience of deaning/directing, as well as actively exploring new opportunities in which the integrated identity can be expressed (Meleis, 2016). Typically, former nursing deans/directors reclaim their professional voice as academics, consultants, administrators, and retired volunteers and activists. According to Meleis (2016), the work of building an integrated identity is paramount and involves identifying goals and roles for the new professional voice; becoming invisible and inaccessible within the organization except to honor requests for consultation by the new dean/director; and generating a daily or weekly schedule around short-term goals that require immediate action, which helps to fill the void of an empty calendar during the initial postexit period. An additional best practice during this period involves hitting the "pause" button frequently to think, reflect, and listen to your inner voice and to significant others, which should be valued as a vital and productive investment of time. Continuous engagement in the revision of behaviors, skills, and goals is also recommended, with a constant eye toward tangible, new learning opportunities that can be accessed (Meleis, 2016).

In the context of a transition to retirement, Hart (2005) emphasizes the importance of building professional goals and activities into a comprehensive postretirement plan. As retirement affords the luxury of choice, selecting goals and activities of personal interest and importance is recommended. Examples include part-time teaching, active participation in professional organizations, serving as a reviewer of grants and/or scholarly papers, and serving as a formal and/or informal mentor.

In the context of transition to a professorial role, Edwardson (2005) emphasizes the importance of dedicating a negotiated sabbatical to the work of renewal and "retooling." According to Edwardson (2005), best practices for retooling in preparation for a teacher/scholar role involve *tuning up* in the interest of integrating the deaning/directing experience into your new role and catching up on professorial issues, trends, skills, and strategies; *tuning in* to the reality of the "we/they" divide between faculty and administration and planning strategies that will facilitate your move from "they" to "we"; and *tuning out* administrative matters but remaining available for consultation with the new dean/director when requested.

Best Practices in Cataclysmic Professional Role Transitions

If your leadership journey takes you to the dark side of deaning/directing—involuntary role transition—it is important to recognize that sudden job loss typically triggers a grief reaction (Justice, 2018; Martin, 2005a). As a nursing dean/director, your focus has no doubt been on caring for the organization and living by the mantra, "It's not about me." At this point, however, understand that self-care is paramount, and best practices should focus on your recovery and the work of reclaiming your professional voice.

Indeed, the negative impact of involuntary transition from a dean/director position is well documented, and best practices for mitigating risk factors and supporting affected parties have been proposed. However, few best practices have been described for the individual who is stepping up from a dean/director role under cataclysmic circumstances.

For example, Martin (2005a) highlights the "downward spiral of bitterness and career withdrawal" (p. 233) that dismissed deans and directors often experience and goes on to emphasize a variety of best practices for adoption by professional organizations and dean/director colleagues. These include outreach, continued connection and support, offers of part-time employment and professional references, information about job opportunities, and preventive education about risk factors and warning signs of involuntary termination for both aspiring and sitting deans.

Justice (2018) offers one of the few—or perhaps only—published personal account of involuntary transition from a deanship that includes practical, albeit terse, advice for navigating the process. A former humanities dean, Justice's emotional trajectory following sudden notification of his dismissal involved numbness and fear for the first 48 hours, followed by shame, rage, and anxiety about his family's financial future. A mixed bag of emotions ensued thereafter, which was dominated by lingering rage comingled with bemusement. Commencement of the search process for a new dean triggered renewed anger and disappointment, which intensified at the outset of each phase of the search. Justice (2018) credits the distraction and perspective provided by a life-threatening health crisis with the engagement and feelings of success that he now experiences in the professorial role at his institution. The following advice is offered to others who face involuntary transition from a dean/director role: Invest in a good therapist, allow time to run its course, detach, and rebuild.

My own experience with the misfortune of cataclysmic role transition from a deanship qualifies me to offer additional guidance for navigating the process. In my case, the request for my resignation was unexpected, undeserved, political, and vicious. As founding dean of the school, the experience was painful, insulting, and infuriating, which I liken to being on the receiving end of a sucker punch:

> *A punch made without warning or while the recipient is distracted, allowing no time for preparation or defense on the part of the recipient...The term is generally used in situations where the way in which the punch has been delivered is considered unfair or unethical, and is done using deception or distraction.* ("Sucker punch," n.d.)

Following a sabbatical year dedicated to self-care, renewal, and redirection, I am poised to reclaim my professional voice in a new administrative position that promises to be ideal for my skill set, values, and vision for the advancement of nursing and healthcare. Based on personal reflection, reading, and shared wisdom from family, friends, colleagues, and mentors, I am pleased to offer several important "lessons learned" during my journey back from the dark side of deaning/directing:

- *Keep your head and hold your tongue if your resignation is ever requested.* A cool head will maximize your dignity, credibility, and negotiating power.

- *Keep a detailed, objective log of the transition process that starts with when you are asked or told to vacate your post.* If possible, conduct all conversation/business pertaining to your transition by email so that you have a ready-made record of interactions and can launder emotional or otherwise inappropriate messages on your part prior to sending them.

- *Consult a labor attorney, particularly if wrongdoing against you is evident or suspected.* Protecting your rights and reputation is always wise, and exposing breaches in organizational policy and/or practice serves the best interest of those who come after you. Keep in mind that seeking legal consultation will yield personal satisfaction that you have explored all options available to you, as well as expert guidance and/or assistance with negotiation if you decide that this meets your needs. The larger-than-life prospect of suing the university is a last resort that neither the attorney nor you will likely be anxious to pursue; however, a variety of other plausible and appealing legal options may be available for exposing wrongdoing and recovering damage to your reputation and finances.

- *Consult past and present deans/directors in your institution about the norms for role transition with an emphasis on perks.* Your goal is to uncover policies and past precedents to guide your own negotiation strategy.

- *Negotiate the content, mode, timing, and flow of your exit message and adhere to the terms of the agreement.* Push for the right to craft, or at least approve, the exit message. For example, you may prefer that the message links your departure to a desire to return to research and/or teaching. Aim for an authentic and transparent message that you can reduce to a 20- to 30-second sound bite as needed.

- *Negotiate perks associated with your transition* (e.g., new role, salary and benefits, sabbatical, funding for research/scholarship). At all costs, push for a sabbatical to recover, refresh, and provide time to explore your next career move.

- *Take care of your organization.* If you are able and inclined, offer to provide selected operational information to the interim leader at her or his discretion. Refrain from responding to gossip or feeding those on fishing expeditions for "gory details." Restrict candid conversations to no more than one or two trusted insiders who have always been reliable keepers of confidential information.

- *Take care of yourself.* You will likely be living with subclinical anger, recurrent dreams, uncertainty, worry, curiosity calls/emails, an abundance of well wishes, and self-doubt. Be intentional about building diversion into your life such as time with family and friends, regular exercise/sports, reading for pleasure, hobbies, and mini vacations. Pamper yourself without guilt and enjoy your freedom; you will likely realize how drained and tired you actually are! At all costs, release any feelings of shame or guilt about your leadership and recognize the culpability of your supervisor and/or others in this temporary setback in your career journey.

- *Keep busy.* Be intentional about nurturing your scholarly and spiritual/existential sides with reflection, writing, and systematic inquiry. Your usual area(s) of interest/expertise, your leadership journey, and your experience with transition from a leadership role are good places to start. In addition, use some energy to accept invitations to participate in scholarly, professional, and community activities that appeal to you, including leadership opportunities that you previously had to forego due to the time constraints of deaning/directing.

- *Seek and accept support.* Decide to trust at least one colleague or friend as your "go-to" confidant with the expectation that the selected party(s) will signal you if the burden becomes excessive or if they lose the capacity or desire to be a vault; a good therapist is also an option (Justice, 2018). Let your gut be your guide as you detach from the organization, its members, and selected professional associations and activities in the interest of self-care; however, be certain to replace what you decide to cut off. Consider the following advice from a very wise and generous nursing leader and mentor: "Leadership is a journey… Along the way, leaders fall down and leaders get up, but leaders do not have to get up alone" (J. Brewington, personal communication, July 13, 2017).

- *Meet with your financial advisor.* If you do not have one, now is the time to get one to obtain a clear picture of your short- and long-term financial status. This will reduce the uncertainty of your situation and help you to figure out options and goals for your next career move.

- *Reboot and rebuild.* Decision points include where, what, when, and how to reboot and rebuild your career within the parameters of your skill set, values, and vision for yourself and nursing. Now is the time to think broadly and boldly about your options and to consider a range of possible goals, roles, settings, and responsibilities for the next phase of your career journey. Keep in mind that job interviews are a two-way street in terms of assessing your fit in a particular role and setting. Do not settle for less than your heart's desire and what you are worth.

Former deans are highly desirable prospects for interim deanships, deanships in new settings, associate deanships, and even higher level administrative positions such as provost, vice president, and president.

- *Interview with candor.* If you decide to seek employment in a new setting, be honest and matter-of-fact about the circumstances of your departure, but refrain from focusing on ugly details or personalities. Being cast aside by new leadership or by jealousy is unfortunately so common today that few consider it a deal breaker for future employment, provided that the candidate is honest during the interview process.
- *Thank all who help you early and often.* Personalized tokens of your appreciation with a hand-written note will always be well received.

CONCLUSION

Leading as a nursing dean/director is a golden opportunity to advance the discipline of nursing and delivery of healthcare. Stepping up from a nursing dean/director role is a difficult decision and lengthy process, whether under normal or cataclysmic circumstances. Although it might seem counterintuitive, best practice is to think about the end of your dean/director role from the beginning and develop a tentative, appealing, and exciting plan for your next career move, including retirement. Frameworks for the processes of normative and cataclysmic "undeaning" are useful to understand in advance and to consider when the time comes, as are best practices for navigating each phase of the transition from the nursing dean/director role. Anyone who serves as a nursing dean or director deserves no less than safe, healthy, and productive passage to the next destination in her or his career journey.

RESOURCES

Clarke, P. N., & Dreher, M. (2017). Transitions and transformations in nursing leadership. *Nursing Science Quarterly, 30*(1), 34–37. doi:10.1177/0894318416680532

Justice, G. (2018, March 25). I was a dean and now I'm not. *The Chronicle of Higher Education.* Retrieved from https://www.chronicle.com/article/I-Was-a-DeanNow-I'm/-242865

McDaniel, T. R. (2015, September 17). The on-going life of one retired dean and professor. *Faculty Focus.* Retrieved from https://www.facultyfocus.com/articles/teaching-careers/the-on-going-life-of-one-retired-dean-and-professor/

Pardun, C. J. (2013, October 1). Why I am dropping out of administration. *The Chronicle of Higher Education.* Retrieved from https://www.chronicle.com/article/Why-I-Am-Dropping-Out-of/142027

Sandvich, C. M. (n.d.). How to find an employment lawyer. *wikiHow to do anything…* Retrieved from https://www.wikihow.com/Find-an-Employment-Lawyer

REFERENCES

Adams, L. T. (2008). Nursing leadership. In L. T. Adams & E. H. O'Neil (Eds.), *Nurse executive: The four principles of management* (pp. 15–20). New York, NY: Springer Publishing Company.

Adams, L. T., & O'Neil, E. H. (2008). Current issues in the education industry. In L. T. Adams & E. H. O'Neil (Eds.), *Nurse executive: The four principles of management* (pp. 89–91). New York, NY: Springer Publishing Company.

Anderson, C. A. (2005). Career progression: Moving beyond the deanship. In *Academic leadership in nursing: Making the journey* (pp. 225–230). Washington, DC: American Association of Colleges of Nursing.

Borwick, J. (2013, June 5). Revolutionary vs. evolutionary organizational change. *HEIT Management.* Retrieved from http://www.heitmanagment.com/blog/2013/06/revolutionary-vs-evolutionary-organizational-change/

Bouws, M. (2017). The nursing dean role: An integrative review. *Nursing Education Perspectives, 39*(2), 80–84. doi:10.1097/01.NEP.0000000000000277

Clarke, P. N. (2005). Career planning and role transition. In *Academic leadership in nursing: Making the journey* (pp. 213–223). Washington, DC: American Association of Colleges of Nursing.

Donnelly, G. F. (2017). Normative and cataclysmic career transitions: A nurse's memoir. *Nursing Administration Quarterly, 41*(3), 223–232. doi:10.1097/NAQ.0000000000000232

Edwardson, S. R. (2005). Returning to the faculty. In *Academic leadership in nursing: Making the journey* (pp. 207–212). Washington, DC: American Association of Colleges of Nursing.

Emory, J., Lee, P., Miller, M. T., Kippenbrock, T., & Rosen, C. (2017). Academic nursing administrators' workplace satisfaction and intent to stay. *Nursing Outlook, 65*(1), 77–83. doi:10.1016/j.outlook.2016.07.003

Giddens, J., & Morton, P. (2018). Pearls of wisdom for chief academic nursing leaders. *Journal of Professional Nursing, 34*(2), 75–81. doi:10.1016/j.profnurs.2017.10.002

Hannah, S., Sweeney, P., & Lester, P. (2007). Toward a courageous mindset: The subjective act and experience of courage. *Journal of Positive Psychology, 2*(2), 129–135. doi:10.1080/17439760701228854

Hart, A. L. (2005). Retirement: The promise of a different life. In *Academic leadership in nursing: Making the journey* (pp. 199–206). Washington, DC: American Association of Colleges of Nursing.

Justice, G. (2018, April 23). What it felt like to lose my deanship. *Chronicle Vitae*. Retrieved from https://chroniclevitae.com/news/2040-what-it-felt-like-to-lose-my-deanship?cid=VTEVPMSED1

Martin, E. J. (2005a). Involuntary termination: Peril of the deanship. In *Academic leadership in nursing: Making the journey* (pp. 231–239). Washington, DC: American Association of Colleges of Nursing.

Martin, E. J. (2005b). Moving on: Introduction. In *Academic leadership in nursing: Making the journey* (pp. 197–198). Washington, DC: American Association of Colleges of Nursing.

Meleis, A. I. (2016). The undeaning transition: Toward becoming a former dean. *Nursing Outlook, 64*(2), 186–196. doi:10.1016/j.outlook.2015.11.013

Posttraumatic Growth. (2018). In *Wikipedia*. Retrieved from https://en.wikipedia.org/w/index.php?title=Posttraumatic_growth&oldid=845858681

Sanaghan, P., & Lohndorf, J. (2018). *How higher-ed leaders derail: A survival guide for leaders*. Denver, CO: Academic Impressions.

Sanaghan, P., Mrig, A., & Fusch, D. (2018). The peril of smartship. In P. Sanaghan & J. Lohndorf, *How higher-ed leaders derail: A survival guide for leaders* (pp. 1–8). Denver, CO: Academic Impressions.

Schwartz, A. J. (2013, February). Searching for courage: Exploring the idea of a courageous mindset. *Widener University Oskin Leadership Institute*. Retrieved from http://www.widener.edu/about/widener_values/leadership/oskin_leadership/about/OLI_CourageWP_13.pdf

Sucker punch. (n.d.). Retrieved from Wikipedia, https://en.wikipedia.org/wiki/Sucker_punch

GENERAL RESPONSIBILITIES OF NURSING DEANS AND DIRECTORS

ENROLLMENT MANAGEMENT

LINDA D. SCOTT | JULIE J. ZERWIC

INTRODUCTION

Enrollment management is a predetermined plan to recruit, enroll, and successfully graduate a group of students. An enrollment management plan contains goals about the type of students desired, including the number, quality, and other characteristics such as percentage of in-state versus out-of-state students. The enrollment management plan also contains information about the resources that are needed to support the students admitted (faculty and staff, physical, financial), the length of time that they will be in the program and when they will graduate, and the revenue that they will generate. A well-developed and communicated enrollment management plan is critical to ensure that a college has the resources needed to manage current and future students.

Before a plan is developed, it is important to identify the variables to consider when creating an enrollment management strategy. In Table 7.1, please rate each variable by order of importance to your institution.

Enrollment management provides a comprehensive approach that requires deans to understand the entire cycle, which includes the pipeline, recruitment strategies, admission, cost of attendance, financial support, retention, graduation, and NCLEX®/certification success rate. The concept of enrollment/strategic enrollment management originated in the 1970s (Hossler & Bontrager, 2015). It was a factor of a competitive environment at a time of a predicted declining pool of traditional college students. Enrollment management was seen as a strategy that integrated academic advising, admissions, financial aid, and orientation into a comprehensive approach that allowed administration greater control over factors that shaped their student enrollment. Nursing programs have been slow to adopt enrollment management planning as an important strategy, likely due to

TABLE 7.1 Higher Education Enrollment Management Strategy Exercise

VARIABLE	LOW 1	2	3	4	HIGH 5	NA
University's mission, vision, and goals	Low 1	2	3	4	High 5	NA
College's mission, vision, and goals	Low 1	2	3	4	High 5	NA
Student recruitment and retention	Low 1	2	3	4	High 5	NA
Student demographics	Low 1	2	3	4	High 5	NA
Financial aid	Low 1	2	3	4	High 5	NA
Market demand	Low 1	2	3	4	High 5	NA
Tuition revenue	Low 1	2	3	4	High 5	NA
Graduation rate	Low 1	2	3	4	High 5	NA
Faculty: student ratio	Low 1	2	3	4	High 5	NA
Clinical placement availability	Low 1	2	3	4	High 5	NA
Classroom/simulation/lab capacity	Low 1	2	3	4	High 5	NA
Faculty availability and qualifications	Low 1	2	3	4	High 5	NA
Level of student	Low 1	2	3	4	High 5	NA
Type of course delivery	Low 1	2	3	4	High 5	NA

a continuing large pool of applicants or minimal involvement in the enrollment management process at the college or university level. However, financial pressures, lack of diversity in the nursing profession, and faculty shortages require savvy deans to advocate for involvement in strategic planning for admissions and to develop and implement enrollment management in their programs.

COST OF NURSING EDUCATION

Prelicensure and graduate nursing degrees are programs that are typically costlier than other university degrees. This is due to multiple factors including the cost of expensive equipment such as simulation labs, the low faculty-to-student ratios required by boards of nursing and accrediting bodies, as well as faculty salaries. Many institutions allow nursing programs to set higher tuition levels than other academic programs using supplemental tuition or course fees. This higher tuition is then routed directly to the college to support the higher costs.

It is critical that the dean and the leadership team understand the budget model that governs their nursing program. The budget must directly factor into decisions around increasing or decreasing enrollment. If an institution has a historical budget model, the dean will need to negotiate an increased budget before enrolling additional students, otherwise the college will be left managing the increased number of students without a change in revenue to support hiring additional staff or faculty. Responsibility Center Management, commonly referred to as the RCM budget model, requires the college to be wholly responsible for the management of revenue and expense. If student enrollment increases and generates additional tuition revenue, the revenue to the school also increases; and if enrollment/tuition revenue decreases, so does the allocation to the college. Deans can therefore increase their budgets by increasing student enrollment, increasing tuition revenue through tuition increases, generating other revenue streams, or reducing expenses. If the college is considering a tuition increase, the budget officer should explore the tuition charged by other competitors. This information will help to determine if enrollment will suffer because the institution is priced higher than the market will bear. If enrollment decreases because the program is now priced higher than competitors, the program may actually have a reduction in tuition generated rather than the goal of increased revenue.

There are often competing pressures in enrollment management in nursing that are not understood by the rest of the campus. There is tension between the number of qualified applicants and the number of individuals admitted to the nursing major. According to the American Association of Colleges of Nursing (AACN), more than 56,000 qualified applicants to generic prelicensure nursing programs were denied admission in 2017–2018 due to capacity issues (i.e., insufficient faculty and/or preceptors, clinical sites, classroom space) and budgetary constraints (American Association Colleges of Nursing [AACN], 2018). Although this reflects an improvement from 2011 when admission denials exceeded 75,000, it continues to be a challenge for current administrators of nursing programs (Kenner & Pressler, 2012) because nursing is projected to remain among the top occupations of job growth through 2024 (Bureau of Labor

Statistics, 2015) and the demand for admission into nursing programs consistently remains high. Nevertheless, campus administrators, legislators, and parents may not understand why a nursing program has a limit on the number of students admitted. If students are initially admitted to a prenursing major and unsuccessful in being admitted to the nursing major, there needs to be alternative desirable majors if the student is to remain on the campus. This puts pressure on other colleges to provide degree options to help facilitate timely graduation, especially for universities that have time-to-degree as a performance metric.

CAPACITY TO INCREASE ENROLLMENT

There are a number of factors that should be considered in determining the appropriate enrollment for your nursing program. These include competitive forces, the pipeline of interested individuals, and resources available to the program. The enrollment management plan must be based on an understanding of the capacity to maintain or increase enrollment given the local situation. In addition, it is important to bring your faculty and staff into the conversation very early so that you have buy-in about the direction of your strategic enrollment plan.

External competitors can influence your enrollment plan. Knowing what your competitors offer in terms of resources (physical, financial, and academic) can help you identify any pressure points that might impact your strategic plan to manage your enrollment. If you lack adequate simulation/learning lab space, you may find it increasingly challenging to recruit applicants. Potential applicants may want to tour the learning environment prior to making decisions about where they will apply. Knowing what other nursing programs in your area, as well as other competitors in your region, charge for tuition is very important; this includes fees as well as living expenses. *Cost of attendance* is a standard term that reflects tuition, fees, books, transportation, and housing for each institution. You may be able to justify a higher tuition cost, but you will want to be able to articulate the added benefits that students achieve at your institution.

The quality outcomes of your program will also determine how successful you will be in recruiting and retaining students. Applicants and their families are savvy consumers and will have researched your institution's pass rate for the NCLEX exam. If you are below the national average, or below the average of your competitors, you will find it increasingly challenging to recruit students. In addition, your ability to retain and successfully graduate the students that you admit can have a significant impact on your enrollment management plan as well as resources. It is much less expensive to spend resources to keep the students you have than to have students exit your program prior to graduation. The tuition income that is lost from students who exit early can have a substantial negative impact on your budget.

It will be important to determine whether you admit students directly from high school into your program as freshman or if you admit them at a later point, such as juniors. There are many highly qualified students who will only apply to colleges that have direct admit as a freshman. There are several benefits to admitting as a freshman. The first is that you are able to start socializing and interacting with students from their first days on your campus. Secondly, if your budget model is based on the number of students who are in your major, then you may receive some or all of the tuition (based on the type of budget model in place) that these students generate from their first semester. The disadvantage to freshman admits is that you are not able to determine how well they will do in their prerequisite courses. Students may struggle in their initial courses and not be able to progress to their nursing courses. This can complicate your prediction of the number of students that will actually end up in your clinical courses, resulting in very uneven numbers over the cohorts as well as open seats that cannot be filled even in a situation of high demand for admission. Providing admission of students in their junior year allows you the opportunity to accept students who have already shown they can be successful in college courses and allows you to tightly control the number of students who will matriculate into the nursing courses. In addition, you may see more diversity in your class if you admit students later since many racial and ethnic minorities, low income, and first-generation students start course work at a community college and transfer after completing their prerequisites. However, you have lost the tuition these students generate over their first 2 years taking college courses. The important takeaway from this discussion is that the greater the handle that you have on the budget model in your institution, the better you will understand the impact different decisions will have on your revenue.

Resources will impact your enrollment. These include classroom, lab, and clinical space, as well as availability of faculty. Changing enrollment in the nursing program will impact other courses at the university so a change should be planned in advance with all university partners. If a prerequisite course is already full, then an additional eight nursing students may strain the system beyond capacity.

Nursing courses are often scheduled on a limited number of days in a week. This means that classrooms are tightly scheduled on certain days and may not be used at all on days when students are typically in clinical. This requires that the registrar and/or classroom scheduler understand the complexities of scheduling nursing courses, and the need for flexibility in course scheduling, especially if a block course scheduling system is used. Adding additional students may require a change in the venue where classes are held, so consulting with the registrar in advance is critical. Likewise, it is important to know room capacity because there may not be physical space available within the school or across campus.

Determining which courses will be impacted by a change in enrollment is important. A theory course may be able to absorb a decrease or increase with little impact in strategy or resources. However, adding students may require that additional faculty be hired to teach clinical courses. The boards of nursing and accrediting bodies often identify the maximum number of students that can be accommodated in a clinical course. Typically, increases in enrollment are done in groups that correspond to a clinical group size. For example, if your ratio of faculty to students in clinical is 1:8, then you will want to increase enrollment by a group of 8 to maximize efficient use of your resources. For some institutions, you may want to increase enrollment in groups of 16 depending on how you assign faculty to courses.

The ability to accommodate additional students in existing laboratory space as well as clinical settings will also need to be determined. You may want to map out whether your simulation lab can accommodate additional students or whether you will need to add additional lab times in nonpeak hours. Similarly, conversations with your clinical partners are essential to make sure that they are prepared for the additional students as well.

The availability of qualified faculty is extremely important when determining the type of programs offered as well as the number of students in the programs. Boards of Higher Education, as well as most Boards of Nursing, specify that faculty must have a degree higher than the level they are teaching or the terminal degree in their field. For example, if someone is teaching baccalaureate students, they must have at least a master's degree. If they are teaching in a doctor of nursing practice (DNP) program, they must have either a DNP or PhD. As programs transition advanced practice programs to the DNP, it is critical to ensure sufficient faculty that are also doctorally prepared. In addition, you need to confirm that you have faculty with the experience and the credentials to teach the content of specialty courses. Accrediting organizations will examine faculty credentials to ensure that there is a match between faculty expertise and courses taught. It will continue to be challenging to recruit and retain doctorally prepared faculty given the insufficient numbers of doctorally prepared faculty being produced (AACN, 2017a). Your current faculty qualifications, as well as your ability to recruit faculty with the needed credentials, are important considerations as you make enrollment decisions.

Likewise, the delivery method, pedagogy, and timing can impact your enrollment management strategy. For example, class size enrollment decisions for effective teaching and learning will vary based on the type of course (didactic, clinical, lab, seminar), level (undergraduate, graduate), delivery mechanism (in-person, online), offering (required, elective), or semester (academic year, summer). Equally important is that the decisions you make can affect the timely progression of students, the quality of teaching–learning practices, students' overall experience, and your financial bottom line.

BEST PRACTICES IN ENROLLMENT MANAGEMENT

Recommended Best Practice #1

Despite the use of strategic enrollment management frameworks in higher education for more than four decades (Hossler & Bontrager, 2015; Hossler & Hoezee, 2001), their use in nursing has been limited, yet critical. Administrators of nursing programs must take an active role in creating strategic enrollment plans across their degree programs to meet their mission, vision, and goals, anticipate change, and manage resources effectively. With best practices in mind, deans must become knowledgeable about theory-based frameworks to engage in strategic enrollment discussions and to guide enrollment decisions. Deans who do not directly control enrollment management can have an impact through regular conversations with those campus administrators who do make these decisions.

Recommended Best Practice #2

Combining strategic enrollment management with educational frameworks can also inform class size determinations. Taft, Perkowski, and Martin (2011) recommend three dominant educational frameworks as useful in determining online class sizes: the objectivist–constructivist continuum (amount of interaction), community of inquiry (COI) model (amount of faculty, student, and social presence), and Bloom's taxonomy (levels of learning). Depending on the amount of required interaction, presence, and levels of learning, Taft et al. recommend the following number of students per faculty member to ensure quality of education in online classes:

> *Small*: less than or equal to 15 students when using constructivist (all interactive) teaching strategies, full implementation of COI principles, and higher levels of learning

Medium: less than or equal to 16 to 30 students when combining middle levels of all three educational frameworks

Large: greater than or equal to 30 students when using objectivist (all one-way interaction) teaching strategies, full implementation of COI principles, and lower levels of learning in Bloom's taxonomy

Recommended Best Practice #3

Increasingly, the nursing profession has been challenged about the lack of diversity among nurses in practice settings (AACN, 2017b). This has trickled down to nursing programs, which are now being scrutinized about the strategies they are using to graduate individuals who mirror the society in terms of race, ethnicity, religion, geographic locations, socioeconomic backgrounds, sexual minorities, and many other characteristics. Strategic enrollment management principles can facilitate building a pipeline of individuals who choose to pursue nursing as a career as well as principles to admit a diverse class or students. A holistic admissions strategy within a strategic enrollment management plan can be used to increase diversity in the students that are admitted (DeWitty, 2018; Glazer et al., 2016; Scott & Zerwic, 2015). Holistic admissions require those involved in admission decisions to value an applicant's experiences and attributes in addition to academic metrics (Witzburg & Sondheimer, 2013). This creates a balance that recognizes that qualified applicants can bring a background to nursing that is as important as having a perfect grade point average. Institutions that utilize holistic admissions have found positive outcomes including a more diverse class, successful retention and graduation rates, and positive outcomes for the entire class, such as an enriched learning environment with exposure to different perspectives (Zerwic, Scott, McCreary, & Corte, 2018). A holistic admission process that values experiences and attributes along with academic metrics may help to reduce applicants' multiple attempts at repeating successfully completed courses or standardized exams in order to raise grades, GPA, or test scores. Holistic admissions allow applicants to demonstrate through a variety of different means their strengths as an applicant beyond a focus on academic metrics.

CONCLUSION

Enrollment management is an important strategy for deans to use to achieve financial stability, manage either increasing or decreasing enrollment, and create a class that enhances the diversity of the nursing profession. Enrollment management includes the entire process, from developing the pipeline to graduating students who successfully pass the NCLEX certification exam. The enrollment plan should be developed with your leadership team and university officials and then communicated and shared with faculty, staff, and clinical partners. This will ensure that your institution is able to survive and thrive in an increasingly competitive environment.

RESOURCES

EMS. 5 Strategies for Increased Community College Nursing Program Enrollment. Retrieved from https://www.simulationiq.com/blog/content/5-strategies-increased-community-college-nursing-program-enrollment

Hassmiller, S. B., & Reinhard, S. C. Nursing Education and the Decade of Change: Strategies to Meet America's Health Needs. Retrieved from https://campaignforaction.org/wp-content/uploads/2017/12/NursingEducationDecadeOfChange-H508.pdf

Nursing CAS. The Centralized Application Service for Nursing Programs. Developing a Recruitment Plan & Strategy. Retrieved from https://www.nursingcas.org/wp-content/uploads/2016/01/developing_a_recruitment_plan_and_strategy_worksheet.pdf

REFERENCES

American Association Colleges of Nursing. (2017a). Nursing faculty shortage fact sheet. Retrieved from https://www.aacnnursing.org/Portals/42/News/Factsheets/Faculty-Shortage-Factsheet-2017.pdf

American Association Colleges of Nursing. (2017b). Enhancing diversity in the nursing workforce fact sheet. Retrieved from https://www.aacnnursing.org/Portals/42/News/Factsheets/Enhancing-Diversity-Factsheet-2017.pdf

American Association Colleges of Nursing. (2018). *2017-2018 Enrollment and Graduations in Baccalaureate and Graduate Programs in Nursing.* Washington, DC: Author.

Bureau of Labor Statistics. (2015). Occupational projections to 2024. Retrieved from https://www.bls.gov/opub/mlr/2015/article/occupational-employment-projections-to-2024.htm

DeWitty, V. (2018). Holistic review in admissions: A strategy to diversify the nursing workforce. *Journal of Nursing Education, 57,* 195–196.

Glazer, G., Clark, A., Bankston, K., Danek, J., Fair, M., & Michaels, J. (2016). Holistic admissions in nursing: We can do this. *Journal of Professional Nursing, 32,* 306–313. doi:10.1016/j.profnurs.2016.01.001

Hossler, D., Bontrager, B. (2015). *Handbook of strategic enrollment management.* San Francisco: Jossey-Bass.

Hossler, D., & Hoezee, L. (2001). Conceptual and theoretical thinking about enrollment management. In J. Black (Ed.), *Strategic enrollment management revolution*. Washington, DC: AACRAO.

Kenner, C. A., & Pressler, J. L. (2012). Deans' concerns about turning away qualified applicants. *Nurse Educator, 37*(5), 183–184. doi:10.1097/NNE.0b013e318262ebd5

Scott, L., & Zerwic, J. J. (2015). Holistic review in admissions: A strategy to diversify the nursing workforce. *Nursing Outlook, 63*(4), 488–495. doi:10.1016/j.outlook.2015.01.001

Taft, S. H., Perkowski, T., & Martin, L. S. (2011). A framework for evaluating class size in online education. *The Quarterly Review of Distance Education, 12,* 181–197.

Witzburg, R. A., & Sondheimer, H. M. (2013). Holistic review: Shaping the medical profession one applicant at a time. *New England Journal of Medicine, 368,* 1565–1567. doi:0.1056/NEJMp1300411

Zerwic, J. J., Scott, L., McCreary, L., & Corte, C. (2018). Programmatic evaluation of holistic admissions: The impact on students. *Journal of Nursing Education, 57*(7), 416–421. doi:10.3928/01484834-20180618-06

STUDENT SUCCESS

JANA L. PRESSLER | CAROLE KENNER

INTRODUCTION

Deans/directors need to realize that their success is highly dependent on the success of students in their school/college/department. First and foremost, for a dean/director to be successful, students enrolling in all of the school/college/department's nursing programs must succeed in graduating. Programs and deans are evaluated on "time to graduation" and student retention. Passing courses is the first hurdle; finishing entire programs and graduating are the next hurdles. Graduates must then be successful in passing licensure and/or certification exams. It cannot be overemphasized that the administrative and academic success of a dean/director is manifested through her or his students. This chapter describes approaches for fostering academic success among nursing students.

ADMISSION AND ENROLLMENT

It is critical that only qualified applicants be accepted into nursing programs. Some schools are lenient with admission criteria and end up having students drop out or fail out of programs because the level of difficulty is more than the students can handle. In many settings, applications for entry level nursing programs are abundant, so there tends to be more qualified applicants than available space. It makes for smoother course progression if, for example, entry level students who are admitted have a 3.0 or higher cumulative grade point average (GPA). The science GPA should also be examined, as this metric indicates that the student has foundational science knowledge that undergirds nursing courses.

Use of holistic admissions is a helpful tool to increase diversity; it also takes into account the fact that some students are not "good standardized test takers."

Admission criteria based solely on the Scholastic Assessment Test (SAT) or American College Testing (ACT) tests do not always reflect the capability of a student in an applied profession such as nursing. See Chapter 7, Enrollment Management, for more information on holistic admissions.

STUDY HABITS

Before a nursing student officially enrolls in any nursing courses for credit, she or he needs to have developed an array of study habits that work. Having a well-defined study schedule helps students to budget their time and efforts. Formulas have been devised for determining the number of hours a college student must allow for studying per week based on the number of credits for which they are enrolled. Not unlike financial budgets, students need to stay within the study time schedule and use the time allotted to their best advantage.

Sometimes students look at the number of credit hours allocated to a college course and expect to allow time for reading about 50 pages per credit per week. The student then adds up the number of pages she or he expects to read each week and totals that as their scheduled study hours. Another popular formula suggests that for each college credit, students should plan to study 3 hours per week to learn the material.

Students might want to plan for extra time to review their class notes, as well as notes from their readings, to help them understand content presented in class and to be able to sit back and think about how the content fits in with the course in the long term. For example, if students are enrolled in a health assessment course and are studying the anatomy and physiology of the ear, they might want to think about how important the sense of hearing is to a person throughout her or his lifetime to gain insight into the importance of protecting hearing acuity.

For some students, using commercial study and test materials throughout a curriculum reinforces the need to set up study schedules. These materials encourage students to keep up their reviews and to determine how well they grasp the content on an ongoing basis. Some programs require these learning materials as part of the course requirements. In either situation, the student learns how to review material and to use their extent of understanding about specific topics to shape their study strategy.

TIME MANAGEMENT

Time is a resource that each student must allocate wisely. It is very important that students go back to their planned study schedule and determine when, where, and for how long at any one time they will study each week. Some students will want to study for a couple of hours, take a 10-minute break to collect their thoughts, and then study for another hour or two. To be able to have sufficient time to get everything done definitely requires the student to be competent at managing her or his time.

Some students will be cognizant that the wisest use of their time is to allocate daytime hours for studying, whereas others will think that they are more productive at studying in the evening. Students will have a pretty reliable idea about when they feel they are the most receptive to reading and understanding course materials. Students might be able to read while on public transportation if they live a long distance from the school/college/department where they are enrolled. For others, reading while in motion or commuting might not work at all.

Having a plan for managing one's time only works if one adheres to it. If students adhere to their study schedules, they can pace themselves and be able to see their progress as well as the anticipated end goal. Not leaving all of the reading and reviewing until the day before a scheduled exam will give students time to process information and generate questions they might still have about content that was presented. If students are disciplined and maintain ongoing lists of questions that come up when reading course content, they will feel more prepared to ask questions about the content either in class or at review sessions.

TEST-TAKING STRATEGIES

To be successful in college coursework, students must be competent at taking quizzes, tests, and final exams. Because licensure and certification exams primarily comprise objective, multiple-choice questions, students must know how to read a test question and determine which of the possible responses is/are correct. At times students will be asked questions and prompted to "select all that apply," meaning that there is a good possibility of more than one correct response. Selecting the correct response(s) is not always easy because competent test item writers are generally also proficient at coming up with plausible wrong answers or distracters. Students might find themselves reviewing their test responses and going back to change an answer(s) because a distracter(s) seems like it "might" be more correct. Our experience suggests that students often provide their best response the first time they answer a test question and thus should be discouraged from going back and changing their answer at a later point during the exam.

When taking a quiz, test, or final exam, students must pace themselves and not spend too much time on questions about which they are unsure. In some nursing programs, there is a time limit established for each test question, for example, 1.3 to 1.5 minutes per question. If students spend too much time on early exam questions, they might not have enough time to finish the entire test. The National Council Licensure Examination for Registered Nurses (NCLEX-RN®) allows approximately 1.3 minutes per exam item. Many programs throughout the country try to be consistent with this time allocation for nursing students' exams in order to prepare them for the NCLEX-RN.

Most tests will contain some difficult questions. Difficult questions help to differentiate students with "better" mastery of the material from those whose mastery is "average" or "below average." Most nursing schools/colleges/departments have test banks to collect and store test questions so that a variety of items based on level of difficulty can be included on exams. Test bank questions must be reviewed periodically, given the frequency of changes in treatment modalities and other aspects of healthcare delivery. Test banks can, unfortunately, influence the decision keep obsolete textbooks and other course materials. Students become dissatisfied quickly if what they see in the clinical setting is different from what appears in their textbooks and on their tests. In these situations, test scores will drop.

Teaching/learning strategies, such as the flipped classroom and unfolding case study, help students to develop clinical reasoning/critical thinking skills and thus enhance student success. These strategies can also be used in testing situations to a degree. For example, answering essay questions relative to a case study requires students to develop compelling responses to questions. Teaching students to create a bulleted outline of what they want to say prior to responding to an essay question helps to ensure that the answer is relevant and on point. Unfolding case studies are particularly well suited to essay exams.

APPOINTMENTS WITH ADVISERS

Even though students and faculty have busy schedules, it is highly advisable for students to schedule and keep regular appointments with their advisers. Students should be encouraged to meet with their advisers once per semester or once per quarter. Students can review their plan of study with their adviser, make course plans for subsequent semesters, and access additional resources if the need is anticipated. At times, obtaining an additional workbook or reference can be worthwhile. Other times, it is helpful to develop a "plan B" in case the student finds one or more courses more challenging than anticipated and a slower pace of progression is desired.

Advisers can help struggling students to weigh their options and determine the best method for securing additional resources (e.g., a tutor). If advisers are faculty members, they may also be able to help struggling students by reviewing tests, suggesting study strategies, and reviewing content. When the student is truly able to problem-solve with her or his adviser, she or he is more likely to be successful in getting additional needed resources.

Students should also meet with advisers to review their career or clinical specialty choices. Advisers can be highly knowledgeable about career options and offer valuable suggestions to students. Advisers are also a frequent source for letters of reference, which tend to be most authentic and compelling when genuine familiarity with the student is evident. This is particularly important when an adviser is asked to write a letter of reference for a student aiming to pursue graduate study.

In the absence of a professional advisement staff, deans/directors should encourage and incentivize faculty to be strong advisers. How? Advisers can be allocated credit for advising activity that is included in course loads and/or toward service in reappointment, promotion, and tenure reviews. Deans/directors should also ensure that faculty advisers are encouraged to share what is working or not working with the current advisement model that the institution uses. If students are not regularly coming to meet with their advisers, the dean/director should meet with student leaders to find out why. Advisement is crucial to student success. It is also a method for identifying gaps between the curriculum, student learning, and faculty performance.

Psychological factors greatly impact academic performance no matter where students are enrolled; examples include self-perception, motivation, self-regulated learning, and anxiety (Fong, Davis, Kim, Marriott, & Kim, 2017). These factors can be addressed by faculty advisers and teaching faculty. Students tend to build resilience or "grit" when some of these psychological factors are addressed (Duckworth, 2016). Developing "grit" helps the student to power through difficult situations by learning strategies for success, including use of institutional resources as outlined in the next section.

INSTITUTIONAL RESOURCES

Academic Success Coaches

Some schools/colleges/departments have an academic success coach on staff to assist students. This staff member might report to a variety of program directors and meet with students in small groups. An academic success coach might or might not be a registered nurse. A coach's main responsibility is to monitor student progression to ensure that students are on track with their plans of study.

Academic success coaches are experts at following the academic trajectories of students. They help to anticipate when students will graduate and project numbers of open spaces for new students based on numbers of students graduating.

Academic success coaches are familiar with resources, such as the best review books for the Graduate Record Exam (GRE); user-friendly online tutorials for anatomy and physiology; and developing goal statements for admission to a graduate school. If they are registered nurses and/or hold a graduate degree in a nursing specialty, they are probably also familiar with a variety of review courses to prepare for licensure and certification exams.

Tutors

Tutors are typically needed by nursing students for core courses, such as pathophysiology and pharmacology. Students can use tutors in core nursing courses as well, particularly if they are not grasping central concepts. Tutors might be used to answer questions that students have from their readings or to help explain how organ or body systems function. Tutors also might provide additional case examples to help place a concept into a more understandable context.

Sometimes, tutors are called upon to provide review sessions prior to a unit test or final exam. Students might be comfortable asking questions of a tutor that they would be embarrassed to pose to a course faculty member. Tutors might look at the content covered in a given unit and identify in a brief period of time the key or critical knowledge to be gleaned. For many students, confidence is knowing that a tutor is available to answer "11th hour" questions before quizzes and tests.

Writing centers have knowledgeable individuals who can assist students who have trouble developing a scholarly/scientific paper. These resources may be online and offer advice about formatting and grammar. Writing centers are especially helpful to students who are not native English speakers.

Navigating Online Platforms

With more colleges/universities/programs offering hybrid and fully online courses, students must become familiar and comfortable using online platforms to access course content, submit assignments, and take exams. Many recent high school graduates have been exposed to or used learning management systems, such as Blackboard, Desire to Learn (D2L), and Canvas. If not, students should consider taking a workshop at a local community college to become literate in using these products. Many times, students are enrolled at a distance and take an entire course online using a university-supported learning management system. For students to be successful in this venue, they need to know how to use the system's drop box, post comments on a discussion board, and access course content in the system. Use of short tutorial videos or screen shots illustrating certain aspects of the system can be very helpful. Students for whom English is a second language (ESL) sometimes express difficulty with online courses because they rely on facial expressions to understand some verbiage and phrases. ESL students might need extra assistance from course faculty. Deans/directors should consider how to offer help to ESL students as well as to students who have never used a learning management system.

Readiness and Preparing for the NCLEX-RN

Lippincott Pass Point® (Philadelphia, PA, Wolters Kluwer), Health Education Systems, Inc. (HESI)® (St. Louis, MO, Elsevier), and Assessment Technology Institute (ATI)® (Leawood, KS, ATI) are examples of tests that can be used to evaluate the readiness of students to take the NCLEX-RN. These readiness tests evaluate essential nursing knowledge and skills and are usually administered at strategic points during and upon completion of an undergraduate nursing program. Specific recommendations for remediation are offered as indicated. Some programs substitute the "free practice exam questions" from NCLEX-RN to assess readiness for testing.

There are also NCLEX-RN review books and flash cards available for students to purchase. Some programs offer the virtual NCLEX-RN coach and/or live reviews. Such resources have been shown to produce NCLEX-RN pass rates of 97% to 98%, which is highly desirable for any undergraduate nursing program. Health Education Systems, Inc., overseen by Elsevier, has produced a software-based practice exam called the HESI A2®. This is another example of an integrated test that provides students with more structured testing to evaluate their readiness for the NCLEX-RN.

Employment Following Graduation

The Commission on Collegiate Nursing Education (CCNE) requires that nursing programs show at least a 70% employment rate of graduates 1 year following completion of a CCNE-accredited nursing program. Thus, it is important that students have a job-seeking plan prior to graduation. The dean/director must track the employment data of their graduates for accreditation reports. If the graduates' employment rate falls below 70%, the dean/director should poll clinical agencies affiliated with the nursing program to determine what might be done differently to make graduates more attractive in the marketplace. We hold career and job fairs where graduating students and prospective employers can meet. We also hold mock interviews with senior students. At the end of the interview, we give feedback to the student regarding strategies to strengthen their interviewing skills. Some institutions now have career centers that can also assist students with interviewing skills, connect students with potential employers, and survey graduates and employers 1 year after graduation. These data help the dean/director to identify areas of strength and opportunities for improvement.

CONCLUSION

Student success drives dean/director success—and vice versa. Many factors interact to ensure nursing student success in any given nursing program. The dean/director must pay close attention to student progression and well-being to ensure that nursing students get access to the resources they need to progress in the curriculum, graduate, and prosper in our profession.

RESOURCES

Dear Loved Ones of Nursing Students: What It Feels Like Going Through Nursing School: https://www.nrsng.com/dear-loved-ones-nursing-students-feels-like-going-nursing-school/?gclid=EAIaIQobChMIi_XylOWk3wIVE4_ICh2UtgGYEAAYASAAEgJzyfD_BwE

Lippincott Nursing Student Success Resources: http://nursingeducation.lww.com/student/lp/newslettersignup.html?pid=&audience=students&agency=morevis&gclid=EAIaIQobChMIi_XylOWk3wIVE4_ICh2UtgGYEAAYAiAAEgLwNPD_BwE

3 Websites Every Nursing Student Should Bookmark: https://onlinenursepractitionerprograms.com/2017/3-web-sites-every-nursing-student-should-bookmark/

REFERENCES

Duckworth, A. (2016). *Grit: The power of passion and perseverance.* New York, NY: Charles Scribner's Sons.

Fong, C. J., Davis, C. W., Kim, Y. W., Marriott, L., & Kim, S-Y. (2017). Psychosocial factors and community college student success: A meta-analytic investigation. *Review of Educational Research, 87*(2), 388–424. doi:10.3102/0034654316653479

RECRUITMENT AND RETENTION OF QUALIFIED FACULTY AND STAFF

CAROLE KENNER | JANA L. PRESSLER

INTRODUCTION

Recruitment of talented, high-caliber faculty and staff is one of the most important aspects of leading a nursing program. Recruitment is also one of the most difficult aspects of the job of deans/directors. Retention of faculty and staff is often directly related to the relationship they have with the unit's leader (Lee, Miller, Kippenbrock, Rosen, & Emory, 2017). This chapter addresses issues regarding recruitment and retention of faculty and staff as well as strategies to tackle the challenges. Best practices for faculty and staff recruitment and retention are shared from the experience and perspective of the first author (CK).

BACKGROUND

In 2016, the American Association of Colleges of Nursing (AACN; 2017) reported that there were 1,567 faculty openings across 821 schools of nursing. These vacancies are hard to fill due to an increase in retirements among members of an aging nursing workforce; low faculty salaries compared with clinical and corporate salaries; and lower numbers of master's and doctorally prepared nurses (AACN, 2017). In addition, younger nurses want work–life balance rather than working 80 hours per week—like many faculty typically devote to their jobs (The Work/Life Blog of the Clinician Reviews Center, n.d.). Younger nurses do not want to enter environments that appear toxic, that is, highly competitive with little mentorship for newcomers. Another challenge is related to the allocation of faculty lines. For example, some faculty positions could be designated solely for teaching or research, whereas others could comprise a combination of teaching, research, service, and/or clinical practice, with portions of the salary paid for by a specific research center, outpatient clinic, or hospital. Indeed, allocation of faculty lines can be complex in terms of job expectations and who is paying for what responsibilities. Despite these challenges, there are many opportunities for attracting innovative, energetic faculty and staff. Leadership of the dean/director is key to making this happen.

FACULTY RECRUITMENT

In general, requests for additional faculty are considered by universities/colleges/schools on an annual basis. The need for additional faculty might reflect new programmatic options, vacant lines due to resignations or retirements, or a need to cover expanding enrollments. Whatever the driver, determining the need for additional faculty requires input from relevant department chairs, assistant deans, and/or faculty. If you are a dean/director in a research-intensive institution, you might need to hire a researcher with extramural funding, a researcher with a specific research focus, or someone who uses a specific research approach. If you are the dean/director in a teaching institution, the hiring emphasis might be on teaching and scholarship related to educational programs, program evaluations, and educational or training grants.

While faculty searches are usually faculty driven, particularly in the context of a strong shared governance model, it is still up to the leader to drive the direction of the search. This means that the dean/director must be clear about the desired skillset of applicants (e.g., someone who can teach pediatric nursing) and their expected contribution(s) to current faculty and the organization. This could be related to an area of research or to the scholarship opportunities that an applicant brings to the table—for example, an editor who can open doors for faculty who need additional scholarly publications.

Another factor for deans/directors to consider when searching for faculty is the maturity profile of their faculty (Hersey, Blanchard, & Natemeyer, 1979; Roberto, 2011). The maturity level of faculty members, a function of organizational experience rather than age, can be classified as low, moderate, or high. Low maturity is typical of the novice, who is a "follower" and focuses on task completion. Faculty members with moderate maturity are experienced and value relationships, whereas those with high maturity need to be empowered. As a leader, you need a mix of maturity levels within your faculty; otherwise, you might end up intensifying your involvement in day-to-day operations or managing too many faculty with similar needs and thought perspectives.

Deans/directors should not fall into the trap of hiring someone simply to fill a vacancy. If your interview with a prospective faculty member leaves you

9 Recruitment and Retention of Qualified Faculty and Staff

with more questions than answers, or there is a nagging feeling that this faculty applicant is not a good fit with the organization, then it is best not to make a job offer and hire that applicant. Faculty who have been hired essentially to avoid losing a faculty line often leave the job within 1 to 2 years. This turnover, if it becomes a trend, sends a message to the community that the environment is not friendly, which could result in making it more difficult to attract highly qualified faculty. A "convenience hire" is neither fair to the individual nor the organization; in both cases, morale suffers.

In the current tight job market for nursing faculty, advertising for positions is only one part of recruitment. A more successful way to recruit and hire qualified faculty involves relationship building—the personal touch, word-of-mouth, and working alongside your faculty in their professional network.

STAFF RECRUITMENT

In most institutions, staff recruitment is just as critical as hiring faculty. Staff are the ones who keep day-to-day operations moving forward and free faculty to complete teaching and curricular leadership tasks. Staff positions can also come with teaching responsibilities. In my experience, I have always tried to hire staff members who are also qualified to teach. For example, a person who oversees a simulation lab or serves as a clinical placement officer can be a registered nurse (RN) who at the very least can also teach in the undergraduate program. Do RN staff members "cost" more than non-RN staff? The answer is "sometimes," but they definitely function more effectively in some roles. Staff who are also RNs can reduce the use of adjunct faculty and give more consistency to teaching. Staff who are also RNs extend the faculty without having to rely on faculty line allocations. It is important that the teaching that staff perform be included in the job description. I usually include "teaching as needed" in certain staff job requirements and job descriptions.

Like faculty recruitment, staff recruitment must be based on specific job requirements, what the staff member brings to the institution, and the staff member's level of maturity. I also look for staff who might aspire to ultimately become faculty. While this underlying goal can lead to staff turnover, it sends a message that the person's needs come first and that you, as dean/director, want them to succeed.

As with faculty recruitment, staff recruitment must rely on written and online advertisement. Personal recruitment can also be very pivotal in recruiting the needed individual. I have encouraged my institutions to seek designation as a National League for Nursing (NLN) Center of Excellence in Nursing Education (n.d.). This designation is attractive to prospective faculty and staff and enhances recruitment. People are drawn to and want to work in an institution that demonstrates excellence in nursing education. In institutions where I have been the nursing dean, we have achieved this designation, which, in turn, has enhanced student learning and professional development. Another strategy for recruitment-friendly messaging involves highlighting the mission and/or goals of the organization; for example, to advance the science of nursing education, promote academic progression of nurses, and promote the pedagogical expertise of faculty (NLN Mission and Strategic Plan, n.d.).

RECRUITING AND HIRING A "MIX OF PEOPLE"

Another consideration when hiring is to obtain "a mix of people." A "mix of people" is what Doris Kearns Goodwin (2006) describes as the "team of rivals" approach. It means that you need people with different styles, whether it is personality types, such as a mix of introverts and extraverts or a mix of early innovation adopters and laggards (MBTI®, n.d.; Rogers, 2003). Why? Decisions will be too easy if there are no differing viewpoints—if all people think alike. Other points of view can slow down the acceptance process for an idea, but they will get to the core of some challenges to the prevailing notion before a flawed idea moves forward. For example, I was having trouble moving ideas from the concept phase to implementation in one organization. Working with an executive coach, we found that my leadership team was a great dream team, but we only had one person who really could execute an implementation plan. From that point on, I tried to be intentional in my hiring of faculty and staff to ensure a mix of personality and thinking styles. This method of recruitment and hiring is not easy, given that an interview does not always give you a feel for exactly how the person makes decisions; however, if you use an interactive approach to the interview, you can often get close to understanding how the person thinks.

LINE ALLOCATION

Line allocation for faculty positions depends on the type of institution in which you work. If you work at a state institution, lines are based on state funds. There may be a finite number of lines that your institution can have. That does not always mean that your institution cannot fund other lines in addition to state lines; however, few employers are in a financial position to take on extra long-term lines. If you are in a private or corporate for-profit organization, there may not be "true" lines but rather monies allocated to support faculty expenses; these may be dependent on revenues to the institution or net income realized at the school or unit level. As dean or director, determine what model and what flexibility there are for faculty lines. Also ask how staff positions can be increased. Again, these are generally not discussed as lines but allocated according to revenues or specific accreditation needs. Use your state board of nursing regulations, accrediting body requirements, and clinical agency guidelines for faculty/student ratios to leverage new lines for faculty and staff positions.

Line allocation can also occur by type of faculty track, typically tenure or clinical. For example, in one institution where I worked, the union contract required that 60% of all faculty positions be tenure track. Clinical track positions might be 1-year renewable positions that give an organization more flexibility to expand and contract on a short-term basis. Other institutions have either multiyear contracts for clinical positions or automatic rollovers if teaching evaluations are strong. Know your institution's policies on line allocation and determine whether a clinical or tenure track position is better for your unit in the long run.

CHALLENGES AND OPPORTUNITIES

Today's tight job market presents both challenges and opportunities associated with recruitment. In general, these consist of financial considerations, incentives for hiring, use of temporary lines, visa issues, and diversification of revenue streams.

Money, Money, Money

Money is the key driver of recruitment and retention. Most institutional marketing budgets are very tight and include recruitment materials for mailing, advertisement, or attending conferences where recruitment tables are available. I tend to use more online advertisements to cast a wider net for faculty and staff. I also tend to travel with recruitment materials or position information—sometimes meaning only my business card to guide a person to our human resources website. Again, although it is labor intensive, personal recruitment is a good strategy. Encourage your faculty and staff to "talk up" your organization. Support faculty and staff to write articles about your institution, programs, and successes. Using an online newsletter is another cost-effective strategy for recruitment. Not all of these tools require a large budget. All do require intentionality and strategic thinking about how to stretch your recruitment and retention dollars.

The opportunities for telling your story are endless and also help faculty and staff retain their jobs or gain promotions. These approaches are not easy or timely if you need faculty/staff today; however, they do contribute to long-term success.

Incentives

Start-up funds for new recruits are offered by some institutions but are less common in public institutions and very uncommon in community colleges. Sometimes start-up funds are only available to tenure track faculty and cannot be offered as part of the recruitment package for clinical or staff positions. If available, start-up funds are very attractive to recruits, especially to individuals who have never had funds for use at their discretion. Other incentives involve ways to earn extra money, such as faculty practice, providing continuing education and/or external consultation, and free or reduced tuition for faculty and/or their families. Seed grants to support scholarly clinical, educational, policy, or research projects act as powerful recruitment and retention incentives. For example, I negotiated some monies from one of our revenue streams to be used for faculty seed grants to jump start their scholarship. These have afforded faculty and staff a mechanism for internal funding, which, in turn, facilitated their funding for external grants. While these internal seed grants were modest, they served the faculty well and sent the message that the institution was invested in their success. Universities and colleges have to compete with high clinical salaries, especially for nurse practitioner (NP) faculty. Most NPs earn six figures in clinical settings; however, in academe, few NP faculty will start this high.

Temporary Lines

Temporary lines can result from a variety of resources. They may be tied to grants or other external funding. They may be allocated as a visiting line for 1 year when a line is in the process of being approved. In other words, a visiting faculty member is placed in the tenure or clinical track position during the time of the search. It should be made clear to the visiting faculty that there is no guarantee of continued employment. If the option of hiring visiting faculty is available, it gives an institution the opportunity to hire a full-time faculty member a year before the budget line is officially allocated and allows the dean/director to test the fit of a faculty member before a full-time commitment is made. Visiting faculty lines are often solely dependent on the availability of soft money or contracts. So again, the person hired into such a position needs to understand the parameters of the position. In my experience, temporary lines have been a way to build a new program before enrollments are sufficient to support a full-time, tenure, or clinical track position. Find out whether temporary lines are available in your institution as a working resource.

Visa Issues

Today's climate for international hires is fraught with challenges. Consult your human resource department to know how you can determine whether or not a visa/sponsorship is required to hire faculty and staff who are not U.S. citizens. Also find out who pays for visa sponsorship. Is it paid for at the institution or unit level? In addition, determine whom you must work with to obtain work visas. In many institutions, working with the legal department, an outside immigration attorney, and human resources is necessary. If a person is already on a visa and is changing employers, make sure you know the type of visa that the person holds. Hiring international talent adds a new dimension to your organization, but it is not easy and takes considerable time and patience. In some cases, I have had to start a year in advance to hire an international faculty/staff member. The dean/director does not need to be an immigration specialist; however, it does help if you learn some of the processes, the time it takes, and any barriers the person might meet once hired. This process takes a good team and open communication among internal team members, as well as with the person you are attempting to hire.

Revenue Streams

Building a variety of distinct revenue streams not only fortifies the fiscal health of your organization, it supports the growth of faculty and staff resources. My entire career has been built around entrepreneurial activities. I have worked most of my years in state institutions where very tight budgets were the norm. I realized very early in my career as a dean that there were sometimes ways to work around this constraint. Some successful examples I have used include starting programs in collaboration with other institutions; sharing a set of courses; using soft money to share the costs of faculty; working with corporations, hospital entities, or for-profit companies to support growing programs, enrollments, faculty, and staff; and negotiating a third-tier tuition for fully online courses/programs or off-campus programs. How do these work?

The first example of expanding resources without straining the budget involves creating a specialty track in a graduate program, such as a neonatal nurse practitioner (NNP) track, that can be offered and shared between two universities. The neonatal courses can be taught by faculty from another institution or co-led with faculty from each institution. The university that matriculates the student collects their tuition and fees and grants the degree, eliminating any argument about whose tuition and fees are paid or who is academically responsible. For a track like the NNP that is in demand but costly and labor intensive, this type of sharing provides each university with the opportunity to increase enrollment, share faculty, and offer a track that neither organization could afford on its own.

Another way of creating a new revenue stream is to collaborate with healthcare agencies and/or other universities to start off-campus cohorts of undergraduate and graduate programs. In my case, healthcare agencies wanted more baccalaureate-prepared nurses as well as, in some instances, advanced practice nurses. I negotiated agreements with the agencies to provide classrooms, IT support, and faculty for teaching. One agency even built a facility to house continued competency education for their staff and associate and baccalaureate degree programs from two colleges/universities. I had a for-profit partner that provided funds to build a simulation lab for use by both programs and agency staff. We all decided to go one step further and share faculty and staff. Thus, the associate and baccalaureate degree programs, each from a separate institution, shared a receptionist/program assistant, simulation lab coordinator, and faculty who covered for each other during exam times.

Another agency, a third-party for-profit company, found healthcare partners and paid for staff and faculty at their site, as well as at our home institution, to assist in managing the enrollment process and academic progression. These staff and faculty had to receive training from our home institution, follow our policies, and work at our direction. We interviewed and evaluated the staff and faculty; if they did not meet our standards, their contracts were terminated. Our undergraduate outcomes included 100% first attempt pass rates for the NCLEX-RN® exam. For the graduate program, we only offered a few courses at healthcare institutions since there were several different specialty tracks.

Our off-campus programs had a different tuition rate and fewer fees since off-campus students did not use campus resources to the same degree as on-campus students. Even when a third party was not involved, I was able to obtain an agreement that a certain percentage of revenue would come back to the unit rather than being swept at the end of a year. I used these funds to support the hiring of several faculty and staff. They were all on soft money, so if revenue decreased, they understood that it might mean the end of their employment. However, these people also understood that they had a good chance of competing favorably for full-time staff and faculty positions as they became available.

Another potential revenue stream, third-tier tuition, is not possible in all institutions beyond what was already described with off-campus programs. However, I had the good fortune to gain support for a different tuition and fee structure for fully online programs. Sometimes these types of tuition agreements must receive approval from a board of trustees and/or state officials. Yet, while tuition for off-campus programs and courses may be higher, the cost of attendance for most off-campus students is usually less as there is no commute, that is, no car, fuel, public transportation, parking, or childcare costs.

The final example of a revenue stream that assists in supporting staff and faculty hires is the shared service agreement with one or more community health partners; that is, a faculty member shared with the clinical agency but hired through the university. Shared faculty can oversee students in the clinical agency and also serve as adjunct faculty for classroom teaching. Shared service contracts can realize true cost savings and expand faculty resources.

RETENTION OF FACULTY

Retention of qualified faculty is key to a successful nursing education enterprise. Today, it is particularly critical to retain faculty of color to inform our curricula and serve as "like role models" for students of color. This will advance our profession's efforts to diversify the nursing workforce in the interest of social justice and changing societal demographics. Non-Hispanic White persons will be fewer in number compared with other races and ethnicities by 2042 (Hamilton & Haozous, 2017). Faculty of color often experience discriminatory practices, bias, and racism (Hamilton & Haozous, 2017). Leadership must be intentional about supporting all faculty, but especially those from diverse backgrounds. Promoting inclusiveness is important (Hamilton & Haozous, 2017). How can this be done? A first step is to intentionally recruit faculty who resemble the community that your college/school/department serves. If you are not of color yourself, tap into your network of dean/director colleagues to find appropriate mentors for new faculty of color. Understanding ethnic backgrounds as well as the expectations of academia is important for successful retention. As a dean or director, you must also ensure that the higher administration supports faculty of color through initiatives such as mentorship, professional development, and salary equity (Hamilton & Haozous, 2017).

I have encouraged my faculty of color to be active in the Black Nurses Association, National Association of Hispanic Nurses, and/or National Alaska Native American Indian Nurses Association (NANAINA) for mentorship, funding for teaching and research, and professional development. We must be deliberate in building a pipeline for students of color to become faculty of color. Mentorship programs with our nursing students are a good way to start. For example, at my institution, one of my staff, now faculty, started a mentorship program for undergraduate Black nursing students called, *"Moving Forward Together"* (Y. Nelson, personal communication, April, 13, 2018). This pilot program, now in its second year, has received rave reviews from both mentors and mentees.

The program involves students entering into an exercise similar to speed dating, during which they interview nurses to see who they think might be a "best fit" mentor relative to their needs. Mentors commit to working with their students throughout the year and come together two to three times annually as a group to share what is and what is not working. This program hopes to expand to other students of color in the future.

Retention is often related to perceptions. These perceptions focus on workloads, competing faculty expectations, and pay. Other factors that impact recruitment and retention include "personal and family policies, collaboration, tenure clarity, institutional leadership, shared governance, and departmental engagement" (Lee et al., 2017, p. 264); all have been shown to influence satisfaction with the work environment and, in turn, retention (Lee et al., 2017).

RETENTION OF STAFF

Retention of competent staff is also key to a successful nursing education enterprise. Working to promote the success of your staff members facilitates their retention. Salary, benefits, working conditions, respectful coworkers and supervisors, and having a variety of responsibilities can contribute to retaining staff. Staff are usually happier working in areas that do not involve confined cubicle space and monotonous tasks. Offering staff a variety of activities to complete can make their jobs more interesting and challenging. Acknowledging staff members' excellent performance and being flexible with their requests demonstrate both trust in individuals and that staff are truly appreciated. Further, staff tend to take pride in the place where they work; otherwise, they would be seeking employment elsewhere.

CONCLUSION

Recruitment and retention of qualified faculty and staff challenge even the most experienced nursing dean/director. There are many opportunities and strategies to effectively address these challenges.

RESOURCES

Columbia University. Guide to Best Practices in Faculty Retention—Draft Outline: https://provost.columbia.edu/sites/default/files/content/RetentionGuide.pdf

National League for Nursing. Centers of Excellence in Nursing Education: http://www.nln.org/recognition-programs/centers-of-excellence-in-nursing-education

REFERENCES

American Association of Colleges of Nursing. (2017). *Nursing faculty shortage fact sheet.* Washington, DC: AACN.

Goodwin, D. K. (2006). *Team of rivals: The political genius of Abraham Lincoln.* New York, NY: Simon & Schuster.

Hamilton, N., & Haozous, E. A. (2017). Retention of faculty of color in academic nursing. *Nursing Outlook, 65*(2), 212–221. doi:10.1016/j.outlook.2016.11.003

Hersey, P., Blanchard, K. H., & Natemeyer, W. E. (1979). Situational leadership, perception, and the impact of power. *Group & Organizational Management, 4*(4), 418–428. doi:10.1177/105960117900400404

Lee, P., Miller, M. T., Kippenbrock, T. A., Rosen, C., & Emory, J. (2017). College nursing faculty job satisfaction and retention: A national perspective. *Journal of Professional Nursing, 33*(4), 261–266. doi:10.1016/j.profnurs.2017.01.001

MBTI® Basics. (n.d.). Retrieved from the Myers and Briggs Foundation website, https://www.myersbriggs.org/my-mbti-personality-type/mbtibasics/home.htm?bhcp=1

National League for Nursing Centers of Excellence in Nursing Education. (n.d.). Retrieved from National League for Nursing website, http://www.nln.org/recognition-programs/centers-of-excellence-in-nursing-education

National League for Nursing Mission and Strategic Plan. (n.d.). Retrieved from the National League for Nursing website, http://www.nln.org/about/mission-goals

Roberto, M. A. (2011). *Transformational leadership: How leaders change teams, companies, and organizations.* Chantilly, VA: The Great Courses and The Teaching Company.

Rogers, E. M. (2003). *Diffusion of innovations* (5th ed.). New York, NY: The Free Press.

The Work/Life Blog of the Clinician Reviews Career Center. (n.d.). Retrieved from the Clinician Reviews Career Center website, http://www.clinicianreviews.directory/misc-category/announcement-new-work-life-blog-for-advanced-practice-clinicians/

10

ACADEMIC POLICIES AND PROGRAMS

LYNNETTE LEESEBERG STAMLER

INTRODUCTION

Academic polices can be a significant factor in the success of programs and, therefore, students in nursing education programs. These policies arise from, and are governed by, a variety of bodies that are external or internal to nursing programs. Some may come from accreditation/approval bodies, such as state Boards of Nursing, Commission on Collegiate Nursing Education (CCNE), or Accreditation Commission for Education in Nursing (ACEN). Some may come from regional or national bodies, such as the U.S. Department of Education or Higher Learning Commission. Still others may arise from the Board of Regents or Board of Governors. They may be exclusive to an institution (especially for private universities) or part of a group of policies that govern all higher education institutions in a particular state.

From those external policies will flow the policies that are internal to your institution but external to your school, faculty, college, or department. Finally, there are policies that arise within your own school, faculty, college, or department. Academic policies can be grouped loosely into two categories—student and faculty. Student policies are further categorized into areas such as admissions, progression through programs, graduation, conduct, academic dishonesty and discipline, and grade appeals. Faculty policies cover such topics as organization, committees, governance, travel, and promotion and tenure.

In most universities, schools, and colleges, faculties and departments may have policies that are separate but mirror policies of the institution or state. In that case, the school policies are often more stringent that those of the larger body, which is usually allowed. Examples of such policies may include admission grade point average (GPA) requirements, requirements for English language proficiency for international students, the grade required for successful completion of a course, or the number of times a student may repeat a given required course within a plan of study. More rarely, an individual program may have even more stringent policies—for example, requiring a certain amount of clinical experience as an RN prior to admission to a specific graduate nursing program, or a dress code policy for clinical experiences in the undergraduate nursing program. The reality is that, in many cases, especially at the school or program level, new policies are created in response to a difficult situation, in order to prevent "*x* problem" from ever happening again. As the new dean or administrator, your "go-to" sentence in many situations is "Do we have a policy on that?" The dean must ensure that policies are followed and work with faculty and administrators to create new policies when the need arises. This chapter gives examples of policies and the dean's role in this process.

CASES

There are many case examples of policies; however, two very broad categories are problem solving and new programs. The following cases illustrate these areas and the types of policies that would inform your resolution of these issues.

Case #1: What Is the Policy?

One of the most common problem-solving situations is the student who is unhappy with her or his grade in a given assignment or course. The logical extension of this issue is: When does the student "run out of chances" in a given program of study? In these cases, policies most frequently come from within your university and within your school, faculty, college, or department and then within the individual programs. In general, faculty committees are the first to hear grade appeals and determine their merit. Deans should avoid getting involved too early in the process because active engagement by the dean may muddy the waters, especially if it turns into a legal matter. That said, the first policy to seek is the grade appeal policy for the program—either undergraduate or graduate. This policy should be well known to faculty and students and include a procedure and timeline so that the student and the faculty both know exactly what to do and who bears the responsibility for certain activities. Questions to be asked might include the following:

- Is there a deadline for a grade appeal?
- Can a student appeal an assignment grade or only the final course grade?

- What grade must the student achieve in order to be successful?
- Can course grades be rounded up in that program?
- What are the steps the student and faculty must follow?
- Does the student progress while an appeal is in progress?
- How is the student notified of the outcome of the appeal?

Once the policy has been followed, assuming the grade is upheld, other questions arise, including the following:

- Does this failure place the student in jeopardy in terms of the program of study?
- If the course needs to be repeated, when will the next offering be, and what happens in the meantime?
- How does this timeline fit with the maximum time allowed for completion of the program?
- If the result leads to dismissal, are more appeals possible?
- If this is a graduate course, does the nursing program or graduate studies department have jurisdiction? How is this communicated to the student and the faculty?

Case #2: Let Us Start a (Fill in the Blank) Program Next Semester

As I looked at this, coming from a public university, I nearly laughed out loud. The probability of actually beginning a program in that length of time is highly unlikely; however, sometimes deans are asked to create a program very quickly. In my almost three decades of academic administration, I have been part of only one program proposal that was approved at the (public) university level within 90 days. In that case, it was a post-master's certificate version of an already existing and approved nurse practitioner program. All other programs that I have been part of have taken 6 to 9 months for a speedy result, but often much longer. It is true that in this area, private universities often have the advantage of fewer administrative layers but still need to answer to requirements from state, regional, or national authorities and/or professional accreditation agencies.

Different bodies will require different types of information, but several key questions will be asked at some level when proposing a new program. These questions and related considerations are listed in Table 10.1.

Some larger institutions may have a generic procedure for proposing a new program, which is very helpful. Look to your institutional academic leader

TABLE 10.1 Key Questions and Considerations for New Academic Nursing Program Proposals

KEY QUESTION	CONSIDERATIONS
1. Does this program comply with legislated and/or approved privileges granted to your school?	A. For example, your school grants MSN degrees, but can your school grant doctoral degrees? B. Is this another track in an already existing program, e.g., a women's health NP program when you already have an approved family NP program? C. Is the new program an accelerated version of an already existing undergraduate program?
2. Can you demonstrate immediate need for the program?	A. Who is encouraging you to open this program? B. Who else has a similar program in the geographic area? Will it influence your program's viability? C. What are the various approvals you need? What are the outlines/forms for the proposals for the various approving bodies? In what order must the approvals be sought? D. Are the resources in place or available? If not, can the groups pushing for the new program assist with resources? E. Can you demonstrate ongoing need for the program that is financially feasible? If not, can you partner with others? F. Do you need faculty with specific education and credentials? Do they need to be full-time academic hires or can you share with a clinical partner?
3. How will you plan the curriculum?	A. Are there criteria/guidelines for this program to meet? If it is undergraduate, what about your state Board of Nursing? If graduate, what about credentialing bodies? B. Do you have faculty who can do the planning or do you need a consultant? C. What is required for accreditation of this program?
4. How do you get buy-in from your faculty and clinical partners?	A. Who needs to approve this at a program level? B. If a clinical program, where will you get clinical spaces and/or preceptors? C. What will be the reaction of other nursing schools in your area? D. How will you demonstrate that the needed resources will be available when required?
5. Will someone need to go to various meetings to put forth your plan in person?	A. Who will represent you? B. If you personally need to begin the process, when, and to whom, can you hand it off?

(e.g., provost office) for advice in seeking those documents. In all cases, the new program must demonstrably fit within the strategic plan of the school, college, faculty, and department, as well as with larger bodies such as the university and beyond. A good first step is to find out what is needed for the proposal process and then create a flowchart that also outlines timeframes, meetings of the various approval committees, and other important dates. Your needs assessment can be very formal or more anecdotal in nature, but it must be compelling, you must demonstrate support, and the committees will insist that you have "done your homework." If this is a new direction for your school, the cost of a consultant may pay for itself many times over. If the resources do not materialize, what is your Plan B?

KEY PROGRAM AND POLICY ISSUES

Program innovation and quality are critical to the success of an academic nursing enterprise. Program innovations such as online learning, competency-based programs, and stackable certificates are attractive to today's learners, and nursing students are no exception. At the end of the day, academic policies drive program quality, outcomes, and the reputation of the department or school and its graduates.

Program Innovation

Online Learning

It is beyond the purview of this chapter to engage in a lengthy discussion about online learning; however, there are at least two issues that are worth thinking about. The first is admissions. By definition, if you are teaching an online program and you have students enrolled from "X" state, you are deemed to be teaching in "X" state. Thus, you or your school need to have acquired permission to "teach" from the Departments of Education in each state in which you are planning to enroll students. Given that nursing programs include clinical experiences, you are also required to gain permission from the state Board of Nursing in each of the same states. The Board may require that the faculty supervisors are licensed in their state, which is not a great problem if state "X" is a compact state, and so are you. These permissions will affect who you can admit to your online programs. The second issue pertains to the quality of online teaching. Like all nursing education programs, online programs require ongoing and planned evaluation and revision. If your university has multiple online offerings, it may have purchased membership in a quality assurance enterprise such as "Quality Matters" (https://www.qualitymatters.org/). Quality Matters is a peer-reviewed consortium for online and blended programs that is dedicated to ensuring quality in online learning. If your university does not belong to such a group, your college, faculty, school, or department will need to create documents and policies to ensure consistency and excellence across all online courses.

Competency-Based Movement

The competency-based movement is relatively new in health professions education. Originally conceived as competency-based medical education (CBME; NEJM Knowledge+ Team, 2019), it has moved further into the mainstream of health professions education and literature for nursing education is beginning to appear (Schumacher & Risco, 2017). Different from learning objectives embedded in a traditional course, competency-based education is founded on demonstration of achieved competencies, with a variable pace for the learning rather than a specified time period (e.g., clinical hours) or number of credits. This new way of thinking about education will need to be reconciled with state Boards of Nursing and the requirements of credentialing bodies.

Stackable Certificates

More and more students are finding they are unable to complete all requirements of a degree at one time. The idea behind stackable certificates is that they are short programs which, when taken in sequence and combined, result in an overall credential, like a degree. One example of this is the student who first becomes a certified nursing assistant (CNA), then a licensed practical nurse (LPN), then an RN, and finally a nurse with a bachelor of science degree (BSN). In the context of a stackable certificate, the entire educational pathway is planned in advance. Thus, the student can choose to take only courses toward the certificate that she or he is seeking, or can add additional certificates to complete a degree or other credential. Also, with advance planning and pathways, the number of "extra" requirements should be much less, making every course count toward the final goal.

Program Quality

Accreditation

Currently, the accreditation of U.S. nursing education programs is shared primarily by two organizations: the ACEN and the CCNE. The ACEN is dedicated to the support of nursing education and transition to practice; promotion of peer review and self-regulation; advancement of quality, equity, access, opportunity, mobility, and preparation for practice or transition to practice at all levels of nursing preparation; and development of standards and criteria for accreditation (ACEN, 2013). The CCNE is described as "an autonomous accrediting agency contributing to the improvement of the public's health" that is dedicated to ensuring "the quality and integrity of baccalaureate, graduate and residency programs in nursing" (CCNE, 2019). The U.S. Secretary of Education recognizes both, and both use self-study and peer review through site visitation as hallmarks of their accreditation programs. The ACEN works with some practical nursing programs as well as hospital-based programs and all levels of RN nursing education, whereas CCNE's focus is on baccalaureate and higher degree nursing education programs. Schools can choose which accreditation program they wish to follow. While accreditation programs are voluntary, most graduate nursing programs do not accept students who have graduated from a basic nursing program that is not accredited.

NCLEX-RN®

This is the national licensure examination for graduates of approved nursing schools. A passing score on the NCLEX-RN must be achieved to be designated as an RN and licensed to practice nursing. Each state Board of Nursing certifies the individual to write the NCLEX-RN, based in part on certification of their graduation from an approved school of nursing. Internationally educated nurses must also be certified by their state of residence to take the NCLEX-RN in order to be licensed in the United States. The National Council of State Boards of Nursing (NCSBN), which is "dedicated to developing psychometrically sound and legally defensible nurse licensure and certification examinations consistent with current practice," administers the NCLEX-RN (NCSBN, 2019).

While applicants have multiple opportunities to take the NCLEX-RN (depending on the state), a school's reputation and demonstrated outcomes are frequently measured by the percentage of graduates who pass the NCLEX-RN on the first try. Statistics on first-time NCLEX-RN pass rates are available for individual schools and as national and state averages. State Boards of Nursing and accreditation agencies require reporting of these statistics by the school. Schools that fall below the expected standards for either their state board of nursing or accrediting agency are required to document what led to their failure to meet the standard and must engage in remedial work to raise the pass rate, usually within a given timeframe. NCLEX-RN pass rates are often used to market nursing schools as well.

Certification

Certification is generally granted on a postgraduate basis. A nurse can achieve certification as a nurse practitioner, clinical nurse specialist, or entry-level nurse in a variety of clinical specialties through the American Nurses Credentialing Center (ANCC). Eligibility requirements generally include education and clinical experience. Nursing schools are required to note on their advertising material if a specific program qualifies for graduate certification eligibility. More than one organization may certify graduates of several NP specialties; for example, pediatric nurse practitioners may be certified by ANCC or the Pediatric Nursing Certification Board (PNCB). Most certifications must be renewed periodically with requirements such as clinical experience and/or continuing nursing education in the specialty.

Comprehensives

Comprehensive examinations can serve two purposes. One is as an entrance examination. Some graduate programs may employ this type of exam. The more common is at the end of a degree program. If the comprehensive examination is prepared by an outside organization for an undergraduate program, it may serve as a predictor of success on the NCLEX-RN. In graduate programs, comprehensive examinations are given in-house and serve as a demonstration of what the student has learned. The most common program to use comprehensive examinations is the PhD program. The school or department that houses graduate studies will have policies governing the use of comprehensives, but each program—for example, nursing, chemistry—will also have policies and procedures that mirror those of the school or department, although they may be more stringent. The comprehensive examination may be in the form of a typical exam, a series of publishable manuscripts related to given topics, a student-written research proposal following national guidelines, or a combination of the aforementioned. PhD comprehensive examinations are generally written after coursework is completed but before the dissertation proposal is defended.

Completion Rates

The completion or graduation rate for each program is another statistic that is commonly required by universities, state Boards of Nursing, and accreditation bodies. The goal is to have a given percentage of enrolled students successfully complete a program within a given amount of time, generally 1.5 times the number of months or years expected for a full-time plan of study. For example, if an MSN program is planned to be completed in 2 years of full-time study, we would be looking at the percentage of students who enrolled in a given year and completed the program within 3 years of their first enrollment. If the percentage rate falls below a given standard, the school is required to show why this happened and what is being done to address it. In extreme circumstances, the program/school may be placed on probation while the issue is being addressed.

Rankings

Rankings refer to metrics that show how a given school/program compares with similar programs across the nation. The most well-known metric in academic circles is published by *U.S. News & World Report*. Schools choose to complete a survey about their program(s) and their knowledge of other programs in the same program area, for example, MSN programs. There is no cost for taking part in the surveys; however, if you are ranked positively and choose to use their logo in your advertising materials, there is an annual fee.

CONCLUSION

It is clear that policies enhance and support programs, faculty, and students. As such, both program and policy review and revision should be part of a systematic evaluation plan. How the evaluation plan is developed and implemented may be influenced by institutional, state Board of Nursing, or accreditation requirements. The final actions in any evaluation involve feedback to students and faculty about the data, conclusions reached, and resulting revisions.

Through policies, programs have structure and equity for all concerned. One of the hallmarks of an excellent program is that all students within the school, college, faculty, or department are treated equitably, whether in-person or at a distance; on one campus or across multiple campuses. By ensuring that polices at a program- or school-level mirror polices at higher (e.g., institutional) levels, nursing students are treated comparably with other types of students. Evidence of equitable treatment of nursing students and regular evaluation of academic policies and programs must be documented in annual reports and self-study documents to secure ongoing program approval and accreditation.

RESOURCES

Accreditation Commission for Education in Nursing (ACEN): https://www.acenursing.org

Commission on Collegiate Nursing Education (CCNE): https://www.aacnnursing.org/CCNE

Kenner, C. A., & Pressler, J. L. (2011). Trends in nursing education. *Nurse Educator, 36*(5), 179–180.

Lucey, C. R., Thibault, G. E., & Ten Cate, O. (2018). Competency-based, time-variable education in the health Professions. *Academic Medicine, 93*, S1-S5. doi:10.1097/ACM.0000000000002080

National Council of State Boards of Nursing (NCSBN): https://www.ncsbn.org/nclex.htm

Pressler, J. L., & Kenner, C. A. (2013). Thoughts regarding innovations in nursing education, part 1. *Nurse Educator, 38*(5), 181–183.

Pressler, J. L., & Kenner, C. A. (2013). Thoughts regarding innovations in nursing education, part 2. *Nurse Educator, 38*(6), 230–232.

Quality Matters: https://www.qualitymatters.org/

Ruff, C. (2016). More colleges turn to "stackable" degrees as entries to graduate programs. *The Chronicle of Higher Education*. Retrieved from https://www.chronicle.com/article/More-Colleges-Turn-to/235886

REFERENCES

Accreditation Commission for Education in Nursing. (2013). Mission, purpose, goals. Retrieved from https://www.acenursing.org/mission-purpose-goals/

Commission on Collegiate Nursing Education. (2019). CCNE Home Page. Retrieved from https://www.aacnnursing.org/CCNE

National Council of State Boards of Nursing. (2019). NCLEX and other exams. Retrieved from https://www.ncsbn.org/nclex.htm

NEJM Knowledge+ Team. (2019). What is competency-based medical education? Retrieved from https://knowledgeplus.nejm.org/blog/what-is-competency-based-medical-education/

Schumacher, G., & Risco, K. (2017). Competency-based nurse practitioner education: An overview for the preceptor. *The Journal for Nurse Practitioners, 13*(9), 596–602.

FUNDRAISING
Mission Critical

JOANNE P. ROBINSON

INTRODUCTION

As dean or director of an academic nursing program, it is expected that your tool kit contains a set of skills on fundraising. At minimum, you will be asked to represent and/or market your unit to external constituents, including prospective donors. However, you might also be given a target amount of money to raise, either with or without advice or assistance from a development professional. If the idea of asking for money on anyone's behalf causes you to cringe or cower, read on and consider that you have probably done this before. Were you ever a girl/boy scout, member of a parent–teacher organization (PTO), church, political party, civic organization, or professional association that raised money for self-support or a good cause? Have you ever applied for funds to support your education, research, scholarship, or a project to enhance student, faculty, staff, or patient experiences? If so, a set of fundraising skills is already in your toolbox.

PHILANTHROPY: AN AMERICAN TRADITION

Philanthropy has been a universal dimension of the human experience for centuries. Confucius exhorted his followers to distribute their wealth for the common good. The Prophet Muhammad encouraged good works in this world to assure wealth in the hereafter. Early Quaker and English colonial leader William Penn advised, "Do good with what thou hast, or it will do thee no good."

Likewise, giving is integral to American culture. Henry David Thoreau, John D. Rockefeller, and Conrad Hilton regarded philanthropy as a virtue and religious duty. Andrew Carnegie, Henry Ford, Franklin D. Roosevelt,

John F. Kennedy, and Martin Luther King all emphasized the obligation of those with wealth to help those without. American entertainers have long been public advocates and models of charitable giving. For example, show business legends Bob Hope and George Burns observed, respectively, "If you haven't got any charity in your heart, you have the worst kind of heart trouble," and "When you stop giving and offering something to the rest of the world, it's time to turn out the lights."

Like their predecessors, contemporary American leaders regard philanthropy as both a virtue and an obligation. Angel investor and philanthropist Ron Conway explained, "I believe that we all have a responsibility to give back. No one becomes successful without lots of hard work, support from others, and a little luck. Giving back creates a virtuous cycle that makes everyone more successful." Ted Turner and Warren Buffett remarked, respectively, about the obligation to give: "As I started getting rich, I started thinking, 'What the hell am I going to do with all this money?'... You have to learn to give," and "If you're in the luckiest 1 percent of humanity, you owe it to the rest of humanity to think about the other 99 percent." New to the list of reasons for giving are *Whole Foods* founder John Mackey's notion of corporate philanthropy as "simply good business," Oprah Winfrey's emphasis on the power of philanthropy "to touch somebody's life," and Mark Zuckerburg's observation on the "big opportunity" for himself and other young successful Silicon Valley entrepreneurs "to give back earlier in our lifetime and see the impact of philanthropic efforts."

FUNDRAISING IN HIGHER EDUCATION

Over the past few decades, the pursuit of philanthropic support has become big business in higher education as costs continue to rise in the context of dwindling government support and skyrocketing tuition. Today, most institutions of higher education have an office of development dedicated to the pursuit of funding from private sources—individuals, foundations, and corporations. Often, development offices are housed within larger offices of advancement, which typically include alumni relations and communication units as well. Advancement offices are dedicated to the broader mission of promoting the causes of particular projects, programs, schools, colleges, and/or the university-at-large to the outside world (Hunt, 2012). In large institutions, development officers may be housed in schools or colleges but usually have dual reporting to the chief officers of both the academic unit and the institution's office of development or advancement.

Strategically, development professionals focus much of their efforts on individual donor prospects, considered the best source for transformational gifts—funding that can dramatically change an organization's future (Judge, 2014). The notion of philanthropy as *relational* rather than transactional (Yoon, 2014) informs the common practice of courting individual donor prospects, especially those capable of high impact gifts, in the interest of building long-term relationships characterized by genuine care and concern (Allers, 2013). In fact, development professionals regard giving as a continuum that extends and repeats itself over time as relationships with donors evolve. The giving continuum is conceptualized as a cycle with five stages: identification of a prospect; prospect qualification in terms of inclination and capacity to give; cultivation of a relationship; solicitation; and stewardship (Hunt, 2012). Similarly, there is a continuum in types of gifts that begins with small, renewable *annual gifts*; progresses to *major gifts* of sizeable amounts and *principal* or *transformational* gifts of even larger amounts; and ends with *planned gifts* involving estate plans and income-producing vehicles (Hunt, 2012). A dean/director plays a critical role in all five stages of the giving continuum and with all types of gifts.

Education is second only to religion as a destination for gifts from private sources (*Giving USA 2017 Highlights, n.d.*). Traditionally, the most "gifted" higher education institutions had greater endowment values, educational and general expenditures, tuition, alumni on record, expenditures per student, and institutional age (Duronio & Loessin, 1990). Today, a game change may be in progress as philanthropy becomes "less about creating a legacy chiseled in granite and more about affecting meaningful change in one's lifetime" (Comstock, n.d.).

Like healthcare, fundraising in higher education is a team sport. Historically, the main players have been development professionals and volunteers, including alumni, community leaders, and board members. Today, fundraising is also an "all in" activity for deans/directors, albeit a new skill set for most (Masterson, 2017). As the point person most often requested by donors, deans/directors typically facilitate the work of development staff by courting wealthy alumni, shaping potential gifts, and articulating the school's mission and the impact of a gift (Masterson, 2017). In the context of a capital campaign, however, deans/directors are often required to develop and lead fundraising initiatives for their school. Many institutions also participate in an annual "Day of Giving," usually toward a targeted project. The dean/director typically works with a development officer on project creation and acts as head cheerleader to maximize participation with even the smallest gift because challenge gifts are generally unlocked only when a specified number of donors make contributions, regardless of amount.

Investment in fundraising activities will benefit your school, our profession, and you. Budget support, enhanced recognition of nursing as an academic discipline and profession, and better understanding of the business world are a few examples of the payoffs (Fitzpatrick, 2005). As a nurse, remember that you bring several organic assets to the table, including membership in the most trusted profession and your stories about what healthcare is like today. Your experience with teamwork as a team member, coordinator, leader, and coach will also serve you well, as will the exquisite interpersonal and observational skills that are second nature to most nurses as the chief architects of caring relationships.

CHALLENGES FOR DEANS AND DIRECTORS

Deans and directors can face personal, contextual, and donor-centric challenges that inhibit their ability to engage effectively in fundraising. On a personal level, finding time for donors and their courtship, access to training, and keeping up with best practices and trends in fundraising can be daunting (Masterson, 2017). Fear of "selling out"—allowing money to drive the mission—can also be a paralyzing force (Perlmutter, 2016).

Contextual challenges include the economic climate, which sets the stage for today's reality of more competition for less dollars (Comstock, n.d.) as well as tough questions from donors and the public about the current quality, value, and delivery of higher education (Duronio & Loessin, 1990). The impact of technology on the speed, ease, and reach of communication can also overwhelm a busy dean/director, as can the demands of strategic collaboration to attract today's donor with less disposable resources but a myriad of philanthropic options (Judge, 2014). Finally, a *one-size-fits-all* approach to fundraising has been replaced by approaches that vary in relation to the donor pool. For example, effective approaches for donor prospects of limited means, such as recent graduates, will be different than those for wealthy prospects ("Donor 3.0," n.d.). All of these factors translate into a steeper learning curve and more time-on-task for the dean/director.

Studies of donor demographics suggest a variety of additional challenges—and opportunities—that are donor-centric. Women, the traditional soldiers of fundraising campaigns, have become independent sources of wealth with philanthropic motives fueled by both their heads and hearts. Women are recognized especially for their responsiveness to crisis situations and expectations of greater stewardship, involvement, and an ongoing relationship with the organization (Fitzpatrick, 2005).

In general, experts portray today's donor as an *active* philanthropist, who is motivated by the opportunity to *define* rather than merely "rubber stamp" institutional priorities ("Donor 3.0," n.d.). Today's donor also expects to see tangible value for their money (Kreimer, 2009) and will soon lose the benefit of a tax deduction for their charitable gifts. The current generation of donors differs from past generations of wealthy and well-connected donors whose gifts were generally inspired by a sense of altruism and causes near and dear to the heart. Today's donor also differs from recent generations of middle-class donors whose philanthropic motives have typically been both altruistic and strategic in terms of enabling their own personal goals ("Donor 3.0," n.d.). The evolution of a "sharing economy"—individual trading of assets and services via the internet—honors the preferences of the current generation of informed, connected, and time-crunched donors for crowdfunding and other online mechanisms for charitable giving (Lamphere, 2018). Online approaches are especially good for very specific projects or for an annual "Day of Giving."

BEST PRACTICES

Time-Tested Principles of Fundraising

Relationships, teamwork, communication, and credibility are cornerstones of four time-tested principles of fundraising (see Box 11.1). Of these, most development professionals contend that fundraising is essentially about relationships ("Donor 3.0," n.d.; Judge, 2014).

An ongoing relationship of genuine care and collaboration is expected by today's donors and prospects. Similarly, mutual respect, collaboration, and adherence to the rules of engagement are expectations of members of your fundraising team, which should include development staff, selected community members (e.g., alumni, advisory board), and perhaps nursing faculty and administrators (e.g., assistant deans, department chairs, program coordinators) who are close to the student experience.

Fortunately, fundraising is a team sport. A solid understanding of the development model used by your institution is an essential step in determining parameters for your own development team (Hunt, 2012). You will need a

---

BOX 11.1

TIME-TESTED PRINCIPLES OF FUNDRAISING

Fundraising is about relationships.
Fundraising is a team sport.
Make a strong case for your cause, and communicate it effectively.
Credibility demands careful stewardship.

knowledgeable, nimble, and dedicated team to meet the expectations of today's donor for personalized, ongoing communication about the organization's mission and goals, and specific impact of their gift. Your fundraising team can also assist you to identify donor prospects, navigate their demands for periods of your undivided attention to discuss personal passions and proposals, and manage their expectations for swift feedback and follow-up.

Nothing has changed in the fundraising world concerning the importance of making a strong case for your cause and communicating it effectively (Judge, 2014). Today, effective communication means respectful, easy, and fast using print, electronic, and social media as well as public and private forums for discussion. Focused case statements for various initiatives should be "ready to go" for both planned and unplanned encounters with donor prospects. Ongoing communication about the mission and vision of your organization is also a mechanism for engaging the community-at-large in your work in the interest of cultivating an "army of friends" who would "never dream of letting the mission die" (Allers, 2013).

Likewise, credibility in the form of careful stewardship of gifts remains essential. In fact, today's donor is very focused on seeing value for their money (Kreimer, 2009) and a meaningful ongoing relationship with the organization. Continued gifts are often contingent on donor satisfaction, connection to their hearts and goals, and a solid stake in the organization's mission ("Donor 3.0," n.d.; Masterson, 2017). For example, a handwritten letter from a scholarship recipient about the impact of the money on their academic journey goes a long way to solidify the relationship with the donor and pave the way for continued gifts.

Setting the Stage

For the novice dean/director or incoming dean/director to a new setting, homework should be your first order of business (Fitzpatrick, 2005). Get to know the players on your school's fundraising team as well as fundraising champions on your campus. Bond with your school's dedicated development officer if this position is already in place; if not, either hire the dedicated development officer that you had the foresight to negotiate when you accepted the deanship/directorship or find a resident expert on your campus who can serve as your fundraising point person or mentor. Next, learn the fundraising history of your school, expectations of deans/directors, and rules of engagement for your setting. Set goals in collaboration with your development officer/fundraising mentor and other members of your fundraising team. Start-up activities should include working with your fundraising team to access or create a database of donors and prospects; connecting with alumni and previous donors; and creating case statements for important initiatives. Public relations specialists in your school or on your campus can assist with the development of case statements, press releases, newsletters, and other forms of communication to engage donors, alumni, and other prospects. In addition, alumni officers can help to arrange "meet and greet" events for local alumni, as well as meetings or social events for distant alumni that correspond to your planned travel.

Hunt's (2012) classification of development priorities for academic leaders is worth considering in terms of strategic investment of your time (see Table 11.1). According to Hunt, success involves *always* investing time in A-level activities, *usually* investing time in B-level activities, and *never* engaging in C-level activities as this is the work of development staff.

If all of this is new to you, formal training may be a worthwhile endeavor. Table 11.2 lists a number of organizations that provide basic training and professional development in the art and science of fundraising. In particular, the Council for Advancement and Support of Education (CASE) has a well-established and highly acclaimed program on *Development for Deans and Academic Leaders*.

Likewise, if your development officer has not covered nursing before or has not had a network of colleagues to discuss strategies for nursing-focused giving programs, suggest they join the Leadership Network for Nursing Advancement Professionals sponsored by the American Association of Colleges of Nursing (https://www.aacnnursing.org/Leadership-Networks/NAP). This is a good way for them to learn about best practices in similar institutions.

TABLE 11.1 Development Priorities for Academic Leaders: Strategies for Fundraising

A Level	■ Building relationships with highest-level donors and prospects ■ Setting development priorities for your unit ■ Collaborating with development staff on strategies
B Level	■ Personalizing annual giving and other messages ■ Attending events ■ General donor relations
C Level	■ Gift processing ■ Writing mailings and phone scripts ■ Prospect research ■ Cold calls to low-level prospects or suspects

SOURCE: Hunt, P. C. (2012). *Development for academic leaders: A practical guide for fundraising success*. San Francisco, CA: Jossey-Bass.

TABLE 11.2 Resources for Training and Professional Development in Academic Fundraising

Council for Advancement and Support of Education (CASE) https://www.case.org/Conferences_and_Training.html	Professional development (conferences, training, publications, and products); highly acclaimed program on *Development for Deans and Academic Leaders*
Georgia Center for Nonprofits https://www.gcn.org/Nonprofit-University	Policy, advocacy, consultation, and professional development (publications, training, conferences) for nonprofit universities
Giving USA https://givingusa.org/	Publications (data-based reports) on the state of philanthropy in the United States
Indiana University Purdue University of Indiana (IUPUI) Lilly Family School of Philanthropy https://philanthropy.iupui.edu/professional-development/courses-seminars/index.html	Professional development (courses and seminars)
Sametz Blackstone Associates https://sametz.com	Consultation and professional development (training, publications)

Your homework and start-up activities should yield a stage set for cultivating a culture of philanthropy in your school. Organizations with a culture of philanthropy embrace donors as full partners in the mission and ongoing journey of the organization and expect engagement by all members of the organization in the pursuit of philanthropic support (Yoon, 2014). Essentially, a culture of philanthropy nurtures lasting relationships and a habit of giving among donors ("Donor 3.0," n.d.), ultimately yielding more support for the mission (Yoon, 2014). To get on the road toward a culture of philanthropy in your school, experts suggest a few steps: invest in the necessary infrastructure and training to support your fundraising goals; market your mission internally and externally at every opportunity; actively seek opportunities to engage donors and prospects in your school's activities; and appreciate donors publicly and privately at every turn (Yoon, 2014). Experts also caution against several common pitfalls, including asking for a donation "on the first date;" making assumptions about a prospect's motivations; making "prn only" contacts and requests; forgetting thank you notes; focusing on new prospects rather than old friends; having a "one-size-fits-all" approach to fundraising; and assuming that courting connectors to money will automatically attract funding (Yoon, 2014).

Next Steps

Commitment to a culture of philanthropy will naturally lead you to evolving philosophies and best practices on fundraising. Development professionals contend that a paradigm shift for communicating with donors is in progress, including migration from one-way to two-way communication; cyclic to iterative strategic planning; "one and done" generic annual campaigns to "high frequency, low volume" appeals that are topical, focused, personalized, and include a mechanism for feedback; reliance on print media transmitted by mail to digital media transmitted electronically; and independent to unified brand messaging across all units of an organization ("Donor 3.0," n.d.). Thus, current best practices for communicating with donors and prospects include branding your school in alignment with the brand of the parent organization; attentive listening and observation to "know thy donors"; sharing your school's short-term tactical goals along with its long-term strategic goals; and actively participating in communities of like-minded people and organizations to showcase your school and its mission and discover possible avenues for collaboration and support.

Today's development professionals live by the code of "friend-raising before fundraising" and embrace the philosophy that "building friends, not funds" yields lasting rewards (Comstock, n.d.). If done well, friend-raising results in a cadre of loyal friends and supporters through careful cultivation of mutually beneficial, trusting, and credible relationships. Best practices for cultivating these relationships include finding common ground that links your brand (i.e., vision, mission, and values) with the vision and values of prospective friends of your organization; connecting with prospects on both rational and emotional levels; focusing start-up conversations on your school's values and strengths relative to what prospects care about and want to invest in; and incorporating generous portions of listening and patience into subsequent conversations about opportunities to support your school's mission (Comstock, n.d.). To cultivate a relationship with a prospect, get them to tell their story. Why are they interested in your school/college? Then take that information and link it to your strategic initiatives. Find their passion and make a connection to what your school/college or institution is doing. That is how deals are made.

Development-focused boards are not new; however, they remain an important mechanism for deepening the engagement of friends and supporters as well as a great source of organizational ambassadors and fundraising team members. Successful boards are informed, dedicated, focused, and supported. They have members who are passionate about nursing and knowledgeable about the school and its programs; bylaws that outline their structure, function, responsibilities, and privileges; and deans, faculty, and development staff who are committed to their effectiveness (Appel, Campbell, Lynch, & Novotny, 2007).

If you do not have access to a development-focused board, find out if you can create one to help you with fundraising. Be strategic about recruiting members. For example, putting a journalist on the board helps get the word out about your events and what you are doing as a school. Putting a banker on the board helps to solicit community and corporate support. Beyond this, Appel et al. (2007) suggest several considerations to guide start-up of a development-focused board, including a clear charge; criteria for board size, term of appointment, membership, and philanthropic support; frequency, focus, and standing agenda for meetings and retreats; criteria and process for selection of a board chair; expectations of board members; orientation and continuing education agenda; and responsibilities of the dean, faculty, and development staff in facilitating board effectiveness.

CONCLUSION

Fundraising is "mission critical" and big business in today's world of higher education. As a nurse, you have an edge on what it takes to be successful: expertise in cultivating caring relationships; experience in all aspects of teamwork; exquisite interpersonal skills; membership in the most trusted profession; and a mission that should touch the heart of anyone who has ever experienced healthcare. Over 10 years ago, veteran nursing dean and champion fundraiser Joyce Fitzpatrick published one of the few scholarly papers on the nursing dean's role in development activities (Fitzpatrick, 2005). The best practices for nursing deans and directors that she proposed in that paper are timeless and reflect the essence of what it takes to follow in her footsteps as a fundraising superstar:

> Persist and it will pay off.
> Build allies.
> Plan strategically.
> Ask fearlessly and do not leave money on the table.
> Invest in homework and preparation.
> Think creatively.
> Be confident and visible rather than shy and self-effacing.
> Treat everyone as a potential donor.

REFERENCES

Allers, C. (2013, September). *The six p's of successful friend-raising*. Retrieved from Georgia Center for Nonprofits website, https://gcn.org/articles

Appel, N., Campbell, S. H., Lynch, N., & Novotny, J. M. (2007). Creating effective advisory boards for schools of nursing. *Journal of Professional Nursing, 23*(6), 343–350. doi:10.3102/0034654316653479

Comstock, B. (n.d.). *Friend-raising before fund-raising: Connecting your values to those of your constituents can give you a leg up.* Retrieved from Sametz Blackstone Associates website, https://sametz.com/articles

Donor 3.0: Connecting with prospects of today, and tomorrow. (n.d.). Retrieved from SametzBlackstone Associates website, https://sametz.com/articles

Duronio, M. A., & Loessin, B. A. (1990). Fund-raising outcomes and institutional characteristics in ten types of higher education institutions. *The Review of Higher Education, 13*(4), 539–556. doi:10.1353/rhe.1990.0013

Fitzpatrick, J. J. (2005). The dean's role in development. In *Academic leadership in nursing: Making the journey* (pp. 129–138). Washington, DC: American Association of Colleges of Nursing.

Hunt, P. C. (2012). *Development for academic leaders: A practical guide for fundraising success.* San Francisco, CA: Jossey-Bass.

IUPUI Lilly School of Philanthropy. (n.d.). *Giving USA 2017 report highlights.* Retrieved from Giving USA website: store.givingusa.org

Judge, K. (2014). What's changed and what's stayed the same: A case study in nursing and philanthropy. *Nursing Administration Quarterly, 38*(4), 312–316. doi:10.1097/NAQ.0000000000000057

Kreimer, S. (2009, June). More than ever, big donors want to see value for their dollars. *H&HN:Hospitals & Health Networks, 83*(6), 20.

Lamphere, C. (2018, March/April). Sharing is caring: Crowdfunding's transformation of fundraising and the rise of the sharing economy. *Online Searcher, 42*(2), 27–29. Retrieved from http://www.infotoday.com/OnlineSearcher/Issue/7835-March-April2018.shtml

Masterson, K. (2017, June 9). What every dean needs to know about fund raising. *Chronicle of Higher Education, 63*(38), A8–A14.

Perlmutter, D. D. (2016, October). Fund raising for deans: How to match donors' passions with your college's needs. In *Focus: How to be a Dean* (pp. 22–24). Washington, DC: Chronicle of Higher Education.

Yoon, C. (2014). Developing a culture of philanthropy to support your mission. *Nursing Administration Quarterly, 38*(4), 299–302. doi:10.1097/NAQ.0000000000000059

12

INTERNAL AND EXTERNAL STAKEHOLDER ENGAGEMENT

EILEEN M. SULLIVAN-MARX | HEATHER M. YOUNG

INTRODUCTION

Increasingly, universities are focusing on their societal role and the multiple constituents critical to their success (Jongbloed, Enders, & Salerno, 2008). Nursing, with its social contract, is committed to serving and reflecting the community in its education, practice, and research missions. This requires a dynamic dialogue with community stakeholders that combines constituent expertise with academic expertise, leading to greater impact (Fitzgerald, Burns, Sonka, Furco, & Swanson, 2012).

The purpose of this chapter is to discuss the role of a dean of a school of nursing in setting strategies and implementing plans to achieve excellence in the mission of the school through engagement of internal and external stakeholders. This chapter uses two case examples to highlight success in relationships with internal and external constituents within a context of the current realities of higher education, that is, affordability, interprofessional education, and preparation of nurses for emerging healthcare changes relative to population health, primary care, and use of technology.

CASE EXAMPLES

The case examples draw from experience at two schools with different perspectives and chronology. The first describes remaking and rebranding a well-established school, New York University (NYU) Rory Meyers College of Nursing. The second describes establishing a new school, Betty Irene Moore School of

Nursing at the University of California Davis, with a powerful mandate from its funder. These case examples will illustrate the major topics of the chapter.

NYU: Refreshing the Vision and Rebranding a School in the Context of a Crisis

As the second dean of the NYU school of nursing, I followed a successful inaugural dean, Terry Fulmer, PhD, RN, FAAN. My initial challenge was to take the success that had been garnered and showcase it to internal stakeholders and external bodies. Importantly, the value of nursing to the university needed to be realized through the contributions that we could make as a leading school of nursing and more engaged participants in university governance and leadership. To achieve this, I needed to fortify faculty structures of governance and incentivize faculty to participate in the internal workings of the university. By doing so, we could attract new senior and beginning faculty to diversify our school portfolio and showcase our excellence to nursing organizations, accrediting bodies, funding agencies, and private donors.

Faculty Governance as a Leading Strategy

As I became dean, the NYU College of Nursing was essentially a "college of nursing within a college of dentistry." Prior to becoming a college, the school was a division of nursing within the school of education. Moving to a college level while growing a research portfolio required partnership with other health schools to facilitate a grants office. Simultaneously, growth in student enrollment was expected in order to generate tuition revenue. NYU was reluctant to establish nursing as an independent college until there was demonstration of a solid fiscal portfolio; however, the university was supportive of a new home for the school of nursing in a new building that was close to the health campus of the university.

Growing Faculty Governance and Reputation

This developmental phase of the school would require strong faculty governance to attract faculty and demonstrate effective faculty leadership, particularly for searches and appointment, promotion, and tenure (APT) committees. Moreover, clinical faculty did not have a coherent role and pathway for career development and promotion. Tuition was the main source of revenue for the school and, as a private school, NYU had high tuition and fees. This was a significant challenge at a time when we were building a new home for the school. While the university was reluctant to allow the school to become independent until financial means of support were clear, we could demonstrate that strong faculty governance would enhance our ability to recruit and retain a strong tenured and clinical faculty.

As background, NYU established a school of nursing in 1935, offering a baccalaureate degree and establishing the world's first PhD program in Nursing Theory and Development. NYU nursing has been known for its early work in nursing theory. Its nursing PhD and master's degree graduates have been and are major nursing leaders since the mid to late 20th century. The school of nursing, however, was situated within other schools and departments at NYU until 2006, when it became a college of nursing albeit "within" the NYU College of Dentistry. In 2006, Dean Terry Fulmer was appointed as the Inaugural Dean for the College of Nursing, reporting to the Dean of the College of Dentistry. In July 2012, I was appointed as the second dean of the NYU College of Nursing, also reporting to the Dean of the College of Dentistry, who reported along with the Dean of the School of Medicine (different person) to an Executive Vice President for Health at NYU. By February 2013, NYU had decided to reorganize the health schools so that the College of Nursing would become an independent college, no longer under Dentistry, and to establish a College of Global Public Health. So, who were the stakeholders, both internal and external, from whom others and I engaged to establish independence in this short span of time? What were the contextual factors that moved this forward? While no one ever wants a crisis, they will inevitably occur; so, how did we take advantage of unforeseen crises to showcase the advantages of an independent nursing college to NYU officials?

At NYU, it was clear that the nursing school had an excellent reputation; however, there was confusion, both within the university and in the larger world, as to how the school functioned within the College of Dentistry and whether the degrees offered were different in any way. As a new dean—and even during the negotiations prior to accepting a deanship—you want to have the opportunity to showcase the school to stakeholders as it currently stands and a plan for creating a future (Collins, 2005). Mission and vision statements ground the work of the school and create frameworks for presenting the school to stakeholders.

As in scholarship and teaching, theoretical frameworks undergird our approach to issues and assist us to establish plans and evaluate our work. This is just as true for your deanship and stakeholder matters. As a family and community health nurse with older adults, the Social Ecology Model (Bronfenbrenner, 1994) has always worked well for me. The model consists of concentric spheres starting with the individual and moving outward to include global communities and high-level organizational and governmental structures. Within these spheres are your stakeholders, what may commonly be called your internal stakeholders—the students, faculty, staff, and peer deans within other units in the university/college where you exist. External stakeholders are your professional community network—clinical practice, regulatory/governmental bodies, accrediting agencies, donors, thought leaders in healthcare and education, the National Institutes of Health (NIH) and other research funding agencies, the surrounding community, and national and global partners. Because of the overlapping functions, roles, and structures of all of these groups, I preferred thinking about them as part of the concentric circles in the context of the Social Ecology Model. This has helped me to think about intersections and how to facilitate new ideas or improvements (e.g., students are internal yet how they perform on NCLEX® examinations certainly connects with your accreditation stakeholders and external donors and peer reviewers).

As part of my early discussions in the search process and early days as a new dean, it was clear to me that faculty governance (internal stakeholders) in the college of nursing was key to operationalizing the mission and vision. Strengthening faculty governance created better visibility and understanding of the college's mission and vision among all stakeholders.

Mission and vision statements are often discounted as less than meaningful unless they are current, dynamic, and specific. These statements must be understood by stakeholders and resonate in repeated conversations, such as in your "elevator speech." In my early days as dean, I noted that the mission and vision statements were quite good and were highlighted in large letters on the walls of the administrative offices; however, nowhere could students, board members, or donors see them as we were in a temporary space while our new building was under construction. You will be asked in your first days as dean, "What is your vision for the school?" When asked this question at my first faculty and staff meeting, I simply replied, "We have a great vision, we just need to make it visible!" That statement resonated with the audience and other stakeholders and it became my motto during the first 100 days of my deanship. We used "making our vision visible" in all new dean communications, on email signatures, social media, stationery, and so on. And indeed, it became a sort of rallying cry for nursing to showcase itself regardless of whether it sat as a division or department or within another college—we are visible and we make a difference.

Then Came Sandy...

Superstorm Sandy hit the east coast on October 30, 2012, 8 weeks into my first semester as a new dean. Heroism was demonstrated by nurses who led evacuations from NYU's Langone Medical Center. Two days later, university administration called me to tap into my experience in community nursing. I was asked if nursing students could assist with visiting tenants of high-rise apartments in the NYU Washington Square area, who were now without running water, electricity, food, and medications. While not every dean experiences such a natural disaster crisis, most deans do have times when they can demonstrate to stakeholders their school's strength. Often nursing students can respond exceedingly well to community needs in emergency situations. These responses, which we might take for granted, can be linked to the larger community of stakeholders.

In the few days following Superstorm Sandy, lower Manhattan, the main location of NYU, remained in darkness. Many older and ill New Yorkers live in multiple high-rise apartment buildings in the Greenwich Village area around NYU, and they remained in place. As a good neighbor and in some cases, as landlord, NYU asked the College of Nursing to assist with checking on residents who were without electricity and water. We did so in teams with the Visiting Nurse Service of New York, assessing residents in three high-rise buildings. The teams of faculty and students impressed university officials with their skills and ability to respond. All data on risk assessments and rescues were shared with the trustees. The president of NYU held a special thank you reception for the nursing school and presented the volunteer responders with pins. In my opinion, this single event did more to coalesce the essence of nursing education and showcase our skills, critical thinking, and distinct body of knowledge than all of our publications or grant funding could ever have done. With our practice partners rescuing babies in the dead of night from neonatal ICUs (Cohen, 2012), our vision became quite visible.

As dean, I used this event to articulate our mission and vision and to showcase the success of our education in every formal and informal venue. For a full year afterward, and at anniversary events, we used the nursing student response during Superstorm Sandy as a representation to our stakeholders of our strength and the reason why our stakeholders should be proud of our college of nursing.

UC Davis Betty Irene Moore School of Nursing: Starting a New School, Establishing a Vision, and Gaining Support From Internal and External Stakeholders

This case example illustrates how internal and external stakeholders contributed to the development and sustainability of a new school of nursing. The major challenges for the founding dean were to identify relevant stakeholders, develop a communication plan including an inspiring vision, and engage stakeholders in making positive contributions during the launch phase of a new organization.

The Founding Grant

In 2007, the Gordon and Betty Moore Foundation announced the largest gift in the history of nursing education: $100 million to establish a new school of nursing at the University of California Davis. I had the privilege of joining the team at UC Davis in 2008 as the founding dean, charged with establishing the Betty Irene Moore School of Nursing. The donor, Betty Irene Moore, had many experiences as a family caregiver and as a patient that fell short of the ideal—she recognized the critical role that nurses play in healthcare delivery, quality, and safety. She believed that if nurses were prepared as leaders and equipped with systems thinking, they could advance quality at a faster pace than the status quo. She wanted a new army of nurses ready to promote person- and family-centered, high-quality, well-coordinated care. This gift was a highly visible gift, with lofty expectations to create a school that could transform the role of nurses in healthcare delivery and quality. It also arrived concurrently with the beginning of a significant economic recession. In short, it was a daunting task.

Engaging Stakeholders and Developing a Plan

Just as my colleague, Dean Sullivan-Marx, approached the challenge, I turned to the social ecological model to guide my thinking around stakeholder engagement. I knew that we would not succeed unless we were successful in engaging supporters and overcoming the objections of detractors. This endeavor had both local and national significance and required the endorsement of multiple stakeholders to move the initiative forward.

I began the process by convening our core team—faculty, staff, and leaders at UC Davis who would be central to the entire process. The founding core team shared several key characteristics: They were creative, bold, willing to take risks, flexible, dedicated, able to multitask, and resilient. We developed a strong project plan, with timelines and key deliverables, and mapped the processes that we would need to pursue to gain approval from the UC Regents to establish the school as a business entity, launch graduate programs, obtain national accreditation, and establish a sustainability plan. We initiated a process of rapid cycle improvement and developed a formal evaluation plan with metrics, regularly reviewing our progress and allowing for course corrections.

In the first month, I hosted a 3-day summit to guide development of the vision and engage external, influential stakeholders as partners. We invited thought leaders in nursing from across the nation to grapple with three key questions: (a) How would you describe the nurse of the future (20 years out)?; (b) Given what nurses will be doing, what should our education include (i.e., curricular elements)?; and (c) What knowledge do we need to generate to support practice and education in the future (i.e., research agenda)? After 3 days, we had a strong vision for the nurse of the future and the essential elements of education and research. We also had gained the support and engagement of key stakeholders—national thought leaders who could advise on an ongoing basis, advocate for the school, and continue to share their ideas as programs developed.

With this strong foundation, we held over a dozen town hall meetings with regional stakeholders, presenting the main ideas from the national summit, and getting their input on the three key questions. The town halls ranged from around 20 attendees to over 200 and targeted specific stakeholders including academic health system and community system leaders and nurses; schools of medicine faculty; consumer groups; nursing faculty from other programs in the region; community providers; and advocacy groups. We built further consensus around the three questions and, again, enlisted support and advocacy from participants.

We formed a National Advisory Council (NAC) comprised of thought leaders in health and healthcare, who provided regular consultation to the founding team, advising on strategy, brand building, key focal areas, and organizational development. The members of the NAC provided advice for our development and also, through their networks, expanded our ability to disseminate our message and gain broader support. We also formed a Regional Advisory Group, including community and health system leaders, who could provide guidance on regional priorities and trends and ensure cultural inclusion in our design and student enrollment.

UC Davis has strong faculty governance, and because we did not have a critical mass of faculty early on, we formed a graduate group in Nursing Science and Health Care Leadership. The group was comprised of faculty who we hired as they arrived, as well as key faculty from relevant disciplines including public health, informatics, medicine, nutrition, psychology, and more. We augmented UC Davis faculty with visiting professors from leading nursing schools who participated in curriculum development. I engaged the UC Davis Faculty Senate early on as partners in helping me to navigate the approval process both at the campus and UC system-wide, developing a strong understanding of their expectations for proposals and criteria for evaluation. With regular, transparent communication, we were able to move the proposals through the lengthy approval process.

The university administration is another key stakeholder group. We established regular meetings with key leaders to update them on progress and enlist support and approvals. Given the recession and cutbacks in state funding, it was critical to communicate with decision makers so that the new school would gain necessary fiscal support. The foundation staff and board were also key stakeholders, and we held regular meetings to address progress with deliverables as well as enlisting input and advice. Having a formalized evaluation process that provided a dashboard of progress, along with specific outcomes, assisted these communications.

Accrediting bodies and the Board of Registered Nursing were additional key stakeholders. As we aimed to innovate in education, new interpretations of existing regulations and guidelines were required. Early conversations and eliciting input all along the way fostered a sense of collaboration that resulted in gaining approval for new approaches.

Because the $100 million was needed to launch the school, we had to develop endowments and capital funds, in addition to securing state funding, for ongoing sustainability. We developed a fundraising plan and engaged potential donors actively to contribute their ideas, volunteer their time and energy, and make financial commitments to the school. We engaged elected officials who were interested in the healthcare workforce, both as part of higher education and also as it related to advancing population health. They were crucial to securing state and national support for many of our priorities.

Finally, our prospective students and their future employers were key stakeholders. We initiated a LISTSERV and developed social media messaging to communicate with both individual prospective students and large employers to brand the school, distribute information relevant to applications, and build the persuasive case to enlist their interest and ultimate enrollment.

Over a 10-year period, these efforts led to the establishment of the Betty Irene Moore School of Nursing with five graduate programs (PhD, Master's in Leadership, Master's for Family Nurse Practitioners, Master's for Physician Assistants, and a Master's Entry Program for new RN graduates), as well as building a 70,000 sq. ft. state-of-the-art educational and research facility.

LISTENING TO YOUR STAKEHOLDERS

These case studies illustrate the array of stakeholders necessary for success and identify the importance of robust relationships. The overarching theme of these cases is the willingness to listen deeply to stakeholders, understand their perspectives, and make visible the ways their advice and input is incorporated into operations. The dean holds the vision and understands what is needed to accomplish that vision; from this perspective, the dean can identify who the relevant stakeholders are and develop the appropriate engagement plan (Kouzes & Posner, 2017). It is incumbent upon the dean to make the issues relevant to the stakeholder, sharing information in ways that reflect their perspective and priorities. Once the intent and perspective of the stakeholder is known, it becomes easier to enlist their support in a meaningful way. For example, one donor may love giving scholarship funds, but another prefers contributing to capital costs and naming spaces in buildings.

Stakeholder engagement is cyclical and must reflect the priorities of the school. At times in university life, accreditation and ranking may be a top priority for your president/chancellor and trustees, whereas other years, it will be the ability to attract top faculty. You need to be aware of these cycles and set your strategic plan to meet these cycles in the context of what is important for the nursing profession at the same time. Research funders will want to know their return on investment since we know that the National Institutes of Health and philanthropic foundations will continue to fund growing programs of successful research that match their priorities.

Ongoing feedback from stakeholders and reflection is important for both short- and long-term success. For example, local elected officials will want to know how you might be developing nursing career opportunities for local high school students. Engaging with the community surrounding your school is a good way to know how you and your students and faculty are viewed. Are you enhancing the community? Is your school/university something that they can speak about with pride? Or is the university viewed as an elite, elusive structure that few people know about? In addition to the usual way to engage with elected and other leaders, we always speak with local neighborhood storeowners, vendors, cab drivers, custodians, and passersby to make sure that they feel we are part of their neighborhood. This goes a long way to hearing reflection about nursing and your school that you would not hear from vested stakeholders.

CREATING AND COMMUNICATING A VISION: BEING THE "FACE" OF THE SCHOOL

The dean is the chief communicator for a school of nursing, and this requires a great message, a strategy to reach the appropriate audiences, and strong communication skills across multiple media. A great message communicates the vision and priorities in a concise and consistent manner. It starts with developing a strong elevator speech for important communications. Elevator speeches—short 1- to 3-minute sound bites—might include the overall vision and current priorities of the school or targeted communications about specific programs or challenges (Sjodin, 2012). Elevator speeches might be proactive or might be crafted to respond in crisis communication. The overall purpose is to provide relevant information in a concise way that keeps the attention of the listener and is memorable. This kind of communication is unlike most academic communication that seeks to explain in detail a concept or finding.

Elevator speech communication is pointed, confident, and purposeful. It is a message that gets repeated over and over again without variation so that the idea is understood and embraced by many stakeholders. Take every opportunity to brand your school with your vision across different audiences.

Communication requires strategy. Invest in a good communication and development team or use your university staff well to develop a strategy that includes defining the priority audiences and messages and the tactics to ensure effective communication. Make sure that both the school of nursing and university communication teams are on message about nursing and the school of nursing at all times by providing relevant updates and information and contributing to framing the message. Student voices on the web, stories in print materials, and thematically putting stories of faculty together are key to the audience you want to reach. Twitter feed and Instagram reach potential student applicants and faculty and require an understanding of the tactics and advantages of each type of social media and how to deploy these resources (Burton, McLemore, Perry, Carrick, & Shattell, 2016; Kenner & Pressler, 2012). Nurses tend to talk with other nurses, and we have not yet broken out of the cycle of doing so on social media; instead, getting "likes" and "followers" from all stakeholders should be our goal.

SETTING STRATEGY AND GUIDING THE MISSION

The dean is responsible for the overall strategy of the school and for ensuring that the operations of the school advance the mission. Effective strategy reflects stakeholder input because it increases the likelihood of widespread adoption of the priorities. Schools and universities vary in how they develop their strategy—from highly structured plans with metrics to guiding frameworks. The dean must understand the overall planning process and strategic priorities of the university as part of school-level planning. In addition, strategic priorities of the profession, funding agencies, and the surrounding community should influence the planning process.

Formal advisors can play a vital role in strategic planning in the form of councils, individual consultants, and key informants. Members should include individuals who can be advocates for nursing and for the school and enhance the network and resources of the school. Effective boards or advisory councils go beyond nursing alumni and include influential members of the broader community (Lott, 2012). At UC Davis, the NAC has provided critical input and guidance on both creating and communicating strategy. Early on, we worked with the NAC co-chairs to define the structure and process for the council so that members could be most effective. After a couple of years, these practices were formalized as bylaws. A key feature is a close partnership between the dean and the co-chairs, who together identify priority discussion topics for the NAC and craft the agenda to accomplish the goals of the conversation.

Since 2006, when NYU nursing became a college within the college of dentistry, the inaugural dean established a Board of Advisors. This group consisted of friends of nursing in the New York City area who had philanthropic networks and a history of supporting nursing. Active members also included alumni and those who would know how to advise the dean on matters as a new college. Since 2012, we have formalized this board as a "Dean's Council," a term used throughout NYU for other such advisory or friendly supportive groups. The Dean's Council does not have governance responsibility for the college of nursing because that responsibility rests with the trustees of NYU. In addition to formalizing terms and expectations of annual giving for each council member, we have grown membership on the council to 25. Council members are engaged with faculty and student activities throughout the year and attend social events where faculty present their work in small sessions. This level of engagement has expanded further interest in support and outreach to others, particularly for scholarship funding. The donor who named the college is a NYU trustee and alumnus of the business school and an active member of the Dean's Council.

ENSURING SUSTAINABILITY THROUGH INFLUENCE

The dean is responsible for the operational and fiscal health of the school of nursing. Increasingly, funding models for schools are more complex, incorporating traditional sources of state support (when available) and tuition/fee revenue, but also adding fundraising, practice revenues, and partnerships with academic health centers and other entities. The annual budget process should follow the strategic plan for the school, and should plan for resources to ensure enactment of the operational and capital goals. Financing involves convincing those who have resources to commit their resources to your priorities. Stakeholder engagement is critical to this process and should consider a variety of players, from the faculty and staff of the school to university decision makers, external funders, and donors. Securing support hinges on effective communication and influence (Kenner, Pressler, & Klepper, 2008). The language of elevator speeches in the fiscal arena must reflect a business case, highlighting how resources support priorities (of the school and of the stakeholder involved), details of revenues and expenses, return on investment, opportunity cost, and the risks of not making the necessary investments. In addition to these elements, donors also want to know how the investment advances their passion and priority. When effective, stakeholders can be instrumental in securing financial support and can also advocate for additional support.

REPUTATION MANAGEMENT

The dean is frequently in the position of communicating in response to external communications, either in the form of crisis communication or by using general news as a way of enhancing the reputation of the school. Successful reputation management presupposes an awareness of external news and information that provides a springboard for communication. The communication team can be charged with monitoring news feeds relevant to the school and developing talking points relevant to important topics. For example, with the release of the National Academies in Science, Engineering, and Medicine report on the Future of Nursing, there were many opportunities to use this highly visible report to advance messages about the schools of nursing at NYU and UC Davis. Having an active plan for stakeholder communication, with ready contact information, facilitates timely communication related to reputation. Media training can be very helpful for deans to develop the skills and composure needed for effective communication under pressure. The public relations department of the university can play a vital role in ensuring success by interacting with reporters prior to interviews, preparing the dean for the interview, and anticipating potential questions and issues that might arise in the conversation (Pressler & Kenner, 2010).

CONCLUSION

In closing, successful engagement of stakeholders is a cornerstone of effective leadership. Stakeholders can play a role in shaping the future of a school of nursing, advancing the mission, and supporting sustainability.

REFERENCES

Bronfenbrenner, U. (1994). Ecological models of human development. In *International Encylopedia of Education* (2nd ed., Vol. 3). Oxford, UK: Elsevier.

Burton, C., McLemore, M., Perry, L., Carrick, J., & Shattell, M. (2016). Social media awareness and implications in nursing leadership: A pilot professional meeting campaign. *Policy, Politics, & Nursing Practice, 17*(4), 187–197. doi:10.1177/1527154417698143

Cohen, E. (2012). *N.Y. hospital staff carry sick babies down 9 flights of stairs during evacuation*. Retrieved from http://www.cnn.com/2012/10/30/health/sandy-hospital/index.html

Collins, J. (2005). *Good to great and the social sectors*. New York, NY: HarperCollins.

Fitzgerald, H., Burns, K., Sonka, S., Furco, A., & Swanson, L. (2012). The centrality of engagement in higher education. *Journal of Higher Education Outreach and Engagement, 16*(3), 7–28.

Jongbloed, B., Enders, J., & Salerno, C. (2008). Higher education and its communities: Interconnections, interdependencies and a research agenda. *Higher Education, 56*(3), 303–324. doi:10.1007/s10734-008-9128-2

Kenner, C., & Pressler, J. (2012). Social media and the dean. *Nurse Educator, 37*(4), 139–140.

Kenner, C., Pressler, J., & Klepper, R. (2008). Managing up. *Nurse Educator, 33*(6), 235–236.

Kouzes, J., & Posner, B. (2017). *The leadership challenge*. Hoboken, NJ: Wiley.

Lott, J. (2012). Creating an effective dean's board. *Nurse Educator, 37*(1), 6–7.

Pressler, J., & Kenner, C. (2010). Speaking with the press. *Nurse Educator, 35*(1), 4–5.

Sjodin, T. (2012). *Small message, big impact: The elevator speech effect*. New York, NY: Penguin.

PERSPECTIVES ON FINANCIAL MANAGEMENT FOR DEANS OF NURSING PROGRAMS

Culture, Policy, and Leadership

GLORIA FERRARO DONNELLY

INTRODUCTION

Managing the finances and resources of a school of nursing (SON) is a critical responsibility of the dean, requiring a deep understanding of how the parent institution and its various constituencies value nursing and support its mission and operations. The technical aspects of financial management, how to construct and track academic budgets, are not the focus of this chapter. Instead, we will explore financial management from three perspectives: (a) the importance of academic culture and how it directly influences the management of finances; (b) culturally driven financial policy and processes, that is, the models and rubrics selected by the institution that guide and determine the allocation of resources and the flow of money; and (c) leadership strategies for deans to promote fair and effective financial management of nursing units. This chapter offers a way of thinking about financial management that will benefit the dean and ultimately the nursing unit.

ACADEMIC CULTURE

The following vignette illustrates how culture creeps into the dean's day-to-day management of and advocacy for resources to manage the school and realize the mission.

Vignette 1: The Food Chain

You have prepared diligently for the planning meeting to finalize the SON's long awaited consolidation in one building, a resource issue that has haunted a growing school for 6 years. There are three attendees from the facilities department—the director, a space planner/designer, and the project manager with whom you have worked to validate the parameters of the consolidation. As a dean, you are the only invited representative from the SON. You present the plan for the dean's office and SON administrators and staff to swap spaces with a nonacademic administrative unit of the university that is currently occupying the space. The spreadsheet that you distribute demonstrates the cost-effectiveness of this plan that can be quickly accomplished with little disruption to the relocating parties—the SON and the university administrative unit. You acknowledge that although the swap will put the university administrative unit into an older building, the consolidation of all SON leadership, faculty, and staff will create conveniences and efficiencies for SON personnel and most importantly for students at a time of growing enrollment. There is dead silence at the end of your presentation. The space planner finally makes direct eye contact with you and asks, "Just where do you think the school of nursing sits in the university's food chain to displace such an important administrative unit?" Without hesitation, you reply, "With respect to the proverbial food chain, the school of nursing is a revenue-generating unit conducting the core business of the university—education, research, and practice. Therefore, it is higher in the food chain than the administrative support unit that it is displacing." Again, the silence is deafening. Eventually, after further substantiation efforts to key senior administrative officials, the consolidation of the SON is realized.

The space planner's question concerning the place of the SON within the metaphorical "food chain" is a reflection of cultural mythologies operating in universities. The dean's understanding of nursing's "place" is contemporary, rational, and business oriented, derived from the school's mission and contribution to the university overall and the school's collective perception of its relative importance. The space planner's remark may reflect the historical view of nursing in society and in the organizational culture of the university.

Martin (1992) explores the complexity of organizational cultures from a variety of perspectives. She asserts that as individuals work in organizations they experience

> *formal rules and procedures…informal codes of behavior, rituals, tasks, pay systems, jargon and jokes only understood by insiders.… When cultural members interpret the meanings of these manifestations, their perceptions, memories, beliefs,*

experiences and values will vary, so interpretations will differ—even of the same phenomenon. **The patterns or configurations of these interpretations, and the ways they are enacted, constitute culture.** (p. 3)

The opening vignette suggests that the university can be considered a metaphorical "food chain," a hierarchy of colleges, schools, and administrative units that have relative status. This status is driven by the longevity of the unit in the university system; the academic pecking order; the societal importance of the disciplines or professions included in schools; the original mission of the university; the tuition or research revenue that the school generates; or the perceived importance that a nonacademic unit such as finance or legal may have in managing and protecting the university.

It is important for a dean to know the university's rationale for including nursing programs among its degree offerings. Offering nursing degrees could be driven by (a) a mission-driven community need documented with a market analysis; (b) the acquisition of a school through a merger or partnership; (c) an administrative champion of nursing who sees nursing's long-term benefits to the university; (d) the need to grow enrollment through a new nursing program and stabilize related departments that provide required courses to nursing students; and (e) a mandate from an external body such as the county or state. Knowledge of nursing's origin in the university can help frame requests by including, for example, a connection to the mission, to growth potential, or to the requirements of an external body. Further, in the disciplinary hierarchy of the university, the dean may discover that nursing is perceived as less important than the sciences, humanities, or other clinical disciplines, as an "emerging discipline," or at worst, as a financial "helper bee" to other programs or to the university in general.

Donnelly (2017) describes her difficulties as a program director in a faith-based university in garnering resources for a new nursing program experiencing explosive growth:

> My attempts at securing resources were often clumsy (i.e., too direct and demanding). My written requests for resources to support program growth were factual and data driven, but that did not seem to matter. In one instance, the Provost responded to my carefully substantiated request with a flat "no" and a critique of my grammar. (p. 226)

After consultation with a "mentor" in senior administration and a concerted effort to understand the history, traditions, and values of the institution, she learned to reframe requests in accordance with cultural norms, for example, "petitioning" instead of "demanding," and was ultimately successful in obtaining resources to meet operational goals. The decision to include nursing degree offerings in this case was both an expression of the university's mission and a response to market opportunity. Understanding the complexity of such decisions within the context of university culture should positively influence the framing of requests for resources.

Collins (2005) asserts that decision-making in social sector organizations such as universities is qualitatively different from decision-making in corporate/business settings. He describes the failed attempts of a corporate CEO-turned-academic dean to move faculty toward his vision and strategy using a top-down, executive style. The faculty responded negatively and frequently stonewalled, which drove the dean back to the corporate sector after realizing that his "executive leadership skills" did not work in academia. Collins (2005) describes two types of leadership skill—executive and legislative:

> In executive leadership, the individual leader has enough concentrated power to simply make the right decisions. In legislative leadership…no individual leader, not even the nominal chief executive—has enough structural power to make the most important decisions by himself or herself. Legislative leadership relies more upon persuasion, political currency and shared interests to create the conditions for the right decisions to happen. (p. 11)

Tierney (1988) defines organizational culture as "the study of particular webs of significance within an organizational setting." Approaching the organization as an anthropologist observing a village or clan deepens a dean's understanding and assists in avoiding the inevitable clashes that occur when management strategies or decisions do not match cultural norms and expectations. University culture is a powerful force in shaping financial policy and practice (Schein, 2010). As Peter Drucker (2007), the iconic expert on management, noted, "culture eats strategy for breakfast and lunch."

Table 13.1 enumerates other cultural themes of the university that may impact the management of finances.

FINANCIAL POLICY AND PROCESSES

Managing the finances of a nursing unit is a mission-driven activity focused on three questions: (a) Are there sufficient resources to fund the delivery of high-quality programs to support students and faculty and to meet external regulatory standards? (b) How does a dean evaluate and promote efficiency, productivity, and innovation? (c) Considering all academic units in the school and the university, is there parity in resource allocation that results in mission fulfillment, excellence, and response to market-driven opportunities?

TABLE 13.1 Cultural Themes of the University Influencing Financial Management

CULTURAL VIEWS OF THE UNIVERSITY'S IMAGE AND MORES	UNIVERSITY'S CULTURAL ARTIFACTS OR EXPRESSIONS OF CULTURE
Elite or Egalitarian Secular or Faith Based Innovative—Entrepreneurial Aggressive—Competitive Team—People—Family Oriented Stable or Fluctuating On the Rise or Trending Down Patriarchal or Androcentric Socially Responsible Hierarchical or Decentralized	The Focus of the Mission Statement Education–Research–Practice Balance The Quality and Sufficiency of the Facilities Degree of Faculty Input Into Financial Matters Type of Budget System Employed Organizational Financial Guidelines—Open or Hidden? Organizational Rituals such as Budget Hearings Stories and Lore, Such as History of Financial Distress or Triumph Ways of Communicating, that Is, a Finance Webpage; Public Rules and Guidelines

Question 1: Are there sufficient resources to fund the delivery of high-quality programs to support students and faculty and to meet external regulatory standards?

Deans must closely examine the sources and uses of financial and other resources earned by and allotted to the school. Table 13.2 itemizes the most common sources of support/funding and typical uses in academic units.

Financial management in universities has evolved over the past five decades. As director of a hospital school of nursing in the 1970s, I never participated in budget development nor did I have a formal budget document. I was not aware that extra funding was provided by the Center for Medicare Services to hospitals that had SONs, nor was I privy to the amount of that funding. I submitted requests that were either approved or rejected. Later as director of a new nursing program in my first university position in the 1980s, financial management and budgeting was highly centralized. I had no input into budget development with the exception of projecting the enrollment of full-time and part-time students, staffing needs, number of classroom and clinical sections, new equipment or upgrades, and instructional supplies. I received an annual departmental expense budget, which I tracked monthly; however, tuition and fee revenue was not reflected in the monthly budget statements. When nursing was refused a budget request to support growth or program enhancement, it was difficult to determine the reason for denial in the absence of knowledge about the revenue/expense ratio. Further, each year a fixed percent increase or decrease was applied to all budgets making it especially difficult for program

TABLE 13.2 Sources and Uses of Financial and Other Resources in Academic Units

SOURCES	USES
* **Net tuition revenue**—revenue after discounts, merit scholarships, and so forth * **Fees**—lab fees, IT fees, and so forth that are assigned to the school's budget * **Grants and gifts** according to specifications (grants may offset salaries; gifts may be used to capitalize the unit, i.e., build labs) * **Endowments**—usually restricted to scholarships or specific uses; endowments earn annual interest and have spending rules * **Other revenue**—continuing education programs, conferences, and so forth; extra university allocations based on incentives; practice revenue * **Designated funds**—used only for specific purposes * **Unrestricted funds**—may be used for reinvestment in the college or special, one-time purposes at the discretion of the dean or a committee	* **Faculty and staff salaries and benefits** (benefit percentage should always be in the expense calculation) * **Instructional and office supplies** * **Capital equipment**—computers, computerized manikins * **Dues, fees, and accreditation costs for external organizations** * **Faculty development**—conference and meeting fees, travel, and lodging * **Rent or depreciation**—includes rent for office/classroom or practice space or for rental contracts for major equipment; if the school resides on a university-owned property, depreciation rather than rent is usually applied * **University allocations and taxes**—the school's share of support for library, student services, enrollment, senior administration, and so forth

IT, information technology.

managers, knowing that some university programs were shrinking while nursing was rapidly growing. It was not until the late 1990s, in an *incremental budgeting system*, that I was required to develop both a revenue and expense budget for a new SON in an academic health center whose mission was to serve the needs of 19 hospitals, to innovate, and to grow. Discounts and merit aid were subtracted from gross revenue to yield the school's *net tuition revenue*, that crucial number that signifies the school's primary contribution to the university. I learned that the key metric in successful financial management is knowing the relationship between net revenue and expense, referred to as the "margin." This revenue margin was ultimately controlled by senior administration who allocated a portion for school expenses. This margin also contributed to supporting non–revenue-generating units of the university such as the library, administrative services, and other strategic initiatives of the university.

The university also incentivized enrollment growth by returning a percentage of new net revenue to the school and in some cases matching newly awarded grant funding to promote further research. Incentives can work effectively if they are used to improve the learning environment for students and faculty; that is, better labs and equipment, balancing teaching load and class size, or additional faculty and staff. However, incentives for growing enrollment can be a double-edged sword if they do not accrue in some tangible way to the faculty, staff, and students.

Finally, I led a large college in a university that adopted Responsibility Center Management (RCM), a highly decentralized budget system, at least theoretically designed to give deans greater control over resources, encourage entrepreneurial efforts to cover direct and indirect costs, and pay the school's share of university administration and strategic initiatives. Revenue remaining after expenses and RCM taxes was returned to the college for reinvestment. Strauss and Curry (2002) studied the results of RCM in universities 25 years after the inception of the model. With respect to the role of deans, RCM requires that "leaders build bases of informed support for explicit and very public bets on the future" (Strauss & Curry, 2002, p. 43). This approach demands collegial rather than "top-down" governance in which the dean "leads," not just "administers," and also can freely employ an entrepreneurial spirit. The move to more decentralized and incentivized budget models by universities has accelerated in recent years; however, it is often difficult for senior administration to relinquish control.

Table 13.3 identifies types of budgeting systems commonly used in universities today, their benefits, and their challenges. Every university has financial policies and processes that reflect cultural beliefs about resource management. The dean's goal is to understand the university's financial management philosophy and budgeting system and to use that information for the benefit of the school. Nurse administrators generally excel at mastering and complying with policy and processes and efficiently managing resources because of their organizational skills and clinical management background. However, in the absence of knowledge about the procedural/cultural interface, deans can fall short in acquiring resources to achieve the school's mission and goals. Box 13.1 lists questions concerning standard financial procedural issues that a dean may find useful in mastering the nuances of the university procedures, in avoiding mistakes, and in accessing crucial financial information.

Through a variety of deanships, I have learned to view budgets as quantitative road maps existing in cultural contexts. If, as one consultant asserted, "a budget is a quantitative expression of how well a unit or organization is managed," the execution of that budget is a qualitative expression of how well the dean understands the "theory" of the budgeting system and the "culture-based practices" of senior administrators responsible for finances. For example, the underlying "theory" of RCM posits that returning control to the school or unit will incentivize the leadership and faculty to innovate, grow, and/or improve. However, it may be difficult "in practice" for senior administrators to let go

TABLE 13.3 Types of Budget Models Employed in Universities

BUDGET MODEL	DEFINITION	BENEFITS AND CHALLENGES
Incremental Budgeting	Base budgets are increased or decreased by a percentage assigned by central administration. Only new revenue is allocated, and budget cuts are usually an across-the-board percentage for all units	Relatively simple, predictable, and inexpensive to implement; the model does not address the need to cut budgets in individual nonperforming units
Zero-Based Budgeting	Previous year's budget is cleared; that is, no revenue carry-over and a new budget is constructed based on tuition, grants, and other income projections and the projected expenses of the unit	Can control unnecessary costs especially legacy appropriations, that is, same annual sum despite changing market conditions; expensive to implement as there is a new start each year
Responsibility Center Management	Operational authority for the budget **resides in the schools** that control generated revenue, pay all expenses, and are assigned percentage allocations to support university offices, services, and strategic initiatives; it is a decentralized budget system; if the school has a deficit at year's end, payback mechanisms in subsequent years are enacted	RCM can work if the subventions (taxes allocated to the schools) have been vetted among school leadership for reasonableness; depending on the allocations, schools could be big winners or losers; can create internal competition for students among schools as well as affect curricular decisions like the elimination of cross-school electives
Activity-Based, Incentive-Based, or Initiative-Based Budgeting	Often driven by the strategic plan of the institution or the school; allocations are made to support initiatives and plans—that is, there may be one-time funds to enhance key facilities or multi-year allocations to support new degree offerings; incentives may include returning a percentage of new initiative revenue back to the school to invest as they see fit; can be applied in centralized or decentralized budgeting systems	Activity- or incentive-based systems often take too much time to implement and are particularly sensitive to the vagaries of the external environment; the initiative that the budget is addressing may not materialize or the incentive may not accrue to those who worked to realize the incentivized rewards
Performance-Based Budgeting	Funding is directly based on a school's or unit's defined outcomes; this type of budgeting is often mandated by legislative bodies that fund public institutions	Tries to determine income based on expected results; attempts to eliminate waste with allocations tied to specific outcomes; analyses to determine credible results are complicated and time-consuming

NOTE: This table was compiled from references/resources in Table 13.4—Key Academic Finance and Budgeting Guides and Resources.

> **BOX 13.1**
>
> ## BASIC ACADEMIC FISCAL MANAGEMENT QUESTIONS FOR DEANS OF NURSING PROGRAMS
>
> Does the university construct budgets on a fiscal (July 1–June 30) or on a calendar year (January 1–December 31)? Knowing the time periods in which revenue is booked can avoid pitfalls such as the capturing of revenue in programs with nonstandard admission cycles.
>
> Who is involved in the development of the school's budget, that is, the dean, financial director, chairs, other administrators, faculty representatives? Who is the final person or approving body of the school budget? The university budget? Are there formal budget hearings?
>
> Does the university have a web-based financial management program and who in the school has access to data? What is the degree of transparency with which the university shares financial data?
>
> What are the spending rules for categories of revenue, that is, if there is a resignation, can the remaining salary be appropriated for expenses other than salary? Does the school have unrestricted accounts in which money in the form of gifts or incentive dollars is placed for discretionary use?
>
> Is the budget centralized in the school or does each chair or program director have and manage a budget? What accountability processes are in place?
>
> If the budget system is decentralized like RCM, is there a university committee with dean representation that sets taxation/subvention percentages?
>
> Does the school of nursing or parts of it (i.e., research labs, practices, learning labs) reside in owned or rented space? If the school's space is rented, is the rent charged to the school's budget? Is the school's budget charged a standard university depreciation tax even if it is paying rent for its facilities?
>
> How are costs for technology shared between the school and the university? (equipment, licenses, etc.)
>
> Who is responsible for tracking expenditures in the school's budget and for determining fiscal health? Is there a school committee that gives input into finances? Does the faculty receive quarterly and annual reports on the fiscal health of the school?
>
> ---
> RCM, Responsibility Center Management.

of centralized control so much so that trust in the new RCM system erodes and new problems evolve. There is no perfect system for managing academic finances. Overreliance on process and procedure to get the best outcome is as dangerous as blind trust and fiscal naiveté given how culture, politics, and tradition influence and complicate financial management.

Question 2: How does a dean evaluate and promote efficiency, productivity, and innovation?

Belt tightening, budget cuts, and "doing more with less" is the new reality in academic settings. Dumestre (2016) asserts that "U.S. universities are either financially at risk or are moving in that direction because the cost of the traditional model is outpacing the middle class family's ability to pay" (p. 12). Over the past few decades, college tuition has increased by nearly 260%, whereas family wages have remained flat. In publicly supported universities, legislatures have reduced support, whereas the demand for higher education is rising. Deans, therefore, need to drive both efficiency and productivity within a framework of innovation and strategic initiatives. In the traditional sense, efficiency is producing results with a minimum of resources, effort, time, or skill, in short, "doing more with less with good outcomes." Productivity is the "rate of output produced by total expenditures"; in short, getting the best results in relation to the level of resources expended. Productivity is not only about teaching and research, it is primarily about quality outcomes: How well are students learning as measured, for example, by NCLEX-RN® scores or certification pass rates; how do students rate the instructional operation, that is, teachers, courses, and clinical sites; are nursing graduates sought by employers; how do faculty fulfill scholarly and service expectations? *With 40 years of experience leading nursing programs, I assert, unequivocally, that the constant monitoring of quality in all school operations is the core of effective financial management, given the inevitable deterioration that occurs in the absence of quality.*

Efficiency is somewhat easier to measure and document as long as we make reasonable comparisons across school programs or across other professional programs in the university. We can benchmark efficiency, for example, by tracking the number of faculty per full-time equivalent student; the number of student credit hours generated by each faculty member each term (note: student credit hours = number of students in a class by number of credits assigned to the course); the number of staff per faculty and students enrolled in each program; the number of square feet occupied by the faculty and staff of each program; and the number of square feet allocated for nursing clinical learning labs. These are normative efficiency rubrics that should be performed routinely and compared across types of faculty and programs, that is, teaching or research faculty, tenure track or nontenure track faculty, and undergraduate and graduate programs. Rubrics concerning the above ratios may be set at the university level by bargaining agreements, or by external bodies that regulate nursing, or by long-held faculty beliefs and traditions about the teaching enterprise in clinical programs.

Senior academic administrators (Cook, 2009) have opined the high cost of nursing education compared with nonclinical programs, referring to nursing programs as "dogs" and not "cash cows" or "stars" in the context of the Boston Consulting Group's (BCG) business model of unit profitability (Reeves, Moose, & Venema, n.d.). However, academic administrators may be misinterpreting the BCG model, which includes four categories: *stars, cash cows, dogs,* and *unknowns*. *Stars* are programs that exist in high-growth markets, as nursing has been and will be through the next decade; however, the parent organization needs to invest in stars to maintain their twinkle. *Cash cows* are programs that may have once been *stars* but now exist in low growth markets and have captured the market share in their region or community. *Dogs* exist in low growth markets, have low market share, and operate at a loss; however, they often persist among university programs because of "mission," legacy, or administrative inertia. Experimental or new programs may be characterized as *unknowns* in the BCG model.

Unlike programs that do not require labs and other direct, supervised experiences, clinical programs can be particularly expensive, especially when full-time nursing faculty teach the majority of clinical sections. Even when "lab fees" are applied to clinical courses to defray costs, clinical instruction contributes to the notion that nursing programs are excessively expensive. However, clinical instruction staffing models can be a point of cost-effective innovation for schools of nursing. Consider Vignette 2 as an example of both programmatic and fiscal innovation.

Vignette 2: Innovating Clinical Instruction—From Experiment to Model

After surviving tough financial times, the market favored nursing enrollment and a new undergraduate nursing program emerged. Enrollment demand was high, and there was an eagerness to admit as many qualified applicants as possible. Faculty–student ratios mandated by clinical affiliates ranged from 1 to 8 in acute care settings to 1 to 6 in pediatric clinical settings. The pro forma budget for the new program revealed enormous instructional expense if clinical teaching was restricted to only full-time faculty. After checking regulations and accreditation standards, the program leadership with faculty input developed a business model wherein full-time nursing faculty did not teach clinical sections as part of teaching loads. Instead, expert clinicians from hospitals and other settings with whom the faculty had close relationships were recruited to be part-time clinical faculty. Clinicians who worked 12-hour shifts, 3 days per week, were particularly interested in clinical teaching for 1 or 2 days per week and on weekends. Affiliates were supportive since their clinicians would be involved in the clinical teaching of future new nursing staff and would have the opportunity to problem-solve through teaching. There were also part-time clinicians interested in the teaching role. An hourly rate was established for clinical teaching. A full-time faculty member teaching the course didactically provided clinical oversight and troubleshooting for all sections and was assigned credit for this activity. Finally, the school initiated a continuing education nursing program focused on didactic and clinical teaching strategies for all faculty, including the part-time clinical faculty. The full-time faculty came to appreciate the model, which gave them not only oversight of the quality of clinical teaching but also deeper insight into the challenges of clinical teaching. The quality of clinical instruction was rated highly by students, and NCLEX results for the program were consistently high, thus documenting the productivity of the model. Cost savings were high—four credits, or one sixth of a faculty member's full-time (24-credit) annual salary (approximately $72,000), would have cost $12,000 per clinical section compared with $75 to $100 dollars per hour per clinical section (usually 8 hours). The adjunct clinical faculty also served as a pool from which to recruit full-time nursing faculty in response to program growth.

This model worked because faculty were deeply involved in researching the issues, crafting the system, and recruiting adjunct clinical faculty. There are many opportunities for innovation in the delivery of nursing education. The dean needs to establish an environment in which faculty can experiment with innovation, occasionally fail, learn from failure, and innovate again.

Question 3: Is there parity in resource allocation in the school and across the university that results in mission fulfillment, excellence, and response to market-driven opportunities?

The movement of nursing programs from hospital-based training schools began in 1908 when the University of Minnesota's hospital-based program was given university status by the efforts of a physician, Dr. Richard Olding Beard (Dock & Stewart, 1938). In 1923, Yale University established the first independent collegiate nursing school supported by an endowment and with its own dean. By 1938, more than 100 colleges and universities offered collegiate nursing degrees, and since the mid-1900s, both undergraduate and graduate academic nursing programs have proliferated in American universities. Nevertheless, academia and its constituencies are often ambivalent or even derisive about the nature and value of nursing as a discipline.

Vignette 3: The Value of Nursing Faculty

The new RN-BSN Program was 2 years old. Enrollment was robust, and five new full-time nursing faculty had been appointed. The curriculum was creative and relevant but needed an infusion of electives. Two faculty from the Women's

Studies Department requested to meet with the nursing chair, who presumed that the meeting would address offering some of the Women's Studies courses as electives in the nursing program. The nursing chair escorted the two English professors into her office which, though new, was very small and had no window. One of the visitors exclaimed that the office was "so enclosed and reminiscent of a uterus." The nursing chair ignored the uterine metaphor and instead moved directly to the meeting's agenda. "We are thrilled at the prospect of offering some of the Women's Studies courses as electives for the nursing students. They are working women and would benefit greatly from these courses." The visitors appeared surprised and explained that "electives" were not the reason for their visit. "We are here to express our grave concern that the addition of nursing faculty has falsely inflated the number of women professors at the university. In a recent meeting with senior administrators, nursing faculty numbers were included as part of the administration's trend data on the appointment of women faculty. We objected since our goal is to promote the appointment of women in traditional male-dominated fields. We are hoping that you will not be adding additional nursing faculty in the near future." The nursing chair asserted that new faculty would be added as enrollment demanded and that the nursing program was contributing crucial financial resources at a time of decline in other programs. "It is likely," the nursing chair added, "that nursing's efforts may save some of the existing positions of women professors at the university and create opportunities for new ones given the increasing demand for electives and cognates that nursing students need." The nursing department went on to develop a prelicense BSN program and graduate programs. The school flourished as a result of the focus and work of the faculty and in light of mission match and the need for new programs.

It may not be surprising that nursing lags behind other university disciplines in the academic hierarchy given the value that society has traditionally assigned to the work of care giving, traditionally thought of as "women's work." Adam Smith (1776), the father of economics, did not include "women's work" (i.e., caregiving, domestic work, child care) in his treatise in 1776 on how the economy works. Smith lived with his mother who cared for him until she died, but he never considered including "women's work" in his economic model that features "self-interest" as a driving principle. A feminist economist, considering the absence of women's work from traditional economic models, points out that the first nurses were nuns who took the vow of poverty: "A nurse's calling was noble and important, it was reasoned. That's why it shouldn't pay" (Marcal, 2016, p. 119). Further, Marcal highlights Nightingale's achievement in legitimizing nursing as compensated work as against all odds for her time given the "unshakeable myth of care as a resource naturally flowing from feminine nature."

> Florence Nightingale's image is still that of a quiet, shy, discreet angel disinterested in money. In reality she was a pugnacious social critic with great interest in economics. Statistics were her weapon in the fight for a new way of thinking about nursing. Not the blushing, self-denying altruism that she has been attributed with…Florence Nightingale fought her entire life for good wages in nursing. (Marcal, 2016, p. 122)

It is imperative that deans of nursing follow Nightingale's lead. Parity, like charity, begins at home, in the SON. Faculty and staff salaries and facilities are elements that require continuous monitoring for parity both in the school and across the university. Faculty and staff salaries are the largest component, 85% to 95%, of most academic budgets. Therefore a large component of the dean's financial management activities should focus on faculty compensation. Salary expenses also include the costs of the benefit package, that is, healthcare and other types of insurance, retirement contribution if any, social security deductions, and other items. For meaningful benchmarking, the dean must know the benefit package percentage so that actual salary can be differentiated from total compensation. Benefit packages can range from 15% to 35% of salaries depending on the institution. Nursing faculty salaries should be benchmarked against those in similarly situated academic institutions and against nursing practice positions in the region. The best source of data on national nursing faculty salaries is published annually by the American Association of Colleges of Nursing (AACN) publication (see Table 13.4). An SON executive council that includes faculty representation and is led by the dean should review the AACN annual faculty salary data and select the best tables for comparison. The dean, chairs, and administrative personnel can then examine current faculty salaries in the school against the most appropriate comparisons in the national database. The results of this exercise should be shared with senior university administrators responsible for budget approvals and adjustments, that is, the provost or VP of academic affairs, the chief financial officer, and so forth. Educating senior university administrators about nursing faculty salary trends, including practice salary comparisons, is the responsibility of the dean, particularly in times of nursing program expansion and nursing faculty shortages.

Benchmarking nursing faculty salaries against those of other disciplines is also necessary. If the school is in a publicly supported university, compensation data are readily available. There are also national databases, such as the Chronicle for Higher Education (Chronicle Data, 2016–17, n.d.), providing data on salaries of full- and part-time faculty and staff by region, type of college/university, and discipline. Regularly monitoring faculty and staff salary trends is essential in crafting data-driven arguments to support compensation trends and requests.

The quality of the nursing school's facilities is also a direct expression of the university's commitment to and valuation of nursing's work. It should be noted that compared with other academic disciplines, nursing is much less equipment or laboratory intensive than disciplines such as computer science, engineering, and other sciences, as the preponderance of student clinical learning takes place in healthcare institutions. However, clinical learning labs, simulation facilities, and web-based technologies are necessary to appropriately prepare students for engaging with real patients in clinical settings and to systematically assess students for summative clinical skills. The most difficult negotiations in my 40 years of "deaning" concerned the acquisition of space for offices, classrooms, and labs, that is, academic real estate. From the acquisition of a nursing learning lab in my first deanship to the consolidation of a large college into one building in my last deanship, process and politics surrounding space acquisition were lengthy and contentious. I kept detailed chronologies of space acquisition efforts that included the rationale for the space request, dates of responses, persons petitioned, and the history of responses. I regularly shared the "space chronologies" with the faculty and senior administration to document progress or regress and to ensure institutional memory accuracy until the goal was met.

STEWARDSHIP, STRATEGY, AND LEADERSHIP

Forty years of experience in academic nursing administration in a variety of colleges and universities underpins the following philosophy and leadership strategies for the financial management of academic nursing programs. These guidelines and recommendations were "hard learned" in environments that ranged from authoritarian to chaotic to innovative and competitive, all with a tinge of ambivalence about high-level female academic administrators and the nursing discipline's place in academia.

Stewardship

By its very nature, the dean's role is one of stewardship. The university entrusts the care, development, quality, and reputation of the school to the dean. De Wolf (2017) defines a steward as one "that is given full responsibility for the valuables of another," in this case, the school, its human resources (i.e., students, faculty, and staff), its fiscal resources, and its future trajectory. Block (1996), an early proponent of leadership as stewardship, emphasized accountability to

TABLE 13.4 Key Academic Finance and Budgeting Guides and Resources

Goldstein. (2012). *A guide to college and university budgeting*. Washington, DC: National Association of Colleges and University Business Officers (NACUBO).	A comprehensive guide addressing academic budgeting models and their interface with strategic planning and the politics of the institution. http://products.nacubo.org/index.php/leadership/a-guide-to-college-and-university-budgeting-foundations-for-institutional-effectiveness-4th-ed.html
Costantinidis, T. (2015). *Higher education budgeting*. A PowerPoint Presentation: Western Association of Colleges and University Business Officers (WACUBO)	This PowerPoint describes the elements of academic budgeting, budget models, and associated issues with each. http://www.wacubo.org/Documents/Business%20Mgmt%20Institute/2015%20Handouts/Track%202%20-%20Costantinidis%20-%20BMI%20Budgeting.pdf
Education Advisory Board. (2014). *Optimizing institutional budget models*. Retrieved from the EAB website: https://eab.com/research/business-affairs/study/optimizing-institutional-budget-models/	Includes data from a dean's survey on the types of academic budgeting models used in higher education. https://www.eab.com/research-and-insights/business-affairs-forum/studies/2014/optimizing-institutional-budget-models
	Also includes the *Periodic Table of Budget Model Elements,* which explains the use of each budget element; helpful for new deans. https://www.eab.com/research-and-insights/business-affairs-forum/resources/infographics/budget-models
Whalen, E. (1991). *Responsibility Center Budgeting: An approach to decentralized management for institutions of higher education*. Bloomington, IN: Indiana University Press.	Academic institutions are increasingly adopting RCM as the budgeting model. This book describes the origin of the model, its rationale, and opportunities and challenges arising through its use.
Curry, J. C. (2002). *Responsibility Center Management: Lessons from 25 years of decentralized management*. Washington, DC: NACUBO.	A data-driven analysis of the successes and challenges of RCM in academic institutions with a chapter on major lessons learned.
Dumestre, M. J. (2016). *Financial sustainability in U.S. higher education*. New York, NY: Palgrave Macmillan.	Addresses the current financial crisis in higher education, including the inability of families to afford a college education and increasing financial pressures on universities since the 2008 financial crash. Explores strategic thinking, innovative practices, and leadership.
American Association of Colleges of Nursing. (2017–18). *Salaries of instructional and administrative nursing faculty in baccalaureate and graduate programs in nursing*. Washington, DC: AACN.	This annual report of national faculty salary data contains 95 tables that report faculty and administrator salaries by region of the country, type of institution, i.e., state, academic health center, or doctoral granting. Salaries are also categorized by calendar year or academic appointment, faculty rank, tenure or nontenure track, and many other useful variables. http://www.aacn-nursing.org/Store/product-info/productcd/IDSR_18SALSINST

RCM, Responsibility Center Management.

the organization and to staff, as well as a dispersion of power and influence throughout the organization, and consistent and documented transparency on the overall status of the school. Donnelly (2005) emphasized the ability to listen and be other oriented, a sense of integrity, and a penchant for directly engaging in the core work of the school, like periodically teaching, as well as the ability to foresee both opportunities and challenges. In short, if as a new dean "decorating your office" and "traveling to meetings" excites you more than the prospect of improving instructional processes, the learning–teaching environment for students, faculty and staff, and the quality of academic programs and research, rethink your career goals.

Risk Management

The dean anticipates and manages risks to the school, which can be both normal and cataclysmic occurrences. For example, the market for undergraduate nursing programs may be at risk if the number of post-secondary applicants is cycling down, suggesting the development of a second degree program or the ramping up of graduate nursing programs. The faculty may resist online programming when other regional schools are swiftly moving in that direction. Morale may be low because of a hostile work environment, which could result in expensive turnover. Effective risk management demands accurate and clear communication to senior administration and to faculty and staff, despite the nature of the problem. Thompson and Clark (2017) caution against the use of "gaslighting" communication strategies, which misalign words with reality: "Conduct in our nursing workplaces remains a curious contrast of overt statements about quality, collegiality and community accompanied too often with the opposite" (p. 995). Nearly every problem or risk that a dean encounters, like the few enumerated, has financial implications. Appointing members of the school leadership, faculty, and staff to an "Asteroid Club" to explore and enumerate external and internal risks and to quantify their effects, if possible, is a useful ongoing risk management strategy.

Humor

I end this chapter with a focus on humor, one of the most important strategies in my 40-year repertoire as a leader of academic nursing programs. Take the work seriously but not yourself, focus on the goal, and pursue it with vigor and humanity. To a provost who refused a reasonable request and shouted, "You are the cash cow. Do not ask me for resources," I made a gift of a portrait of a happy cow in a pasture with an insignia in bold script: "Feed the Cow!" The request was approved. To a provost with whom I was in difficult negotiations concerning a budget cut and who declared that he hated dealing with me as much as he hated brussel sprouts, I compared, in a memo, the high nutritional value of both budgets and brussel sprouts. And to the administrator who scolded and shook his finger at me when I legitimately secured space for the nursing program, I spontaneously declared, "Never speak to me in that tone, I have given birth twice!" The administrator apologized profusely, and we remained good colleagues, always with the expectation of mutual respect.

If you have a self-effacing sense of humor, use it. It is the coping mechanism that I value most. Humor can serve as an empowering cognitive strategy for nursing deans who are regularly subjected to legacy resource management and programmatic elitism in addition to the usual pressures of academic administration.

CONCLUSION

The Gordian knot is a cogent metaphor for the intricacies of academic administration and the place, role, and perspective of academic deans, particularly with respect to financial management. To lead nursing programs requires untangling the "knots" that keep programs from realizing their potential, such as garnering necessary resources internally or externally, enhancing faculty development and engagement, creating a safe and exciting work environment, and ultimately preparing excellent nurses for the future. With a deep understanding of the culture, a knowledge of policy and processes, bidirectional communication and transparency, a sense of stewardship, and a good sense of humor, a dean will succeed in garnering resources and managing the finances of an SON. This final vignette applies to many of the strategies described herein and offers a snapshot of successful financial management.

Vignette 4: The Budget Hearing

You are 1 year into your first nursing deanship. Over the past 2 months, you have worked with the program director/chairs of the school and with your administrative staff to craft the next annual budget. You have examined trends and changes in the external market to determine programming, to meet enrollment demands, and to sufficiently staff according to the criteria set by regulators and accreditors. Enrollment in nursing programs is in a growth cycle because of the aging of the population, the expansion of home care, and the demand for more nurses by healthcare employers. Senior administration of the university is sending a clear message to grow. It is the "school of nursing as nurturer" image that you need to counteract. Your experience is that senior university administrators do not always understand the nuances of budgeting for nursing programs, particularly for the clinical or practicum components, and the budget you are presenting includes an 8% increase in expenses to accommodate growth in enrollment. There are a few areas in this budget where you can tighten up if necessary but decide to leave those areas as is for the time being.

You must present the school's budget at a "hearing" attended by the provost and five of his staff. In order to have deep information at hand and witnesses to the process, you think it best to have a number of SON staff also attend—the administrative/finance director and several associate deans. The provost accepts your rationale and agrees to this plan.

One week before the "hearing," all attendees from the SON have a rehearsal meeting where the group (a) conducts a detailed analysis of budget requests and their rationale; (b) critiques the dean's presentation and proposes adjustments; (c) projects possible counterarguments by the provost group and fall back positions; and (d) delineates roles for SON attendees, that is, who will respond to specific questions.

From your perspective, the "hearing" was productive—you even enjoyed it! The provost's staff seems surprised at the depth of the presentation and at how well the staff responded to questions, concerns, and issues. You know that the external market is aligned with your school's programs and that the projection of significant growth, supported by market trends, provides the school with negotiating leverage, and can contribute to the university's stability. However, you also realize that garnering resources in academia is a function of not only administrative policy and processes but also culture, politics, and leadership. You wait, hope, and have a plan to regroup depending on the administration's formal response.

REFERENCES

Block, P. (1996). *Stewardship: Choosing service over self-interest.* San Francisco, CA: Berrett-Koehler.

Chronicle Data, 2016–17. (n.d.). Retrieved from Chronicle of Higher Education website, https://data.chronicle.com

Collins, J. (2005). *Good to great and the social sectors.* Boulder, CO: Jim Collins.

Cook, J. D. (2009, September 23). *Feed the start, milk the cows, and shoot the dogs.* Retrieved from John D. Cook Consulting website, https://www.johndcook.com/blog/2009/09/23/community-college-finance/

De Wolf, J. (2017, August 1). *Leadership is stewardship*. Retrieved from Wolf Prairie website, https://www.wolfprairie.com/leadership-is-stewardship

Dock, L. L., & Stewart, I. M. (1948). *A short history of nursing*. New York, NY: G.P. Putnam's Sons.

Donnelly, G. (2017). Normative and cataclysmic career transitions: A nurse's memoir. *Nursing Administration Quarterly, 41*(3), 223–232. doi:10.1097/NAQ.0000000000000232

Donnelly, G. F. (2005). The dean's annual review: Transparency and accountability in the dean's role. In *Academic Leadership: Making the Journey* (pp. 175–186). Washington, DC: American Association of Colleges of Nursing.

Drucker, P. (2007, May 23). *Culture eats strategy for breakfast*. Retrieved from Quotation Investigator website, https://quoteinvestigator.com/2017/05/23/culture-eats/

Dumestre, M. J. (2016, September 18). Creative destruction: The new economic reality in higher education. Academic Impressions, 1–9. Retrieved from https://www.academicimpressions.com/how-is-higher-education-changing/

Marcal, K. (2016). *Who cooked Adam Smith's dinner? A story of women and economics*. New York, NY: Pegasus Books, LLC.

Martin, J. (1992). *Cultures in organizations: Three perspectives*. New York, NY: Oxford University Press.

Reeves, M., Moose, S., &Venema, T. (n.d.). *BCG classics revisited: The growth share matrix*. Retrieved from the Boston Consulting Group website, https://www.bcg.com/en-us/publications/2014/growth-share-matrix-bcg-classics-revisited.aspx

Thompson, D. R., & Clark, A. M. (2018). Leading by gaslight? Nursing's academic leadership struggles. *Journal of Advanced Nursing, 74*, 995–997. doi:10.1111/jan.13399

Tierney, W. G. (1988). Organizational culture in higher education: Defining the essentials. *The Journal of Higher Education, 59*(1), 2–21. Retrieved from http://www.jstor.org/stable/1981868

Schein, E. H. (2010). *Organizational culture and leadership* (4th ed.). New York, NY: Jossey-Bass.

Smith, A. (1961). *The wealth of nations: Representative selections*. Indianapolis, IN: The Bobbs Merrill Company, Inc. (*Wealth of Nations* original published 1776)

Strauss, J. C., & Curry, J. R. (2002). *Responsibility Center Management: Lessons from 25 years of decentralized management*. Washington, DC: National Association of Colleges and University Business Officers.

14

STRATEGIC THINKING, PLANNING, AND DOING

KAREN J. KELLY THOMAS

INTRODUCTION

Competencies related to strategic leadership, strategic visioning, and strategic thinking are part of the overall profile of leaders. Leaders are expected to inspire, create, and innovate. How do we acquire these competencies? By doing them. And just what do the words "strategic" and "strategy" mean in your situation? Know that there will be many meanings to many. Simply stated, strategy is an approach to achieving an end. What end? Therein lies the skilled leader's competence to define, describe, and inspire teams, groups, and individuals toward achieving a common future end or goal that is coherent with the organizational mission. Leaders have a wonderful opportunity to create, develop, build, continue, transition, and transform with the effective implementation of changes. All are core components of strategic thinking and planning and change management. Chances are good that you have some knowledge and experience with strategic planning. This chapter provides introductory information about selected elements of strategic thinking and strategic planning and makes suggestions about how nursing deans and directors can acquire skills regarding these desired leadership characteristics.

STRATEGIC PLANNING: PRESENT AND FUTURE

Strategic planning has become a standard of practice in most public and nonprofit organizations for several reasons, including legal, accrediting, and funding body requirements. It serves as a mark of professionalism, and most importantly, *it helps the leader think, act, and learn strategically* (Bryson & Alston, 2011). For some, it is a way of being. For others, it's a time-consuming task. That's quite a range of thought about strategic planning!

A simple search on the term "strategic planning" yields definitions, processes, models, templates, process models, PowerPoint presentations, courses, and endless more. Do-it-yourself resources abound. In practice, nursing leaders bring many well-developed skills in assessing, critical thinking, diagnosing, problem solving, planning, implementing, and evaluating. Applying these same competencies to the systematic process of strategic planning expands the leader's skill set. Though some define levels of organizational planning as strategic, operational, and tactical (Hinton, 2012), for our purposes, strategies are simply the priorities, procedures, and operations to achieve envisioned futures (Hanover Research, 2013).

Strategic thinking is an element of the strategic planning process. Like critical thinking, it is about synthesis and involves intuition, creativity, and innovation (Kelly-Thomas, 1998). Strategic planning and thinking emerged from the military in the 1940s and were adopted in for-profit organizations in the 1950s and higher education settings in the 1990s; many definitions, models, approaches, and ways of doing it have evolved. Most models can be categorized as goals-based, issues-based, organic, or scenario-based (McNamara, n.d.). Gap analysis and forces are other models used in higher education (Lerner, 1999).

Purpose, Benefits, and Definition of Strategic Planning

Strategic planning serves a variety of purposes. Box 14.1 lists the major purposes of strategic planning.

Box 14.2 lists additional benefits of designing a strategic planning process that engages many (Lerner, 1999).

BOX 14.1

MAJOR PURPOSES OF STRATEGIC PLANNING

- Clear definition of mission, vision, values, and goals
- Communication internally and externally
- Development of plan ownership
- Consensus building
- A base from which progress and success measurements can be made
- Improved organizational effectiveness
- Focused use of human, fiscal, and other resources

> **BOX 14.2**
>
> ## BENEFITS OF A STRATEGIC PLANNING PROCESS
>
> - A framework for determining direction
> - A clearer picture of shared goals and directions
> - Stronger and empowered groups and teams
> - Increased productivity and effectiveness
> - Improved alignment
> - Improved satisfaction
> - Problem resolution
>
> SOURCE: Lerner, A. L. (1999). A strategic planning primer for higher education. Retrieved from https://fgcu.edu/Provost/files/Strategic_Planning_Primer.pdf

The approach to strategic planning depends on many variables, including purpose, culture, experience and success with past planning efforts, pace of internal and external organizational change, and organizational preference. Practical guides and handbooks are readily available. Essentially, strategic planning involves formulating goals, objectives, and action steps; monitoring implementation; tracking progress; and revising the plan. Strategies are necessary priorities, procedures, and operations to achieve that vision (Hanover Research, 2013).

For our purposes, a strategic planning initiative is defined as an organized set of group activities designed and implemented systematically to envision a desired future state for the organization and the steps necessary to get there. This definition represents a standard goal-oriented approach that has sustained the test of time. A variety of approaches can be used to create a strategic plan, which typically includes a document delineating the mission, vision, values, goals, and timetable for implementation.

Issues and Challenges: Steps, Leaps, and Bounds

When to start, when to continue, and when to begin anew with a strategic planning initiative are challenges facing leaders. How often is another. Ending or dissolving programs, closing units, and integrating with others are complex tasks confronting leaders that some view as innovation opportunities. Perhaps a new plan is needed for a single program component of a larger program plan. Perhaps the college decides to plan a new interprofessional degree program based on a population health need, and you are asked to lead that effort. Most commonly, an updated strategic plan is needed for an accrediting or licensing body. Some colleges and departments are expected to develop their own strategic plans that are then fit into or integrated into the whole institution's plan. Many have established planning cycles with annual updates. Institutions with strategic planning cycles usually align those cycles with established budget planning cycles. Bottom-up or top-down strategic planning efforts will include a timeline or target date by which a document representing the activities and outcomes needs to be completed. Agreements about these elements are made during the development of the strategic plan.

Another challenge is the scope of the plan. Expectations around depth and breadth of the plan should be clear between the leader and higher-level authorities but often require clarifying conversations to recognize other work accountabilities. Clarity will help define the timeline, scope, and expected outcomes of the planning project. Large or limited in scope, this component of the planning to plan process will help define and delimit other issues. Other institutional plans exist in areas such as IT, academics, facilities, and advancement. Ideally, a large project strategic plan should inform other existing plans. This is often not the case due to parallel planning within today's dynamic organizations. With trust considered the most important factor in the planning process (Sanaghan & Hinton, 2013), frequent communication among leaders is requisite for coherence among multiple plans.

Complex environmental issues, internal and external, and other variables simultaneously confront leaders and require them to think through issues with others and understand the organization's issues. Leaders are then expected to develop a plan to resolve issues and follow through with effective implementation. The rapidity of change, time constraints, and multiple expectations are additional challenges. Strategic thinking and planning activities can help, as they are dynamic, ongoing, and even organic in thriving organizations.

The iterative nature of all strategic thinking and planning activities is a critical characteristic and must be appreciated by all staff, faculty, and other stakeholders involved in strategic planning. Thinking, visioning, and planning *together* are core components of any strategic planning initiative. Returning to stakeholder groups and leaders frequently during the process is key to success for plan acceptance. The frequency and timing of progress reports to stakeholders should be spelled out during the planning to plan activity discussed in the following.

How far out into the future should you go? How often should you plan? There are few evidence-based replies to these questions. For most, it depends on environment, scope, goals, and purpose of the strategic initiative and plan, structure, coordination, management work at hand, stakeholders, and more. It also depends on will, resources, expected outcome, included stakeholders, and several other factors. Sometimes a timeline is imposed. For a whole department or college facing a top-down strategic planning initiative, a 5-year or even 10-year timeline might be prescribed or simply agreed to at the start.

Patrick Sanaghan of the Sanaghan Group provides a "Collaborative" Strategic Planning Process to direct whole university strategic planning. He suggests five phases that take a year and to plan for about 5 years. The phases can be applied to any size project and include (a) getting organized, (b) data gathering, (c) sense making, (d) vision conference(s), and (e) goals conference (Sanaghan, n.d.). Sanaghan also recommends a highly credible internal planning team as the driving mechanism for success.

Depending on people, time, and money, designing an exercise in which participants are asked to imagine the future might yield useful and often unexpected data. This occurs when creative ideas are generated and bounced around a group or several groups, which opens further ideas. Our rapidly evolving knowledge about genomics, climate change, new technologies, and so much more are causes to pause before deciding how many years into the future you will project your strategic plan. Large project timelines should influence timeline estimates, particularly for new services or degree programs that require capital investment. For example, new programs or centers of excellence targeted for opening by a certain date and requiring investment in several high-level faculty positions and technologies will usually require more approvals and are likely planned on a timeline that works backward from target dates. A wise nurse leader (Haller, 2002) once advised developing a timeline for a strategic plan or project and then doubling it! This is not always doable, but that experienced voice is worth heeding.

Many organizations have some form of planning committee(s), and some even have employees dedicated to strategic planning and development to monitor implementation plans and timelines. Some have templates for development of strategic plans and internal facilitators to assist leaders to achieve goals. Use them. New leaders are expected to spend a good deal of time learning about resources. Networking with key individuals and groups is often critical to success with small and large projects. Outreach to surrounding communities is another part of planning and often an end goal as well. Thus, the complexities of leadership and strategic planning proliferate, and with it, the strategic thinking skill set expands.

Toward Shared Strategic Directions and Integration

In making major organizational change, some opt for using strategic direction language to define the general path or chosen direction they wish to go. Changing and improving service perceptions is a common example of a strategic direction that requires change on many levels and in many forms. Specific resources, including staff and sometimes capital or other expenses, may be required. Another example of a strategic direction is transition to a new registration system. In both cases, leaders should welcome and even seek opportunities to participate in planning these large organizational changes *to think, act, and learn strategically* (Bryson & Alston, 2012). As a leader, you may be expected to coordinate, align, and integrate activities of projects like these with other activities.

Further, both large and limited strategic plans require integration of the articulated vision, priorities, and goals with the organization's decision-making, resource allocation, and efficiency systems. Strategic planning can provide a fundamental forum for creating new or continuing conversations about important decisions. It can help organize assessments. The process can also be organized to make assessment, resource allocation, and accreditation easier and to be a source of information about progress and achievement with very real meaning to those associated with the institution (Hinton, 2012). Strategic planning processes can help individuals and groups inspire and learn from each other and further enrich goals and their implementation.

Embedding strategic planning into the systems and actions of the organization is another task in the work of organizing the processes and eventual implementation of the strategic plan. Evidence of integration should be considered. Thus, conversations with individuals from other disciplines, departments, and groups will provide a firm foundation for the strategic planning process. Adding diverse individuals or groups to your strategic planning work group may result in different thinking altogether and potentially better goal identification, integration, and planned implementation.

Innovation, Disruption, and Futuring

Innovation and disruption are words sometimes associated with strategic planning. Each word has a body of knowledge, models, definitions, theories, and consultants willing to help. Depending on the goal or issue being addressed, strategic planning activities can be designed to germinate ideas, create innovations, and generate disruptions to change or improve programs and services. Those designs will likely include bringing together groups with diverse talents, skills, and positions within the organization to create an atmosphere and environment open to disruption for problem solving and change. Experts agree that there is value in being in the same room to brainstorm ideas, identify immediately what is possible, and build connections that deliver unified results. Teams and groups need to work so closely that the term "collaboration" evolves into something bigger still—interdependence. When groups and teams plan together, departments and groups are transformed into a more seamless, integrated, and effective group (Goodspeed, 2018).

Disruptive innovation is another term occasionally associated with strategic planning. First described by Christensen et al. in 1995, the theory of disruptive innovation has been used to predict the likelihood of success in small enterprises that challenge industry leaders (Christensen, Raynor, & McDonald, 2015). Disruption is a *process*, and disruptors often build very different business models compared with their competitors. The wide and sometimes careless use of the term "disruptive innovation" has prompted some to call anything that disrupts a disruptive innovation. In fact, the theory's core concepts have been widely misunderstood, and its basic tenets frequently misapplied. One basic tenet of disruptive innovation is that the product or service originates in the low-end or new-market footholds. The early days of photocopying is a good example of disruptive innovation theory applied. The largest provider of photocopying technology targeted large companies and charged high prices. Schools, clubs, and other small organizations were priced out of the market until new small businesses (disruptors) started offering personal photocopiers (innovation), thus building a market that challenged the mainstream photocopier market. The Internet is another example of a disruptive innovation as are convenient care clinics and online learning. An example of misapplication of the theory is Uber, as it did not start from a low-end or a new-market foothold; rather, it began in San Francisco where taxis were available and customers were already in the habit of hiring rides. Nevertheless, the authors of disruptive innovation theory continue to refine it and are hopeful that it will continue to be a useful predictive model of success in the business world. The initial and subsequent work of Christensen et al. are excellent sources of information about this popular, evolving, and expanding theory and its potential application to your setting.

Futuring is another term of interest that is linked to strategic planning. Futuring can be defined as the field of using a systematic process for thinking about outcomes, picturing possible outcomes, and planning for desired outcomes. Futuring has its roots in the post–World War II era and has evolved to today's profession of futurists. Currently, the World Future Society (www.worldfuture.org) exists to provide a forum for discussion and analysis. Common futuring initiatives include brainstorming about the future of healthcare (e.g., providers and settings) and external environmental scanning based on world predictions.

The need to create better structures and processes to deliver our services and programs is ever present. Beginning or continuing support of innovative thinking and idea development in organizations is helpful to strategic planning. Innovation and creativity group exercises and activities can be embedded into strategic planning initiatives to generate innovative or new ideas applied to your setting. Read how others are applying this systematic approach to engage nurses in achieving significant outcomes (Wadsworth, Felton, & Linus, 2016), building teams (Albert & Priganc, 2014), and creating new models of care through academic–clinical partnerships (McCarthy, Carleton, Krumpholz, & Chow, 2018).

Internal and External Planning Consultants: Yea and Nay

Organizations with development or planning departments are more likely to have resources, both human and material, that are useful to leaders interested in undertaking a strategic planning initiative. New or smaller organizations, as well as institutions without trained facilitators, will want to consider hiring a consultant to help. Likewise, if the organization has a wide range of ideas and issues to be addressed in a plan, an external consultant will be useful. Sometimes the outside or objective voice of a consultant is preferable, as they are less likely to have strong predispositions about the organization's strategic issues and ideas. Involving the external consultant from planning to implementation is the preferred approach. This chapter, designed to give a basic understanding of contemporary strategic planning, will help you hire the right consultant with the right fit. Strategic planning consultants are master facilitators who are focused on process, whereas participants are usually content masters. The bottom line is that it's up to the leader, the resources available, and the outcomes desired. In the interest of developing your own knowledge and skill, Box 14.3 lists selected resources to guide strategic planning initiatives.

BEST PRACTICES: STEP BY STEP

Suppose you, as a new dean, are charged with moving forward a goal that entails development of a strategic plan. You will find many references to steps, stages, and phases in the literature (Barksdale & Lund, 2006; Bryson & Alston, 2012; Hinton, 2012; McKay, 2001). In this section, seven phases of strategic planning are presented (see Box 14.4). These phases are a blend of documented

BOX 14.3

STRATEGIC PLANNING RESOURCES

Hinton, K. E. (2012). *A practical guide to strategic planning in higher education.* Retrieved from Society for College and University Planning website, https://scup.org

McNamara, C. (n.d.). *All about strategic planning.* Retrieved from Management Help website, https://managementhelp.org/strategicplanning

Sanaghan, P. (n.d.). *A "collaborative" strategic planning process.* Retrieved from website http://thesanaghangroup.com/PDFs/planning.pdf

Lerner, A. L. (1999). *A strategic planning primer for higher education.* Retrieved from https://fgcu.edu/Provost/files/Strategic_Planning_Primer.pdf

McKay, E. G. (2001). *Strategic planning: A ten-step guide.* Retrieved from http://siteresources.worldbank.org/INTAFRREGTOPTEIA/Resources/mosaica_10_steps.pdf

BOX 14.4

PHASES OF STRATEGIC PLANNING

1. Laying the groundwork, planning to plan
2. Internal and external environmental scans and data analysis
3. Stating vision, mission, values, and goals
4. SWOT and identifying risks
5. Identifying and prioritizing strategies and identifying resources
6. Documenting and communicating
7. Implementing, managing, and sustaining changes

SWOT, strengths, weaknesses, opportunities, and threats.

best practices, the author's experience, and the critical recognition that time management plays a large role.

The phases are purposefully broad, as institutions, departments, and groups vary in need, nature, and preference for management of large change. Some phases will take longer than expected or predicted. Some phases are completed in differing order from here. Those familiar with grant writing and quality improvement projects will find many of these phases and processes familiar. Some sample applications for the strategic planning process include the following:

- Moving a program or department of nursing up to a college
- Joining with other health disciplines/departments to form a new college
- Creating a brand-new program of nursing within an established health sciences program

Phase 1: Laying the Groundwork: Planning to Plan

During this phase, the leader begins to assess the department or organization's readiness for change in meetings, using available assessment tools, interviews, surveys, and other means. A planning committee with a clearly designated chair/leader is best for a strategic planning initiative. In some settings, a written charge to the strategic planning committee is made as formal authorization. Authentic involvement and engagement of participants is a central element and can make or break a strategic planning process (Sanaghan & Hinton, 2013). Key stakeholders are designated and asked to build broad support among diverse constituents. Champions of the strategic planning process are chosen, elected, or selected. Decisions around scope of plan, timelines, and necessary mandates are made, and resources are acquired. The size and composition of the committee, team, or work group is determined and filled with designated individuals. Committees can range from 10 to 25 members and should allow for broad participation (Hanover Research, 2013). Internal and external political help is required, along with effective decision-making.

Some projects are launched with much fanfare, but most are begun with announcements in meetings and reports. Many strategic planning initiatives begin and end with a retreat. Based on college or university resources, well-designed days of reflection and hard work among key stakeholders, committee members, and others may help yield consensus on stated or revised statements of mission, vision, values, goals; generate consensus; and build relationships necessary to accomplish goals. The interprofessional nature of nursing, medicine, and other health science professions today certainly serves as a clear call for inclusivity. Generating creativity and innovation might be another outcome planned into a strategic planning activity; if so, exercises are designed to reach those outcomes.

Depending on the desired goals and preferred future, it may be useful to plan activities that get at why we do what we do. With today's emphasis on finding joy in work, beginning the work of strategic planning with discussions and story-telling exercises about why we do the work we do will yield important common ground information for futuring and visioning activities.

A general timeline, scope, and goals document should be released to all involved. Most strategic planning initiatives include a time and date for a kickoff activity or retreat. Other meetings may be scheduled with appointed subcommittees or working groups, as the project unfolds and more data are presented. Time is also allotted for follow-up meetings of the overall committee and any subcommittees as needed.

Promoting the strategic planning process and communicating goals and progress are also key to success. Leaders will find that overcommunicating during this time serves a purpose. Gaining wide support and organizational buy-in is required for successful implementation. Feedback acquired during each of these phases is another key to success.

Phase 2: Internal and External Environmental Scans and Data Analysis

Deciding what and how much internal and external environmental scanning to do as part of the initiative is difficult. Much information is readily available. Teasing out relevant information can be an intricate task. The leader should facilitate some group decisions about what data are relevant to include, often working with the organization's departments of planning and/or institutional research. Human resources, student records, medical records, and other departments and schools are good internal environmental scan targets. In some projects, the data pointing to a need for change emerge from routine organizational assessments; in others, very limited data are needed to support the need for change. In some organizations, the ability to search large data sets is assigned to select staff members, who may also be able to provide necessary data for review by the strategic planning group. Also, local, state, and federal websites (e.g., www.CDC.gov, www.NIH.gov, www.USDA.gov, www.state.nj.us, www.county .ocean.nj.us) are a treasure trove of information available at no cost. Professional societies, regulatory agencies, and accrediting bodies are other sources of information.

Depending on the strategic planning project, data may have to be coded, sorted, and analyzed as part of the environmental scanning process. In other situations, a leader may get a mandate to write a plan that will expand and even explode successful programs. Collecting and analyzing data are a part of the environmental scanning process. Decisions and strategic planning should be evidence based. It is safe to say that any leader involved in strategic planning should collect and analyze selected external and internal data as part of the process. Thoughtful, careful, and sensible use of information from environmental scans will ground the decisions of leaders, committees, groups, and others involved in strategic planning processes. Information from environmental scanning is also used in a later phase of the strategic planning process in which strengths, weaknesses, opportunities, and threats are considered relevant to the project at hand. The importance of evidence-based decisions cannot be overstated.

Phase 3: Stating Vision, Mission, Values, and Goals

Organizations are required by various accrediting and regulatory agencies to have mission and goal statements. Some also have vision and values statements. Some strategic planning committees are charged with creating, revising, or updating mission and values statements within the context of an organizational strategic plan. In some highly decorated organizations, the mission established at their origin governs all decisions and goals, even within an increasingly complex and evolving environment. Vision, mission, values, and goal statements serve as the foundation and reason for the strategic planning initiative at hand. Most new strategic plans include a statement that illustrates its coherence and connection with past mission statements and envisioned futures. Some must indicate specifically how the plan will support established mission, vision, and values statements. Final strategic planning documents must include the organizational mission of the institution and other fundamental institution-wide statements.

Mission and vision definitions proliferate. Brief basic definitions are provided here as a foundation for discussion during the strategic planning process:

- Mission statement: a statement of what you do and who benefits
- Vision statement: a statement of your preferred future that describes how the organization will look if it fulfills its mission

Keeping participants' eyes lifted and thinking directed toward mission and vision statements during their deliberations is an important task of the facilitator. Visioning is about imagining it forward. Success as a leader is often grounded in your vision of the future.

Values statements are a newer addition to the strategic planning lexicon. Established, evolving, and new organizations define organizational ethics in their policies and procedures; these are core to how everyone is expected to behave. Values statements are sometimes written to help everyone understand organizational culture and expectations and how to behave when facing difficult and/or controversial issues. Values statements address fundamental beliefs and guiding principles for ethical behavior and mind-sets. Contemporary values statements often address ethical issues confronting organizations today and are used to launch new initiatives or programs. Values statements address issues in the areas of integrity, diversity, social justice, civic responsibilities, respect, caring, culture, accountability, and others. The development of a values statement can be worked into the strategic planning process as a forerunner to the development of a vision statement.

There are many guided exercises that will harvest useful information for strategic planners who are helping an organization build or update their mission, vision, and values statements. As a nursing dean or director, consider using your established organizational mission, vision, and values statements as the launching pad for your strategic planning efforts.

Phase 4: SWOT and Identifying Risks

During this phase, the internal **s**trengths and **w**eaknesses (or limitations) of the organization are identified along with its external **o**pportunities and **t**hreats (or challenges). This so-called *SWOT analysis* is useful in clarifying the situation or context in which the organization exists. Taking a broad look around the organization and using the results of internal and external environmental scanning, this part of the process generates data that put emerging strategic issues into play and helps prioritize needs. Exercises that generate SWOT information are useful for revealing effective strategies. Every successful strategy builds on strengths. Risk identification by groups and individuals is another component of strategic planning that will assist in developing the next phases. In large strategic planning initiatives, a gap analysis exercise helps participants identify gaps between vision statements and current issues. Exercises, worksheets, and group activities are widely available to generate SWOT data for group processing. From these data, a strategic plan is developed in a user-friendly format for implementation.

An alternative to the SWOT framework for strategic thinking and planning has emerged recently. Based on the philosophy of Appreciative Inquiry, the SOAR framework focuses on **s**trengths, **o**pportunities, **a**spirations, and **r**esults and uses a collaborative strategic planning approach that involves stakeholders at all levels. As a framework, the SOAR approach is positive in terms of identifying strengths, building creativity into opportunities, encouraging development of individual and team aspirations, and determining measurable and meaningful results (Stavros, 2013). A strength-based approach, weaknesses, and threats are reframed within the conversations of opportunities and results (Stavros & Hinrichs, 2009). Successful engagement of nurses to achieve significant outcomes has been reported (Wadsworth et al., 2016). The focus of this strategic planning framework on strengths, opportunities, and aspirations is an attractive approach that may yield positive results in settings seeking a strength-based planning strategy.

Phase 5: Identifying and Prioritizing Strategies and Identifying Resources

During this phase, strategic issues are identified and gathered on master lists. Depending on the scope of planning, there may be subissues. Identifying issues, questions, and choices to be addressed is germane to this phase. Issues should be something the organization can do something about. A strategic issue is a fundamental policy choice or change challenge that affects an organization's mandates, mission, services, student and faculty mix, costs, financing, organization, or management (Bryson & Alston, 2012). The scope, purpose, and framework for strategic planning will likely inform the identification of strategic issues and their categorization. Templates for passing the strategic issue through tests of feasibility, desirability, and more are widely available for this stage as well. Decision matrices and other tools are available online and in the business literature for leaders interested in educating staff about strategic planning processes (Barksdale & Lund, 2006). Integrating budget planning and resource acquisition into an evolving strategic plan is a challenge. In some well-developed organizations, it may seem seamless; however, in many, the quest for financial and human resources is competitive on every level.

Phase 6: Documenting and Communicating

Your strategic plan draft will evolve as you move through the processes. At minimum, the strategic planning document should include an introduction; environmental scanning results; mission, vision, and values statements; strategic issues, goals, strategies; and a plan for management, monitoring, and review. In some organizations, an annual plan may be developed separately that coincides with budget cycles and other plans. You may want to communicate summaries widely and personally to those who have key roles in your plan's implementation. Staying focused with competing priorities and seeking coherence will be the primary challenge during this and the next phase.

Phase 7: Implementing, Managing, and Sustaining the Changes

Implementation of a strategic plan involves assigning and tracking actions toward the accomplishment of designated key goals. Implementation is the hard part of strategic planning but essential to its success. Online templates for project management are available and useful to communicate status reports widely. Spreadsheets and software programs designed specifically for strategic plan implementation or project management are available. Capterra, an online resource for software buyers, recently posted best reviewed project management software as Microsoft Project, Atlassian, and Wrike. In addition, their specific list for strategic planning included Balanced Scorecard by Quickscore, Envisio, and more (Capterra.com, 2018). SPOL, for Strategic Planning OnLine, a software product available at SPOL.com, was built by educators for strategic planning, assessment, implementation, accreditation, credentialing, budgeting, and other needs. Charts or spreadsheets are the preferred vehicle for communicating progress toward goals. At minimum, each strategic goal, action step, deadline, and accountable party(s) should be tracked. Build in checkpoints to share the implementation plan and share it widely, particularly during the first 90 days of implementation. Some organizations create dashboards to measure selected key actions. Others use scorecards and other means of tracking. If people know their progress will be monitored and recognized, they are more likely to engage. Sometimes assigning co-leaders for a goal is helpful so that one can help the other (McKay, 2001).

Building a strategic plan is a stimulating, complex, and intense activity. The strategic planning implementation document should be used at all relevant meetings to update and report status and recognize accomplishments. Deviations from the plan happen and need to be documented, so planners and other stakeholders understand them. The strategic planning implementation document can be used for annual and semiannual reviews. When placed in an accessible drive on organizational intranets, the document is a live vehicle that the leader can use to identify organizational priorities, recognize accomplishments, and evaluate outcomes.

CONCLUSION

Leading strategic thinking and planning using guidelines presented in this chapter will equip the nursing dean or director with basic knowledge about developing and implementing a strategic plan. Using strategic leadership and management will help nursing deans and directors achieve success in building direction, setting tone, and developing organizational vitality. The experience of strategic planning need not be dull and drawn out. On the contrary, it should be viewed as an exciting intertwined dynamic process that can stimulate, inspire, innovate, and yield planned change with measurable outcomes unique to your setting.

REFERENCES

Albert, D., & Priganc, D. (2014). Building a team through a strategic planning process. *Nursing Administration Quarterly, 38*(3), 238–237. doi:10.1097/NAQ.0000000000000036

Barksdale, S., & Lund, T. (2006). *Ten steps to successful strategic planning*. Alexandria, VA: American Society for Training and Development Press.

Bryson, J. M., & Alston, F. K. (2011). *Creating your strategic plan: A workbook for public and nonprofit organizations* (3rd ed.). San Francisco: Jossey-Bass.

Capterra.com. (2018, June). *The top 20 most popular project management software*. Retrieved from Capterra.com.

Christensen, C. M., Raynor, M. E., & McDonald, R. (2015). What is disruptive innovation. *Harvard Business Review*, December, 44–53.

Goodspeed, N. (2018). Why media and creative work best under one roof. *Smart Brief for Health Care Marketers*. Retrieved from https://www.smartbrief.com/original/2018/10/why-media-and-creative-work-best-under-one-roof?utm_source=brief

Haller, K. (2002). Personal communication, January 12, 2002.

Hanover Research. (2013). *Best practices for school improvement planning*. Retrieved from Hanover Research website https://hanoverresearch.com/media/Best-Practices-for-School-Improvement-Planning.pdf

Hinton, K. E. (2012). *A practical guide to strategic planning in higher education*. Retrieved from Society for College and University Planning website, https://scup.org

Kelly-Thomas, K. J. (1998). *Clinical and nursing staff development: Current competence, future focus* (2nd ed.). Philadelphia, PA: Lippincott.

Lerner, A. L. (1999). *A strategic planning primer for higher education*. Retrieved from https://fgcu.edu/Provost/files/Strategic_Planning_Primer.pdf

McCarthy, C., Ford Carlton, P., Krumpholz, E., & Chow, M. (2018). Accelerating innovation through competition: The innovation learning network experience. *Nursing Administration Quarterly, 42*(1), 26–34. doi:10.1097/NAQ.0000000000000036

McKay, E. G. (2001). *Strategic planning: A ten-step guide*. Retrieved from http://siteresources.worldbank.org/INTAFRREGTOPTEIA/Resources/mosaica_10_steps.pdf

McNamara, C. (n.d.). *All about strategic planning*. Retrieved from Management Help website, https://managementhelp.org/strategicplanning

Sanaghan, P. (n.d.). *A "collaborative" strategic planning process*. Retrieved from website, http://thesanaghangroup.com/PDFs/planning.pdf

Sanaghan, P., & Hinton, K. E. (2013, July). *Be strategic on strategic planning*. Retrieved from https://insidehighereducation.com/advice/essay-how-to-do-strategic-planning

Stavros, J. (2013). The generative nature of SOAR: Applications, results, and the new SOAR profile. *AI Practitioner: The International Journal of Appreciative Inquiry, 15*(3), 7–30.

Stavros, J., & Hinrichs, G. (2009). *Thin book of SOAR: Building strength-based strategy*. Bend, OR: Thin Book Publishers.

Wadsworth, B., Felton, F., & Linus, R. (2016). Soaring into strategic planning: Engaging nurses to achieve significant outcomes. *Nursing Administration Quarterly, 40*(4), 299–306.

15

DEVELOPING A SUSTAINABLE NURSE-LED CLINICAL ENTERPRISE AND FACULTY PRACTICE

JULIE COWAN NOVAK

INTRODUCTION

Nursing deans and directors are challenged with creating income streams for their schools, as grant attainment becomes increasingly more competitive and state, institutional, and federal resources become more finite. As members of a practice discipline, nursing faculty must maintain clinical expertise and relevance through faculty practice while providing rich clinical educational experiences for students, meeting the school and institutional missions, and community engagement and service. The historical basis and social mandate for nursing's leadership role in health promotion and healthcare delivery is rooted in the work of Florence Nightingale and expanded through the work of public health nurses such as Lillian Wald and Lavinia Dock (Novak, 1988). Just as Nightingale and public health leaders influenced the British and U.S. healthcare delivery systems and military healthcare from the mid-1800s through the 20th century, advanced practice registered nurses (APRNs) have more recently developed, implemented, managed, and evaluated alternatives to the failing U.S. healthcare delivery system. Unfortunately, the majority of these projects were tied to nonsustainable financial models or a single 3- to 5-year grant. This chapter features the integrated nurse-led model for sustainability and innovation (INMSI), a road map for developing a sustainable clinical enterprise, creating an integrated faculty practice, gaining access to research populations, expanding clinical sites, and responding to community needs for accessible, quality, cost-effective, value-based healthcare (Novak, 2007, 2011, 2017, 2019b,

2019c). Over the past decade, a growing number of nursing deans and directors have invested in vice deans or associate deans/directors for practice and engagement to develop, facilitate, oversee, and optimize a sustainable clinical enterprise and/or entrepreneurial faculty practice plan.

THE INTEGRATED NURSE-LED MODEL OF SUSTAINABILITY AND INNOVATION

The earliest iteration of the INMSI was developed by the author in 1994 to address primary care workforce development needs in rural Virginia (Novak & Corbett, 2000). Community assessment, surveys, focus groups, local and state demographic and public health analyses, and direct feedback from patients guided the earliest and subsequent iterations. The model evolved further in rural and urban Indiana and Texas with significant clinic development, expansion, and replication, resulting in 12 nurse-led clinics in a variety of settings, including Head Start, K–12 school systems, college student health, employee health, refugee health, and rural and urban primary care. The model was further refined and expanded in California with the development of a nurse-led specialty clinic. Creation of the Neonatal Intensive Care Unit Follow-up Clinic over a 2-year period (2016–2018) was informed by the INMSI. The clinic was subsequently designated as a California Children's Services (CCS) High-Risk Infant Follow-up Clinic and funded through a variety of foundation grants and billing. Concurrently, the INMSI was used to design a system of care for the Neighborhood House Association's Head Start Health and Wellness Mobile Van. The Head Start health promotion and parent coaching programs are held at Head Start Early Childhood Education sites and further deployed through a mobile health van that offers health screenings, developmental assessments, nutrition and activity counseling, and behavioral health. The van provides a safety net for parents and children who face healthcare access and transportation challenges. Each of the 14 INMSI clinics meets the Institute for Healthcare Improvement (IHI) Triple Aim and Quadruple Aim goals of (a) better healthcare and access; (b) better health with a focus on population health and the patient experience; and (c) lower cost including per capita cost analysis (Berwick, 2013); and (d) joy in work for healthcare providers (Linzer et al., 2017). In addition, each clinic demonstrates integration of the educational, practice, and engagement mission of the parent institution and achieves sustainability through a diverse financial portfolio that includes billing, philanthropy, and grant funding.

The INMSI (Novak, 2007, 2011, 2017, 2019a, 2019b, 2019c) consists of 12 key elements, illustrated in Figure 15.1. The first four elements, in the 12 o'clock to

15 Developing a Sustainable Nurse-Led Clinical Enterprise 179

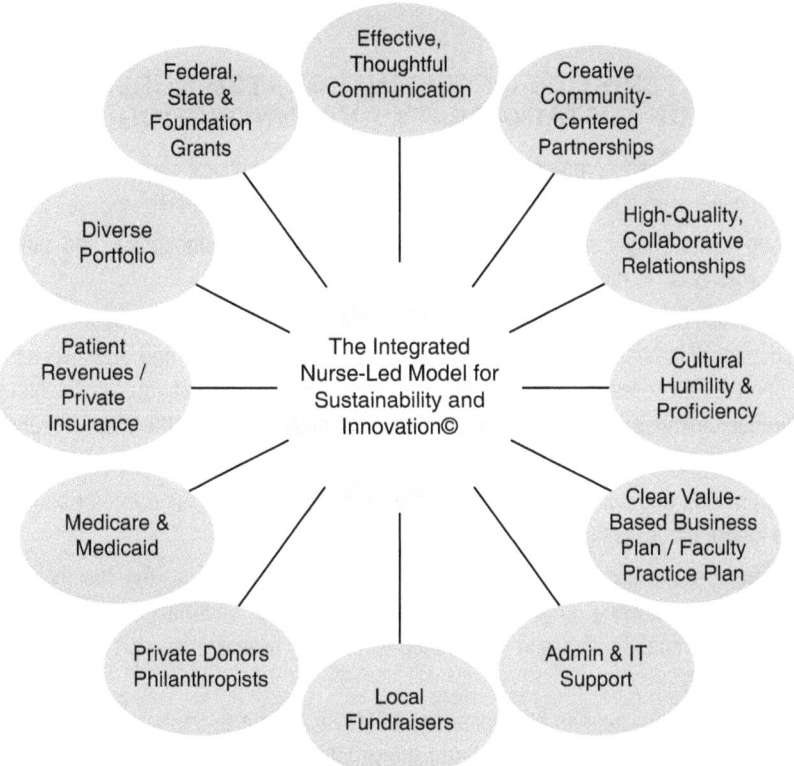

FIGURE 15.1 The integrated nurse-led model of sustainability and innovation.

SOURCE: Created by Julie Cowan Novak, DNSc, RN, CPNP, FAANP, FAAN

3 o'clock positions, focus on relationship-based communication, building community partnerships, and ensuring cultural humility and proficiency as foundational to clinical enterprise development. The remaining eight components focus on the mosaic of support or diverse portfolio for long-term sustainability and innovation. Signature characteristics of the INMSI appear in Box 15.1.

Before developing the business plan for a nurse-led clinical enterprise, nursing deans/directors must carefully lay the groundwork through relationship-based communication, careful selection of community partners, and hiring a team of culturally proficient members across all levels of the project, from clinicians to administrators to billers and coders to engineering support and facilities management. Each of these individuals contributes to the sustainability, innovation, and overall success of the clinical enterprise. The INMSI helps

> **BOX 15.1**
>
> **CHARACTERISTICS OF THE INTEGRATED NURSE-LED MODEL OF SUSTAINABILITY AND INNOVATION**
>
> Relationship-based communication, reflective practice, cultural proficiency, value-based healthcare delivery, and a diverse portfolio/mosaic of support
>
> Strong community partnerships that overcome social circumstances and place resources close to those who need them most
>
> Optimal use of digital innovation, technology, and data analytics, including a customized electronic health record to promote accessibility, efficiency, and effectiveness; support faculty research; enhance care continuity and patient safety/quality; facilitate communication with system and community partners; and track the most frequent presenting concerns and clinical outcomes
>
> Best practice and education that are evidence-based and integrated into promotion and tenure processes for faculty
>
> Interprofessional discovery, learning, and practice/engagement for faculty and students from nursing, engineering, audiology, medicine, pharmacy, physical therapy, occupational therapy, and information technology (Novak et al., 2016; Rapala & Novak, 2007)
>
> Application of engineering principles and LEAN Six Sigma to improve performance by systematically removing waste; reducing variation through cross-training for multiclinic coverage; and using just-in-time purchasing to reduce cost and analyze use and competitive bidding (Novak in Yih, 2011)

to create a diverse and inclusive community of clinical experts, scholars, and leaders for value-based healthcare delivery (Novak, 2019b, 2019c).

BEST PRACTICES FOR APPLICATION OF THE INTEGRATED NURSE-LED MODEL FOR SUSTAINABILITY AND INNOVATION

Six training modules are available to guide application of the INMSI to an academic nursing clinic and/or faculty practice (Novak, 2019b). See Figure 15.2. Each module is described here.

Module 1: Setting the Stage

Module 1 presents the development of the INMSI and the establishment of 14 clinics based on the model. Health promotion for social justice, Brazelton's

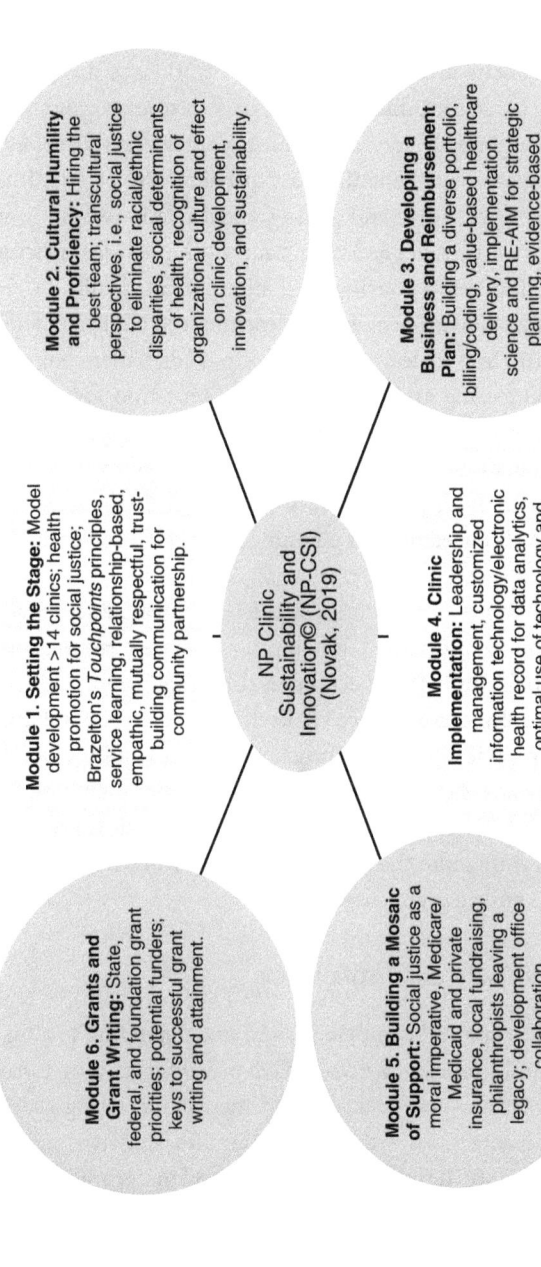

FIGURE 15.2 Training modules for the integrated nurse-led model of sustainability and innovation.

SOURCE: Created by Julie Cowan Novak, DNSc, RN, CPNP, FAANP, FAAN. Novak, J. C. (2019a). Globalization and international health. In M. A. Nies, & M. McEwan, *Community health nursing: Promoting the health of populations* (7th ed., pp. 275–289). St. Louis, MO: Saunders-Elsevier; Novak, J. C. (2019b). Pioneering an integrated NP-led model of clinic sustainability, innovation, and faculty practice. *NAPNAP Annual Conference Workshop*, New Orleans, LA, March 9, 2019.

TouchpointsFramework (Stadtler, Brandt, Novak, & Beauchesne, 2013; Stadtler & Novak, 2010), service learning, and communication principles for building community partnerships are emphasized.

Identification of faculty strengths and interests will guide the dean/director in determining clinical focus areas, faculty practice workforce analysis and hiring needs, planning strategies, metrics, necessary resources, and realistic initial and long-term goals. A service learning framework (Furco, 2011) is ideal for clinic selection, development, and expansion. Projects optimally address community-identified needs and goal-oriented relationships. Consistent with course objectives, a service learning framework provides structured opportunities for reflection before, during, and after patient, family, or community encounters, designed to achieve desired learning and clinical outcomes (Richards & Novak, 2010). Service learning is a required curricular component in many schools of engineering and fosters ideal collaboration for nurse-led clinics. Engineering expertise in human factors (the underpinnings of patient safety and quality), simulation, patient flow, information technology, media use, and Lean Six Sigma methods (Morgan & Breinig-Jones, 2016) are valuable to the dean/director and clinic team when planning the clinical enterprise budget and designing clinic space.

The Brazelton Touchpoints Framework (Stadtler & Novak, 2010; Stadtler et al., 2013) focuses on goal-oriented relationships, shared responsibility/mutual ownership of goals, mutual respect, open communication, and recognition of competence to build confidence. Reflective practice is emphasized. Reflection is essential in understanding various perspectives and the developing relationship among patients, families, and healthcare team members. Since the Touchpoints framework is highly valued by a variety of healthcare foundations, integrating this training into the clinical enterprise will strengthen grant applications and help to ensure grant attainment.

Module 2: Cultural Humility and Proficiency

Cultural proficiency takes cultural competence and understanding to a higher level of empathy. Cultural proficiency involves advocacy for lifelong learning such that you view yourself and your team as instruments for creating a socially just democracy in your interactions with patients, families, students, and communities (Lindsey, Robins, & Terrell, 2013). Working with communities is a dance, and the community always leads the dance (Novak, 2006, 2019a, 2019b, 2019c). If a community partner is not fully engaged, the clinical enterprise will be unsustainable. With community empowerment, the community identifies its problems and a relevant and meaningful plan of action. Practice deans/

directors focus on the clinical enterprise selecting faculty facilitators, connectors, partners, consultants, and team members who recognize the existence of different and widely divergent world views and perspectives. In the INMSI, the clinical enterprise team discusses and evaluates cultural proficiency and challenges in monthly focus groups with patients, families, patient/parent advisory groups, and formal and informal community leaders. A mutually respectful, shared decision-making process builds trust and helps community partners develop interventions that are culturally acceptable while breaking down cultural barriers. Lifestyle choices and social determinants of health and equity, such as poverty, food insecurity, poor access to healthcare, genetics, biology, and behavior, must receive careful consideration, evaluation, and action since all affect clinical outcomes and long-term sustainability of the clinical enterprise.

In 2014, the American Academy of Nursing's Expert Panel for Global Nursing and Health published standards of practice for culturally competent nursing care (Douglas et al., 2014). Based on principles of social justice, culturally competent nursing care involves (a) knowledge of cultures; (b) education and training in culturally competent care; (c) critical reflection; (d) cross-cultural communication; (e) culturally competent practice; (f) cultural competence in healthcare organizations and systems; (g) patient advocacy and empowerment; (h) multicultural workforce; (i) cross-cultural leadership; and (j) evidence-based practice and research. Each standard should be reviewed with all clinic team members. The goal is to balance cultural diversity and proficiency with the universal human experience and common needs of all people. The best team at every level is both clinically and culturally proficient, valuing accessible, continuous, cost-effective, compassionate, and coordinated care (Novak, 2019c). Cultural world views range from seeking to eliminate other cultures to seeking to interact with other cultures in a way that builds on the best of both worlds (Lindsey et al., 2013).

Module 3: Developing a Business and Reimbursement Plan

Module 3 emphasizes the importance of building a diverse portfolio, billing/coding, value-based healthcare delivery, strategic planning, evidence-based practice, and evaluation. Reimbursement through billing and coding is an important component of long-term sustainability. Billers and coders must be hired with care and attention to communication style and cultural proficiency. Billers and coders interface with institutional offices of provider credentialing. Billing can be so fragmented that it obscures overall value. The clinical enterprise team enables patients to learn about and obtain the best care, helps patients prevent illness and manage their chronic conditions, simplifies administrative processes, and eliminates skewed incentives that work against value (Porter & Teisberg, 2006).

As with most small businesses, nurse-led clinics using the INMSI model will take 2 to 3 years to break even financially unless they are fully grant- or university-supported from project inception. By year 3, the clinic should have at least a 10% operating margin. By year 5, the goal is an operating margin of at least 20%. These margins allow growth and development of the clinic team, services, and programs in response to evolving student, patient, family, and community needs. The dean/director must clarify with upper administration how costs will be covered if there is a gap between a grant or contract award letter, start date, and actual arrival of grant/contract funds. For example, how will a delay between a July grant award and launch expectation and the September fund arrival be handled?

The focus of a sustainable clinic should be on value and not merely costs. High-quality care should be less costly (Porter & Teisberg, 2006). The Harvard Business School offers online and week-long courses on value-based healthcare delivery taught by Michael Porter and colleagues. The courses emphasize the importance of rewarding innovations that increase value and encouraging team members to practice more creatively while maintaining efficiency and effectiveness. Team members are encouraged to think and plan strategically on a daily basis and to define the right goal: superior patient value. Publishing an annual report that includes a vision, goals, clinical outcomes, and innovations is essential. Deans/directors and faculty must be ready to tell their story and explain the value of the clinical enterprise in 60- to 90-second sound bites to a variety of audiences, including legislators, prospective donors, university administrators and leaders, community members, and most importantly, the nursing faculty whom they wish to engage in the practice plan.

There have been persistent concerns regarding the science-to-service gap, the movement of research from bench-to-bedside to global health programs (Greenhalgh, Howick, & Maskrey, 2014), and the "quality chasm" resulting from the research to practice gap (Institute of Medicine, 2001). Deans/directors and faculty engaged in the clinical enterprise can use Implementation Science to advance evidence-based practice and evaluation. Implementation Science, the study of factors that influence the full and effective use of innovations in practice, promotes the uptake of consolidated research findings and emphasizes the study of factors that are action-oriented and mission-driven (Madon, Hofman, Kupfer, & Glass, 2007). The RE-AIM model (reach, effectiveness, adoption, implementation, maintenance) for planning, evaluation, and reporting was used to evaluate the 14 clinics (Glasgow, Klesges, Dzewaltowski, Estabrooks, & Vogt, 2006).

The clinical enterprise emphasizes system development while providing faculty practice opportunities, access to research populations, and rich educational experiences for interprofessional students. Sample capstone and research projects included the following:

- The INMSI effects on emergency department (ED) diversion, chronic disease management, and top 10 presenting concerns.
- System quality improvement including medication reconciliation and Team Strategies and Tools to Enhance Performance and Patient Safety (TeamSTEPPs; Rapala & Novak, 2007).
- Analysis of optimal scheduling patterns, patient flow, and root cause analysis (Novak, 2011).
- Health policy effects (Novak in Dreher and Glasgow, 2017; Wall, Novak, & Wilkerson, 2005).
- Telehealth, telepsychology, teleaudiology (Novak et al., 2016), digital monitoring devices for behavioral change, for example, hearing health, smoking cessation, chronic disease management.
- Analysis of scope of practice including Future of Nursing full practice authority (FPA) recommendations.

Module 4: Clinic Implementation, Expansion, and Replication

Module 4 focuses on leadership, management, and customized information technology (e.g., electronic health records) for data analytics and ongoing analysis of revenue growth.

Relationship-based communication among faculty, the clinical team, and community partners is fundamental to clinic development, implementation, expansion, and replication. Clinic site selection should be based on alignment with the school and university missions and the clinic's capacity to facilitate evidence-based practice and education, access to research populations, and faculty practice and service to local communities to ensure accessible, continuous, cost-effective, compassionate, and culturally proficient care.

Faculty must be reminded that working with communities is a dance (Novak, 2014). Electronic health records should be customized with the information technology team to meet specific needs of the clinic, including the ability to easily and consistently input patient data, facilitate linkage with the health home and members of the healthcare referral team, and support population-based data analytics and ongoing analysis of billing/coding to optimize revenue growth, scalability, and expansion.

An X, Y, Z Faculty Practice Plan was originally developed by the author in the 1990s and later refined for use in multiple settings. In the X, Y, Z Model, faculty compensation is a function of three factors: base salary (X); supplemental salary for additional responsibilities, for example, lead nurse practitioner or Magnet® Program consultant (Y); and end of the year productivity bonus (Z). INMSI clinics and the X, Y, Z Faculty Practice Plan created an income stream at Purdue and University of Texas (UT) Health Science Centers at both San Antonio and Houston that exceeded $1 million annually for each campus. Approximately 40% of the UT faculty participated in the X, Y, Z Faculty Practice Plan as APRNs, consultants, or executive leaders (Novak, 2013, 2018, 2019b).

Module 5: Building a Mosaic of Support

Module 5 describes funding mechanisms for clinical enterprises, including Medicare, Medicaid, private insurance, local fundraising, and legacy donations by philanthropists. Collaboration with the university's development office (UDO) is emphasized.

Guided by the INMSI, the dean/director can develop a diverse funding portfolio to support the clinical enterprise. The model's emphasis on community engagement opens doors for a revenue stream. Building a diverse portfolio includes monthly review of potential local, state, federal, and foundation sources of funding. This review is the responsibility of all team members. Grant writing is a team sport. A diverse portfolio can be supported through partnerships with local universities for service learning, for example, industrial, mechanical, or computer engineering graduate student projects. Understanding the range of available third-party payers is critical. For example, the INMSI clinic teams have worked with approximately 50 private insurance vendors.

It is also essential that deans/directors and leaders of clinical enterprises work with the university development office to identify philanthropic community partners who want to leave a meaningful legacy. Local fundraisers, including silent and live auctions, are effective in enhancing revenue streams. Patient revenues are a key component of the portfolio; cash payment on the day of service using a sliding fee scale is the preferred mechanism. A concierge model may be considered for patients who want to pay a flat fee annually for a menu of healthcare services. To enhance the patient-centered focus of service delivery, INMSI clinics may incorporate fee-for-service house calls as another innovation. The response to house calls is especially well received with new parents and seniors.

Social determinants of health are the economic and social conditions that influence individual and group differences in health status (Braveman & Gottlieb, 2014). Funding agencies expect that deans/directors and faculty will address factors unique to a specific patient population in grant proposals. Health disparities within a population can be created by differences in culture, socioeconomic status, literacy, access, language, gender, geography, and religion of its members. Health disparities for a local clinic population can be identified through federal, state, and local health department data, census data, patient and community advisory boards, community focus groups, and interactive community presentations. Use of the INMSI demands an understanding of social determinants of health, the conditions in which people are born, grow, live, work, and age. Thus, clinic priorities can be balanced and informed with input from local community members, who can be gathered in focus groups and/or other forums to identify what they believe influences the health of their community. To promote healthcare equity, nurse-led clinic teams provide health screenings, immunizations, health education, counseling, and other interprofessional outreach opportunities. A deep understanding of private and public insurance is essential to clinical enterprise success. A sustainable clinical enterprise positions schools of nursing to provide innovative and successful alternatives to the current private and public options.

In our experience, the cost of INMSI clinics is 50% to 70% lower than the cost of traditional medical practice models, and outcomes are comparable or better. For example, the INMSI clinic in Indiana achieved designation as a Federally Qualified Health Center (FQHC), which allowed for billing of Medicare and Medicaid at a higher rate. A "pay for performance" contract through the Delivery System Reform Incentive Payment (DSRIP) mechanism of the Centers for Medicare and Medicaid Services (CMS) allowed expansion of an INMSI clinic and faculty practice in Texas. From 2012 to 2017, six states participated in the CMS DSRIP mechanism. New York recently extended their DSRIP contract through 2021. DSRIP contracts can provide substantial funding for clinical enterprises in academic nursing.

In an era of transference of great wealth through wills and trusts and a younger generation with an interest in philanthropy, legacy gifts to support nursing models of care are realistic. It is not uncommon to hear from donors of significant gifts that they would have donated sooner if they had been informed of the need and asked to donate. It is important to work with the university's development office to identify and meet with potential donors, coordinate fundraising activities, and ensure a consistent and clear message regarding the work and needs of the clinical enterprise. A community advisory board helps lead fundraising events. Members can invite potential donors with the time and passion to support fundraising efforts. It is essential to match fundraising events with local community-identified needs and values and to determine potential fundraising capacity of the target audience. It is important to develop a clinic "wish list" that can be shared with potential donors, including items ranging in cost from books and toys to office equipment, such as pediatric exam tables.

Module 6: Grants and Grant Writing

Module 6 enumerates grant priorities, potential funders, and keys to successful grant writing and grant funding. For grant writing success, find one or more mentors with experience in successfully securing both small and large state, federal, and foundation grants. Clarify the research and/or clinical question. Review the funding agency website for upcoming requests for proposals (RFPs), proposal deadlines, agency priorities, strategic plan, and specific details of their proposal format. Create an evidence-based background statement that sets the stage for the objectives or aims of the grant project. Compose three and five objectives or specific aims for the project. Develop a budget with clear justification for each line item.

A mosaic of grant support provides a revenue stream while increasing access to care. State and federal grant funding are obvious resources for initial and ongoing clinic support. Each state public health department identifies priorities based on root cause analysis of top healthcare concerns in each county; examples include mental health, immunizations, tobacco control, obesity prevention, school health, healthy nutrition/active lifestyle, and opioid addiction, prevention, intervention, and treatment. State funding is tied to each of the county and/or state priorities. Grant proposals for state support must be tied to the priorities identified in your particular state. You can usually download specific RFPs at the website of your state health department. State public health priorities are typically consistent with priorities of nurse-led clinics, making clinic or wellness center projects highly fundable. For example, Indiana clinics received annual funding from the Indiana State Health Department to support health promotion/disease prevention programs, chronic disease management, and personnel. Personnel costs (salaries and benefits) comprise 80% of most nurse-led clinic budgets.

The following federal agencies have funded the INMSI and other nurse-led clinic projects: the National Institutes of Health (NIH), National Institute of Nursing Research (NINR), CMS, Department of Health and Human Services/Health Resources and Services Administration (DHHS/HRSA), Agency for Healthcare Research and Quality (AHRQ), and the Department of Justice (DoJ). Federal funding priorities are consistent with state priorities listed previously with an overarching emphasis on social justice, equity, and poverty. Federal funding success is linked to strong proposals tied to the priorities specified in the RFP. Federal health priorities are consistent with nurse-led clinic priorities, which means that clinic operations, projects, and capital improvements are fundable.

Nongovernmental sources of funding should also be explored in the pursuit of a diverse revenue portfolio. A sample of foundations with missions/goals connected to nursing and/or healthcare are listed in Table 15.1. Grant priorities of these and other foundations with similar profiles should be reviewed annually.

TABLE 15.1 Selected Sources of Foundation Funding With Nursing and Healthcare Goals

FOUNDATION	MISSION/GOAL
Rita and Alex Hillman	Cultivate nurse leaders, support nursing research and innovations, and disseminate new models of care. Contact: 212-365-3115; www.rahf.org/grant-programs/innovations.
Helene Fuld Health Trust	Support student nurses and nursing education. Contact: 212-525-2418.
Robert Wood Johnson	Build a national culture of health. Contact: 609-627-5937.
Johnson & Johnson	Access to care and advocacy to advance health globally. Contact: 732-524-0400.
Commonwealth Fund	Promote a high-performing healthcare system that achieves better access, improved quality, and greater efficiency, particularly for societies most vulnerable and the elderly. Contact: 212-606-3800.
Annie E. Casey	Improve the well-being of American children. Contact: 443-438-3579.
Jonas	Scholarships for DNP and PhD doctoral students who commit to a career as nursing faculty or leaders in primary care. Contact: 212-305-9792.
Hartford	Improve the care of older adults. Contact: 212-832-7788.
Gerber	Improve nutrition and/or health of infants and toddlers. Contact: 231-924-3175.
Hervey Family Fund @ San Diego	Scholarships, literacy/libraries, healthcare research. Contact: 619-402-1827.
Alexander and Eva Nemeth	Transform the lives of families in the San Diego Region; human health, animal welfare, and community progress. Contact: 877-412-1145.
Kenneth and Eileen Norris	Southern California: Advance better health and intellectual enlightenment through education, cultivation of the arts, and individual responsibility. Contact: 562-435-8444.
Thrasher Research Fund	Improve children's health through the provision of grants for pediatric research. Contact: 801-240-4753.
Virginia Healthcare	Increase access to primary healthcare for all Virginians. Contact: 804-828-5804.

My own experience with grant funding illustrates the possibilities for building a mosaic of grant support. Through DHHS/HRSA and the Americans for Relief and Recovery Act (ARRA), I was successful in securing FQHC designation for the INMSI clinics in Indiana. This resulted in a $600,000 annual base budget and approval to bill CMS at a significantly higher rate. For the development and expansion of INMSI clinics in San Antonio, a $5.1 million CMS DSRIP contract and $600,000 in Hillman Innovations in Care funding were secured. A diverse portfolio for the Houston INMSI clinics was created with funding from the Hillman Foundation, AVANCE Head Start, contracts with local businesses for employee healthcare, contracts with four local universities for student healthcare, and donations from local philanthropists and private foundations. Finally, Medicaid, private insurance billing, and $12 million in foundation funding (see Table 15.1; Nemeth, Hillman, Hervey, Thrasher) support the INMSI clinics in California.

CONCLUSION

Before one can develop a business plan and build a mosaic of support for an academic nursing clinical enterprise, the dean/director, leadership team, and faculty must carefully lay the groundwork through relationship-based communication, careful selection of community partners, and hiring a team of culturally proficient staff members across all levels of the planned project—from clinicians to administrators, to billers and coders, to engineering support and facilities management. Each of these individuals will contribute to the sustainability, innovation, and overall success of the clinical enterprise. As the dean/director sets the stage with relationship-based communication and cultural proficiency, the INMSI helps to create a diverse and inclusive community of clinical experts, scholars, and leaders for value-based healthcare delivery.

Risks and challenges to long-term sustainability of nurse-led clinics include projects tied to grants that are nonrenewable or highly competitive, grant funding sources that change priorities annually, a lack of diversity in funding sources, and bureaucratic idiosyncrasies or changes in upper administrative personnel that create challenges for innovation, stability, and sustainability. A key threat to the incorporation of faculty practice as an integral component of a university-based INMSI is when community engagement and practice are not consistently embedded or valued in the university and/or school of nursing promotion and tenure process (Novak, 2011).

The benefits of implementing the INMSI are numerous. Clinical enterprises and faculty practices based on this model operate at just 30% to 50% of the cost of a traditional medical practice model and create cost savings and value through health promotion, disease prevention, emergency department diversion, and chronic disease management. INMSI clinics are a replicable, scalable, accessible, safe, patient- and family-centered, cost-effective, and efficient system of care provided by APRNs and an interprofessional team. INMSI clinics have demonstrated effectiveness and sustainability in rural and urban Indiana, rural and urban Texas, and urban San Diego.

RESOURCES

Agency for Heathcare Research and Quality: https://www.ahrq.gov

Commission on Medicare and Medicaid Services: https://www.cms.gov

Duke University Health Innovation Lab: https://hil.nursing.duke.edu

Randall, S., Crawford, T., Currie, J., River, J., & Betihavas, V. (2017). Impact of community based nurse-led clinics on patient outcomes, patient satisfaction, patient access and cost effectiveness: A systematic review. *International Journal of Nursing Studies, 73*, 24–33. doi:10.1016/j.ijnurstu.2017.05.008

Sources of Federal Funding: National Institutes of Health: https://www.nih.gov

University of Minnesota School of Nursing Bentson Healthy Communities Innovation Center: https://nursing.umn.edu/about/our-facilites/bentson-healthy-communities-innovation-center

U.S. Department of Health and Human Services/Health Resources and Services Administration: https://www.hrsa.gov

REFERENCES

Berwick, D. (2013). *Promising care: How we can rescue health care by improving it*. Hoboken, NJ: Wiley–Jossey-Bass.

Braveman, P., & Gottlieb, L. (2014). The social determinants of health: It's time to consider the causes of the causes. *Public Health Reports, 129*(Suppl. 2), 19–31. doi:10.1177/00333549141291S206

Douglas, M. K., Rosenkoetter, M., Pacquiao, D. F., Callister, L. C., Hattar-Pollara, M., Lauderdale, J., … Purnell, L. (2014). Guidelines for implementing culturally competent nursing care. *Journal of Transcultural Nursing, 25*(2), 109–121. doi:10.1177/1043659614520998

Furco, A. (2011). Service learning: A balanced approach to experiential education. *International Journal of Global and Development Education Research*, 71–76. Retrieved from https://digitalcommons.unomaha.edu/cgi/viewcontent.cgi?article=1104&context=slceslgen

Glasgow, R. E., Klesges, L. M., Dzewaltowski, D. A., Estabrooks, P. A., & Vogt, T. M. (2006). Evaluating the Overall impact of health promotion programs: Using the RE-AIM framework for decision making and to consider complex issues. *Health Education Research, 21*(3), 688–694. doi:10.1093/her/cyl081

Greenhalgh, T., Howick, J., & Maskrey, N. (2014). Evidence based medicine: A movement in crisis? *British Medical Journal, 348*, g3725. doi:10.1136/bmj.g3725

Institute of Medicine. (2001). *Crossing the quality chasm: A new health system for the 21st century*. Washington, D.C.: National Academies Press.

Lindsey, R. B., Robins, K. N., & Terrell, R. D. (2013). *Cultural proficiency* (4th ed.). Thousand Oaks, CA: Corwin.

Linzer, M., Sinsky, C. A., Poplau, S., Brown, R., Williams, E., & the Healthy Work Place Investigators. (2017). Joy in medical practice: Clinician satisfaction in the healthy work place trial. *Health Affairs*, 36(10), 1808–1814. doi:10.1377/hlthaff.2017.0790

Madon, T., Hofman, K. J., Kupfer, L., & Glass, R. I. (2007). Public health. Implementation science. *Science, 318*(5857), 1728–1729. doi:10.1126/science.1150009

Morgan, J., & Breining-Jones, M. (2016). *Lean Six Sigma's for dummies* (3th ed.). Chichester, UK: Wiley.

Novak, J. C. (1988). The social mandate and historical basis for nursing's role in health promotion. *Journal of Professional Nursing, 4*(2), 80–87.

Novak, J. C. (2007). Faculty practice plans. In S. J. Real & I. C. Abraham (Eds.), *Business and legal guide for nurse practitioners* (pp. 203–214). Philadelphia, PA: Elsevier.

Novak, J. C. (2011). Designing a nurse-managed healthcare delivery system. In Y. Yih (Ed.), *Handbook of healthcare delivery systems* (pp. 1–9). Boca Raton, FL: CRC Press, Taylor & Francis Group.

Novak, J. C. (2013). UT Nursing Faculty Practice Plan, Presented to University of Texas Board of Regents (approved January 13, 2014).

Novak, J. C. (2014). Partnering and engaging with families. In *Tribute* (pp. 17–19). San Antonio, TX: School of Nursing, UT Health Science Center. Retrieved from https://issuu.com/hscsa_communications/docs/tribute_spring2014_flipbook

Novak, J. C. (2017). Interdisciplinary and interprofessional collaboration. In H. M. Dreher & M. E. Smith Glasgow. (Eds.) *Role development for doctoral advanced nursing practice* (pp. 397–414). New York, NY: Springer Publishing Company.

Novak, J. C. (2018). Pioneering an integrated NP-led model of clinic sustainability, innovation, and faculty practice. *American Association of Nurse Practitioners Annual Conference*, Denver, CO, June 27–29, 2018.

Novak, J. C. (2019a). Globalization and international health. In M. A. Nies, & M. McEwan, *Community health nursing: Promoting the health of populations* (7th ed., pp. 275–289). St. Louis, MO: Saunders-Elsevier.

Novak, J. C. (2019b). Pioneering an integrated NP-led model of clinic sustainability, innovation, and faculty practice. *NAPNAP Annual Conference Workshop*, New Orleans, LA, March 9, 2019.

Novak, J. C. (2019c). Pioneering an integrated NP-led model of clinic sustainability, innovation, and faculty practice. Rita and Hillman Foundation Annual Report.

Novak, J. C., & Corbett, C. (2000). Nurse practitioner education: The Virginia experience. In J. Novotny (Ed.), *Distance education in nursing* (pp. 152–179). New York, NY: Springer Publishing Company.

Novak, R. E., Cantu, A. G., Zappler, A., Coco, L., Champlin, C. A., & Novak, J. C. (2016). The future of healthcare delivery: IPE/IPP audiology and nursing student/faculty collaboration to deliver hearing aids to vulnerable adults via telehealth. *Journal of*

Nursing & Interprofessional Leadership in Quality & Safety, 1(1). Retrieved from http://digitalcommons.library.tmc.edu/uthoustonjqualsafe/vol1/iss1/1

Porter, M. E., & Teisberg, E. O. (2006). *Redefining health care: Creating value-based competition on results*. Boston, MA: Harvard University Press.

Rapala, K., & Novak. J. C. (2007, March/April). Integrating patient safety into curriculum. *Patient Safety & Quality Healthcare, 4*, 16–18, 20–23.

Richards, E., & Novak, J. C. (2010). From Biloxi to Cape Town: Curricular integration of service learning. *Journal of Community Health Nursing, 27*, 46–50. doi:10.1080/07370010903466189

Stadtler, A. C., Brandt, K. A., Novak J. C., & Beauchesne, M. A. (2013). Reflections on T. Berry Brazelton: MD influence on pediatric nursing. *Journal of Child and Adolescent Psychiatric Nursing, 26*(4), 234–238. doi:10.1111/jcap.12057

Stadtler, A. C., & Novak, J. C. (2010). *Improving healthcare service delivery systems and outcomes with relationship-based nursing practices*. Oxford, UK: Wiley-Blackwell.

Wall, B., Novak, J. C., & Wilkerson, S. (2005). Doctor of nursing practice program development: Reengineering health care. *Journal of Nursing Education, 44*(9), 396–403.

16

EXECUTIVE LEADERSHIP

CAROLE KENNER | JANA L. PRESSLER

INTRODUCTION

An executive leader is a senior-level person who guides strategic planning, creates a shared vision, and manages/directs personnel to achieve organizational goals. Competencies for nurse executives exist. There are key traits that executive leaders possess. This chapter explores what executive leadership means in an organization and how one achieves this level of professional development.

WHAT DOES EXECUTIVE LEADERSHIP MEAN?

Executive leadership in an academic setting can refer to the responsibilities of a dean/director who oversees regional deans/directors. It can refer to the responsibilities of a senior-level position that has organizational duties in addition to those of a dean/director at a college/school/department level. In either case, the executive leadership position encompasses strategic thinking, direction of the business activities of the organization or unit, goal setting, and motivation of personnel to move the organization forward.

Executive leaders possess specific traits. They need to "be results oriented, customer focused, have a vision, be strategically focused, effectively get work done through others, be good at dealing with conflict, ask great questions, make high-quality decisions, be trusted leaders, and be incredible communicators" (Hawes, 2014). The executive leaders must provide a road map for their personnel and the organization or unit. This work requires clear, transparent communication; engagement of faculty, staff, and students in the strategic planning process; and documentation of the strategic plan's action steps. Key performance indicators (KPIs) represent the metrics by which the plan's progress can be measured. A strategic plan is not a static document that lives on a shelf and is reviewed every 3 to 5 years. The strategic plan should be used to document your respective progress as well as challenges encountered.

The American Organization of Nurse Executives (AONE) developed nurse executive competencies that are applicable in both practice and academia. These competencies are modeled on core competencies for healthcare leadership that were proposed in 2004 by the Healthcare Leadership Alliance, a group comprised of representatives from the AONE, American College of Healthcare Executives, American Association for Physician Leadership, Healthcare Financial Management Association, Healthcare Information and Management Systems Society, and Medical Group Management Association. Common domains of competencies that were identified include "communication and relationship management; knowledge of the health care environment; leadership; professionalism; and business skills and principles" (AONE, 2015, p. 3). In each of these domains, there are multiple, clearly articulated competencies such as building collaborative relationships; serving as a resource to the community; health economics knowledge; and governance, including performance evaluations, patient safety, risk management, personal journey, succession planning, systems thinking, change management, ethics, financial and strategic management, and information management (AONE, 2015). The nurse executive competencies are tested and refined periodically and now form a useful basis for executive leadership education in nursing.

TEAM APPROACH

In reviewing the key traits and competency domains associated with executive leadership, it becomes clear that a leader cannot lead without followers. Followers do not follow if there is not engagement by the leader. The old adage "There is no I in team" holds true. A team approach must be used for a leader to act strategically. How does one get to the level of executive leader and become an effective strategic thinker? One of the competencies from the AONE model—personal journey—illustrates that there is not just one pathway. I (Kenner) will describe my own professional journey as an exemplar to illustrate some ways a nurse can become an executive leader.

EXECUTIVE LEADER EXEMPLAR

I (Kenner) started my academic career as a master's prepared nurse working on my doctorate. I was told that I had 7 years to complete my doctorate and 7 years to secure tenure. Initially, I had no idea what tenure meant. However, I was already accepted for admission in two doctoral programs so I just needed to decide which one best fit my career goals.

Over the course of the next 7 years, I moved from instructor to assistant professor, earned my doctorate, and then tenure. I progressed quickly to associate professor—a senior-level rank—but the rank itself did not make me feel as though I was senior. I was a newly minted PhD. I was asked if I would serve as department chair. At first, I did not accept the offer. Within several months, I agreed to go ahead and try out the role. I had completed a minor in higher education during my doctoral studies. This coursework gave me a bit of confidence in curriculum design, measurement, and legal issues in higher education. As the department chair, I found that, while my relationship with the team changed, I had been mentored by many of the team members and we had already established trust. Before I accepted this position, I talked with senior faculty at the school to determine if they had any concerns about me taking charge. They told me that they did not have concerns and subsequently served as great mentors to me in my new role. I relied on them and the dean to explain some of the aspects of the union contract in terms of workload, use of tenure track versus clinical track faculty, and asked many questions about clinical rotations. These clinical rotations were ones that I had not been involved in while serving as a faculty member; however, they were assigned to our department.

At this same time, I had become nationally recognized in my specialty area of neonatal nursing. I had served on a neonatal national board and knew trends in both neonatal and pediatric healthcare. This gave me credibility in the department as we examined our curriculum to make changes. Over the course of the next few years, I was promoted to full professor and was elected President of the National Association of Neonatal Nurses (NANN). This gave me insights into trends beyond my specialization as I interacted with national nursing and medical leaders. This professional network opened doors for my junior faculty in terms of serving on committees, obtaining funding for research or education projects, and writing for publication—all activities that would help them gain promotion and/or tenure. More importantly, I learned through my board work how important it was to be strategic, set goals, develop metrics for measurement of these goals, and report our progress each year. I also learned the business model of association work, including relational databases for marketing; customer service for our members; fundraising through our members, foundation, and corporate advisors; and how to build educational product lines, develop clear profit/loss statements, and develop "break even models." These were all things I never learned in nursing school or during doctoral education. I served on the national board and as department chair for 8 years.

Because of my experience in developing product lines, knowledge of nursing education trends, and experience in neonatology at a national level, I was hired as an associate dean to oversee academic programs at five campuses of the large university in which I was employed. The regional dean model was used for general oversight of the campuses, but I had responsibility for day-to-day operations. I worked directly with the regional deans/directors and department chairs to maintain high-quality programs. I also developed short-term educational programs that gave us revenue to support curricular growth. I learned how to write large research and program grants for funding by federal and/or state agencies. My dean at that time was a great mentor to me, encouraging me to take risks and be innovative. My dean was used to working in teams as a researcher. So, I followed her lead and did the same on the education side. I technically served on 27 university/college committees but obviously could not attend all of the meetings. I established a working relationship with my department chairs, directors, and faculty. Those individuals would involve me as needed when special topics were discussed. I reviewed their planned meeting agendas and gave input. I attended meetings when my presence was very much needed. This style of working not only freed me up to do other things but also empowered the faculty and built their trust in each other and me.

After 4 years as associate dean, I was hired for my first deanship at another large university with three campuses and two satellite branches. My first deanship felt very comfortable. Since I had been given so much autonomy as an associate dean, I was confident in moving to the next level. I was secure about my ability to lead and build a team. I worked on communication with the distant campuses, as they requested more face time to get to know and trust me. I traveled many times in the first few months so that I could get to know the faculty individually. I did a listening tour with all faculty and staff so that I could learn their perspectives on the organization—challenges and opportunities they saw, as well as their own professional career goals. I spent 6 years working with state leaders to build a statewide organization for associate degree through doctoral degree programs so that we could discuss and work on seamless academic progression models before these became a hot topic in nursing education. I tried to always admit when I was not familiar with something and was never concerned about asking faculty or staff for help. At the same time, I realized that I had the ultimate decision-making authority and responsibility. I felt that I needed training in some areas of deaning, so I began working with an executive coach. We worked on communication techniques, team building, conflict management, and self-care, an area that I always relegated to last on my priority list. I offered executive coaching services to some of my teams and leaders. This yearlong work helped all of us to recognize strengths and weaknesses and improve communication.

I was selected to participate in the Harvard Kennedy School's *Women and Power* program. This weeklong adventure was exciting and exhausting. It brought together a global group of women from different career paths: sitting senators, staff from ministries of health, three nursing deans, business executives, and relevant others. The program challenged us to problem-solve and think outside of our discipline. Unfolding case studies were used, which required teamwork to develop practical solutions. We quickly found that we had to influence others without use of jargon and to explain the perspective that we were using—for example, the perspective of healthcare as a backdrop for an answer.

Over the course of the next few years, I went from participation in the Harvard course to participation in Oxford University's Round Table (Women's Rights and Leadership: Regaining the Momentum). This weeklong program was similar to the Harvard course but had more global participation. The third program that I completed was the Helene Fuld Leadership and Policy Fellowship at the Health Policy Institute of George Mason University. As intended, the focus was on honing leadership skills with a policy thrust. This work was important since I knew that, as dean, I needed to be more politically active and drive policy changes in the areas of workforce development and educational standards.

The area in which I felt least comfortable was building and working with financial models. I enrolled in the Executive Leadership Program offered by the American Association of Colleges of Nursing (AACN) in collaboration with the Wharton School of Business at the University of Pennsylvania. This weeklong program, taught by Wharton faculty, focused on marketing, trends in higher education, and financial models. All of the participants were assistant deans, associate deans, or deans of schools/colleges of nursing. Classes on strategic thinking, goal setting, and ethical/legal dilemmas in business forced me out of my comfort zone and helped me to start thinking with and using more of a business lens.

All of these focused educational programs helped me over the course of the next few years to accept new deanships, including an appointment as associate dean of a college of pharmacy, nursing, and health professions while simultaneously serving as dean of the nursing school. My current deanship encompasses nursing, exercise science, and public health. Moving out of the nursing discipline forced me to learn about different accreditation standards and new curricular challenges. It also gave me the opportunity to work with more of a mixed faculty in terms of gender, ethnicity, and race. How did my journey prepare me for executive leadership?

LEADER AMONG LEADERS

After more than 30 years in higher education and participation in a number of world-class executive leadership education programs, I have developed a skill set for working at both the school and college level to move a strategic plan forward. I have experience working with information technologists (ITs), registrars, and personnel in enrollment management, student affairs, and academic affairs. I am closely aligned in my work with individuals in the treasurer's office and human resources. I am confident that I have a solid administrative knowledge base with complete understanding of the dean's role. I am also humble in knowing that I still have a lot to learn about operations at the top level of the organization.

CONCLUSION

Executive leaders are considered leaders among leaders. They are individuals who have achieved a high-level leadership position through education and experience, but they coexist among many other organizational leaders. At the executive level, the keys to success are putting the team first, readily admitting to mistakes or lack of knowledge in certain areas, and asking for help without fear of embarrassment or shame. Executive leaders serve as mentors to other dean colleagues as well as to their faculty, staff, and students.

Executive leadership requires a commitment to the team approach, strategic thinking, clear communication, and decisive action. It requires forward thinking and an ability to look to the future. Executive leadership means risk-taking with no guarantee of successful outcomes. Executive leadership is exciting, challenging, and well worth the time and effort involved.

RESOURCES

American Association of Colleges of Nursing Wharton Executive Leadership Program. https://www.aacnnursing.org/Faculty/Professional-Development/Wharton-Executive-Program

George Mason University Health Policy Institute. https://www.internationalroundtablesymposiums.com/Oxford University International

Maxwell, J. C. (2019). *Leader Shift: The 11 essential changes every leader must embrace.* New York: HarperCollins Focus, LLC.

Round Table Symposiums. https://www.internationalroundtablesymposiums.com/

Women and Power: Leadership in a New World. HARVARD Kennedy School. https://www.hks.harvard.edu/educational-programs/executive-education/women-and-power

REFERENCES

American Organization of Nurse Executives. (2015). *Nurse executive competencies.* Chicago, IL: Author. Retrieved from http://www.aone.org/resources/nurse-leader-competencies.shtml

Hawes, R. (2014). *Top ten traits of great leaders.* American Management Association. Retrieved from https://www.amanet.org/training/articles/top-ten-traits-of-great-leaders.aspx

SELF-CARE AND WORK–LIFE INTEGRATION FOR NURSING DEANS AND DIRECTORS

17

CHALLENGES OF DEANING AND DIRECTING IN NURSING

CAROLE KENNER | JANA L. PRESSLER

INTRODUCTION

Deaning and directing takes stamina, grit, and resiliency. Throughout this text, we have discussed many opportunities for leaders. This chapter focuses on common challenges faced by nursing deans/directors. Some of these challenges are not unique to nursing education; however, most are definitely "character-building" moments for nurses (B. Melnyk, personal communication, April 1, 2016).

TRENDS IN HIGHER EDUCATION

The landscape of higher education has changed dramatically during the past 10 years. Students seek education that is fast and easy to access. Students want to earn stackable credentials. What does that mean? They do not only seek full degrees but also want education to meet new occupational trends (Williamson & Pittinsky, 2016). Employers are demanding more certifications to demonstrate competency in specified areas. In nursing, this may be a certificate in palliative care, school nursing, nursing education, informatics, quality and safety, sexual assault nurse examination (SANE), and many other areas. In other instances, this means earning a minor in public health along with a nursing degree, or earning a masters in business administration (MBA) in addition to becoming an advanced practice nurse.

The Chronicle of Higher Education (2018) identified 10 current trends in U.S. higher education (see Box 17.1).

These trends drive a number of the innovative program offerings and new teaching/learning approaches that we see today. For example, competency-based education is an innovation that reflects the current trends of becoming more

> **BOX 17.1**
>
> ## CURRENT TRENDS IN U.S. HIGHER EDUCATION
>
> 1. *The American campus under siege*: More scrutiny over business practices, including admissions.
> 2. *Students in charge*: Student-centric environments.
> 3. *Loss of global prestige*: U.S. schools are not as attractive to international students as in past years.
> 4. *Peer review in flux*: Increasing selection of open-access journals for faculty publications.
> 5. *Era of deregulation*: Changes in guidelines for for-profit schools.
> 6. *Sexual assault*: Title IX regulatory changes.
> 7. *Student success up front*: Emphasis on academic progression and solid graduation rates; use of incentives to improve outcomes.
> 8. *Rebranding the PhD*: Reinventing doctoral education to meet market demands outside academia.
> 9. *Data scientists in demand*: Big data and data mining are growing markets.
> 10. *Black college renaissance*: Increasing enrollments in HBCUs.
>
> HBCUs, historically black colleges and universities.
> SOURCE: Adapted from The Chronicle of Higher Education. (2018, March 4). *Inside the Trends Report, March 04, 2018*. Retrieved from Chronicle of Higher Education website, https://www.chronicle.com/article/Inside-the-Trends-Report/242676?cid=cp188

student-centric and defining student success in terms of academic progression. In a competency-based approach to education, "seat time" is no longer the gold standard enrollment metric for many courses; instead, students must demonstrate attainment of competency. While not new, competency-based education is difficult for nursing programs due to their regulatory and accreditation requirements. Staffing for courses that students move through at their own pace requires much reorganization and planning. Yet, there are institutions of higher education with nursing programs that have used competency-based assessments and educational models for a number of years; Excelsior College in New York and Southern New Hampshire University in New Hampshire are recognized examples (Hansen, 2018). Competency-based education also holds promise as a strategy for increasing enrollment as more students can move through a course or program in a year compared to a traditional "seat time" model.

Online and hybrid learning—including use of simulation—are modalities that have been around for years; however, they are growing at exponential rates in response to the current emphasis on student-centric environments and student success. Even though many students claim that they like the traditional face-to-face classroom approach, others admit that they have to work, even during their undergraduate education. Thus, online or hybrid models fit better with many students' lifestyles. These modalities must be supported through faculty development to fully engage students in the online environment; otherwise, students may resent these courses and view them as self-teaching assignments. The dean/director must advocate for standards and faculty training when using these teaching approaches. The use of simulation and unfolding case studies in risk-free environments is growing as a way to teach psychomotor skills, clinical reasoning, teamwork, and clinical decision-making. Unfortunately, equipping and establishing simulation labs is very costly. The dean or director must seek ways to offset these costs through grants and other fundraising mechanisms.

TRENDS IN NURSING

The landscape of nursing education is changing as part of the changing landscape of higher education. Meanwhile, the landscape of nursing practice is changing as well. For example, it is increasingly difficult to gain access to (a) electronic health records; (b) medication administration systems; (c) clinical rotations; and (d) public health and primary care experiences due to regulations, legal concerns, the emphasis on volume of patients seen, and dwindling staff in practice.

Preceptors and/or practice sites want payment for participating in the education of nursing students at a time when university, college, school, and program budgets are tight. Nursing faculty shortages reduce the ability to flex student rotations and cover didactic courses with full-time faculty. Use of graduate teaching assistants, adjunct faculty, and part-time faculty has the potential to diminish the continuity of curricula and negatively affect accreditation reviews.

Few nursing faculty receive formal education in curriculum design and higher education law in their doctoral programs. This situation leads to the implementation of nursing curricula that do not always follow a clear path in addressing the essential elements of baccalaureate, master's, or doctoral nursing education that are specified by accrediting agencies. Clear connections between course objectives and program outcomes can also be problematic. In some institutions, few faculty understand how to construct solid tests and/or conduct item analyses of faculty-made tests and other student assessments.

Deans/directors must garner resources for continuing professional development of faculty related to issues and trends in nursing education.

State boards of nursing and accrediting bodies require evidence of faculty expertise, adequate staffing ratios, control over budgets, clear systematic evaluation plans, adherence to specialization standards at the graduate level, and clear oversight by a qualified dean/director. Pressures from various higher education organizations and the numbers of reports that are required annually have increased dramatically over the last decade. It is necessary for the dean/director to delegate some or all of these tasks while retaining general oversight. Some institutions now support an evaluation and/or outcomes coordinator for nursing programs so that data are systematically collected on an ongoing basis.

COMPETING PRIORITIES—CAUGHT IN THE MIDDLE

Bouws, Candela, and Bonnema (2016) conducted a qualitative study to examine the lived experience of a novice nursing dean. They found the following four themes: servant leadership; lack of preparation for the role; uniqueness of the nursing dean role; and highly political environments. New deans felt the need to sacrifice their clinical practice and/or research because the leadership position consumed them. To cite some common areas of concern, new deans referred to challenges, such as long work hours; lack of mentorship; inability to talk freely with faculty following transition to the leadership position; difficulty achieving desired connections with peers, especially those from other disciplines; budgets; accreditation requirements; toxic work environments; gender bias; students' lack of respect for hierarchy; and faculty and clinical facility shortages (Bouws et al., 2016). If these issues are not addressed satisfactorily, turnover among new nursing deans will likely increase.

Wabash Center Blogs (2015) identified eight challenges that deans of theological schools face, including student issues; faculty discontent; presidential pressures; budgets; staff changes and conflicts; curricula; legal issues; and personal issues (Galindo, 2015). These challenges are typical and not unique to any one discipline. They are part of a dean's job. Student issues around academic progress, academic integrity, financial hardships, sexual assault, racial bias, hate crimes, bullying, and mental health (e.g., suicide, anxiety) are common. Student deaths from suicide, homicide, accidents, and chronic or life-threatening illnesses are more common today than in years past. Faculty issues center on workload, pay, budget constraints, incivility, bullying, hate crimes, and perceived bias. It may surprise some that a dean's position is truly middle management. Therefore, oftentimes, a dean finds herself or himself caught between faculty and upper administration.

In times of administrative change, there can be a shift in institutional priorities. This shift requires a quick culture change, which is never easy and pressures the dean to change strategic course while concurrently bringing the faculty and staff along the modified path. Budget constraints are a very real part of higher education. Shifts in programs (e.g., program expansion or closure in response to enrollment) are certain to unsettle some faculty, staff, and students. Parallel to this trend is the rising cost of tuition and fees so that students are feeling financially pinched. Fewer scholarships and financial aid are available in many institutions. Nursing students also commonly experience difficulties with time management and priority setting, culminating in substantial stress associated with getting everything completed on time (Wojciechowski, 2017). Finally, today we live in a very litigious society. Threats of lawsuits are commonplace. The dean or director is often the mediator and must seek guidance from legal counsel, human resources, dean of students, or provost on legal matters. All of these challenges, while predictable, take a personal toll on a dean (Galindo, 2015). Extreme exhaustion, development of chronic illnesses, stress, and anxiety are all symptoms of the pressures associated with being a dean.

While many studies have explored staff nurse turnover, there are few large evidence-based studies of nursing dean turnover. Turnover among college administrators was examined, however, in a recent study by Higher Education Publications, Inc. (2018). In this study, a 16% turnover rate was observed among deans/directors of nursing education programs, compared to the 21% turnover rate observed among provosts—their customary supervisors. With provosts, nursing deans/directors were among the top 10 college administrators with the highest rates of job turnover.

CONCLUSION

Many challenges exist for today's nursing deans and directors, especially with the current push to expand and extend opportunities for higher education. Chronic stress and burnout are possibilities for many. Yet, garnering resources for faculty, staff, and students and creating a risk-tolerant environment that nurtures innovative solutions for complex issues and challenges can be rewarding and help deans/directors to survive and thrive.

RESOURCES

American Association of Colleges of Nursing. (2008). *The essentials of baccalaureate education for professional nursing practice.* Washington, D.C.: Author.

American Association of Colleges of Nursing. (2011). *The essentials of master's education in nursing.* Washington, D.C.: Author.

American Association of Colleges of Nursing. (2018). *AACNLEADS: Transforming academic nursing leadership*. Retrieved from https://www.chronicle.com/article/Inside-the-Trends-Report/242676?cid=cp188

Elevating Leaders in Academic Nursing. American Association of Colleges of Nursing. Retrieved from https://www.aacnnursing.org/Academic-Nursing/Professional-Development/AACN-LEADS/ELAN

National League for Nursing. Academy of Nursing Education. Retrieved from http://www.nln.org/recognition-programs/academy-of-nursing-education

National League for Nursing. Certification for Nurse Educators. Retrieved from http://www.nln.org/professional-development-programs/Certification-for-Nurse-Educators

REFERENCES

Bouws, M., Candela, L., & Bonnema, J. (2016). The novice nursing dean: A qualitative study of the lived experience. *Journal of Nursing Education and Practice, 6*(8), 43–51. doi:10.5430/jnep.v6n8p43

The Chronicle of Higher Education. (2018, March 4). *Inside the Trends Report, March 04, 2018*. Retrieved from Chronicle of Higher Education website, https://www.chronicle.com/article/Inside-the-Trends-Report/242676?cid=cp188

Galindo, I. (2015). *Wabash Center Blogs. Theological school deans: Eight challenges you WILL face during your tenure as dean*. Retrieved from Wabash Center Blogs website, https://wabashcenter.typepad.com/wabash_center_deans_blog/2015/09/eight-challenges-you-will-face-during-your-tenure-as-dean.html

Hansen, S. E. W. (2018). Improving educational and financial effectiveness through innovation: A case study of Southern New Hampshire University's College for America. *International Journal of Educational Development, 58*, 149–158. doi:10.1016/j.ijedudev.2017.04.006

Higher Education Publications, Inc. (2018). *College administrator data/turnover rates: 2016-present*. Retrieved from @HigherEd direct website, https://hepinc.com/newsroom/college-administrator-data-turnover-rates-2016-present/

Williamson, J., & Pittinsky, M. (2016). *Making credentials matter*. Retrieved from Inside Higher Ed website, https://www.insidehighered.com/views/2016/05/23/understanding-differences-what-credentials-are-being-stacked-and-why-essay

Wojciechowski, M. (2017). Challenges facing nursing students today. *Minority Nurse*. Retrieved from Minority Nurse website, https://minoritynurse.com/challenges-facing-nursing-students-today/

FINDING THE JOY AND SATISFACTION IN DEANING AND DIRECTING

THEODORA SIROTA | BRENDA PETERSEN

INTRODUCTION

Joy can be defined as the experience of feeling good about yourself as a person (Oxford Living Dictionaries, n.d.-a). Joy also can be defined as a feeling of pleasure or happiness that comes from feeling that you are highly successful or thinking that you have done extremely well at some activity. Satisfaction can be defined as a sense of fulfillment of one's desires, expectations, or needs. Satisfaction can also be defined as the pleasure emanating from fulfillment of one's goals (Oxford Living Dictionaries, n.d.-b).

From our perspective, there are both joys and satisfactions to be found and embraced by those serving in the position of dean/director of a nursing school, college, or department. However, given the many stresses involved, not all nursing deans/directors would concur that there is overwhelming joy and satisfaction in the role. We propose that the joy and satisfaction that a dean/director can experience flows mainly from two sources: (a) building a culture and environment of happiness and joy in the school, college, or department, and (b) implementing and witnessing the fulfillment of their vision for nursing education. This chapter offers an overview of the demands of deaning and directing; qualifications, competencies, and personal qualities of nursing deans and directors; and best practices for finding joy and satisfaction as a nursing dean/director in the context of a very complex, intense, and challenging role.

THE DEMANDS OF DEANING AND DIRECTING IN NURSING

Most nurse educators who ultimately assume the role of dean/director start their careers by developing expertise in teaching along with a solid program of research and/or other forms of scholarship. After years of impressive accomplishments in these areas, opportunities to take on overarching administrative responsibilities present themselves. There are ongoing shortages of nursing deans/directors throughout the United States; thus, administrative job opportunities for nurses in higher education are plentiful. Based on their personalities and goals for career fulfillment, some nurse educators are drawn to administrative opportunities and the corresponding responsibilities associated with these positions. Most nursing deans/directors have experienced academia for an extended period of time prior to stepping into the role of chief nursing officer and have witnessed the myriad challenges that accompany a dean/director position. Thus, it is useful to consider what attracts some nurses to the dean/director role and how they derive joy and satisfaction from the work.

Working as the chief administrator of a nursing school/college/department is not easy, and the work associated with it grows exponentially more complex with increases in the size of the unit, number and scope of didactic programs, breadth of extracurricular activities, and number of students, faculty, and alumni. These factors are just those that are internal to the nursing unit itself. The dean/director must also consider and respond to external demands, such as university mission, culture, management, budget, interdisciplinary educational activities, outside communities of interest, and, most importantly, advancement of the discipline of nursing itself.

Further, deans and directors are continually focused on building competent, confident, and caring nurses who can remain resilient in the face of complex, chaotic, and rapidly changing healthcare environments that can also be unsafe at times for one reason or another. Therefore, to ensure optimal well-being for students, faculty, and staff, deans/directors must seize opportunities to bring joy and happiness into the teaching/learning process and workplace environment. Sikka, Morath, and Leape (2015) describe joy as the feeling of success and fulfillment that results from meaningful work. They maintain that realizing the full potential of individual employees and teams is a generative process that cannot be sustained without continuing joy and meaning in work.

QUALIFICATIONS AND COMPETENCIES OF NURSING DEANS/DIRECTORS

Nursing deans/directors are expected to possess a plethora of personal and professional characteristics that equip them for the position and reflect the nature and quality of their leadership. According to Fagin (1996), educational administrators should have a strong record of scholarly productivity as well as prior experience as a leader and documented management skills. Additionally, outstanding interpersonal skills are quintessential qualifications for the following dean/director responsibilities:

- Promoting the profession within the nursing unit, university, and larger community
- Influencing faculty, students, and alumni to become leaders within the profession and representing the nursing unit to university administration and other on- and off-campus entities

A nursing dean/director must possess the vision and skill of a transformational leader—someone who can create a proactive learning environment that energizes and engages faculty and students and, perhaps more importantly, anticipates future nursing and healthcare needs (Fagin, 2000). In fact, Broome (2013) found that an overwhelming majority of nursing deans described their leadership style as transformational.

No matter how small or how large the school, college, or department, all nursing deans and directors take on a broad array of responsibilities and respond to a wide variety of demands. Moreover, they are expected to accomplish everything with competence, confidence, and a calm demeanor that elicits the respect and cooperation of all with whom they interact. Common responsibilities of nursing deans/directors appear in Box 18.1.

In addition to these responsibilities, somehow the dean/director must balance the ongoing needs and concerns of students (and often their families), faculty, institutional administrators, alumni, accreditors, clinical affiliates, professional boards and organizations, and geographically or academically close communities of interest. All too frequently, there are competing, contradictory, and/or shifting interests and demands among these parties. Nevertheless, it is the responsibility of the dean/director to attend to all with competence, grace, and a sense of ongoing discernment related to priorities and appropriateness. The nursing dean/director must possess a stalwart work ethic since

> **BOX 18.1**
>
> **COMMON RESPONSIBILITIES OF NURSING DEANS/DIRECTORS**
>
> Ensuring that all curricula are sound and adhere to professional, educational, and accreditation standards
>
> Educating students who meet benchmark licensing and certification standards upon graduation
>
> Hiring, supporting, and developing competent and inspiring faculty and staff
>
> Translating a vision for the future of nursing education and practice to faculty and staff
>
> Developing and maintaining successful and mutually satisfying collegial relationships with clinical affiliates
>
> Supporting the continuing development of a scholarly academic community of faculty, students, and staff
>
> Communicating with and eliciting the support of financial donors and alumni
>
> Addressing student issues and "crises," some situational and others based more on the anxiety associated with the rigors of nursing programs of study
>
> Juggling institutional demands or constraints on the school/college/department alongside professional needs for the unit itself
>
> Advocating for the nursing unit with the institution's upper administration

the hours are long and the workload is intense. In fact, it is a common expectation for deans/directors to be "on call" 24-7 to manage and respond to any potential crisis.

PERSONAL QUALITIES OF NURSING DEANS/DIRECTORS

Deans/directors must have and maintain a caring and empathetic nature, a high tolerance for stress and the unexpected, and a strong ability to discern, prioritize, and delegate. The nursing dean/director must be able to remain calm and self-soothe in the moment, while clearly articulating plans and interventions in the face of immediate demands within a sometimes chaotic environment. For example, deans/directors are routinely called upon to manage difficult situations such as a student who is having a panic attack in a clinical setting; a student who passed out while involved in a clinical experience in the operating room; a faculty member's sudden injury, chronic illness, or personal issue that interferes with her or his ability to manage workload; and students and/or parents who are upset about course grades or a particular faculty member's behavior.

To achieve a balance between the demands of the workload and the desire to create joy and satisfaction in the nursing unit, the dean/director must be able to seek and find her or his own individual joy and satisfaction on an ongoing basis. Resilience and self-care are critical to prevent lingering distress and ultimate burnout related to facing a wide variety of daily demands, none of which can be managed with a 100% success rate 100% of the time. Resilience has been defined as the ability to withstand, adapt, and recover from stress and adverse events (U.S. Department of Health and Human Services, 2015). Characteristics that support resilience include optimism, positivity, and the ability to manage strong feelings and control impulses, all of which reduce feelings of aggression and/or frustration. Low resilience can affect motivation, cognitive function, and emotional well-being; it is well known that those who are able to "bounce back" from frustration, negative emotions, or unsuccessful outcomes are those who flourish. Tenacity and the ability to withstand rejection and disappointment are also necessary to remain resilient and to maintain well-being for self, faculty, students, and staff.

For nursing deans/directors, resilience is especially needed in smaller settings, where shared governance typically is minimal or nonexistent, budgets are lean, and numbers of faculty and staff are modest. When deans/directors have limited autonomy and/or lack a trusted and competent administrative leadership team, they should cope by adjusting their goals rather than attempting to single-handedly lead and actualize most or all of a unit's ideal goals and initiatives. Failure to make such adjustments sets the dean/director up for significant frustration and stress.

To serve effectively in the role, nursing deans/directors commonly relinquish some roles and activities that contributed to their happiness and success as nurse educators or scientists and propelled them toward their current administrative positions. Taking on a dean/director position with its multifaceted obligations requires keeping a 24-7 schedule with little downtime. This usually includes the necessity of suspending or postponing most or all teaching and/or scholarly activity due to the demands of administration. The overall schedule of the dean/director is intense, arduous, and consuming, very unlike the more flexible work schedule enjoyed by faculty.

Serving as dean/director also changes the relationship with faculty from colleague and peer to supervisor, and the relationship with students from benevolent teacher/mentor to evaluator/judge. Additionally, there is substantial loneliness experienced at the top. Deans/directors must be able to make complex, sometimes controversial, and often unpopular decisions based on their interpretation of policy and/or understanding of a specific situation or precedent. Furthermore, deans/directors must make such decisions with confidence, clarity, and cogent rationale.

FINDING THE JOY AND SATISFACTION IN DEANING/DIRECTING

Despite the rigors and responsibilities of a very critical, complex, and often lonely job, many nursing deans/directors experience exceptional joy and satisfaction in the role. Deaning/directing offers myriad opportunities to exercise transformational leadership and to operationalize a vision for nursing education that flows from a personal philosophy of nursing. Likewise, satisfaction as a nursing dean/director is also based on the ability to build a joyful milieu within an academic nursing setting. Selected examples of activities that can build joy and personal satisfaction are provided in Box 18.2.

To the extent that the dean/director's vision-in-action takes advantage of these and other opportunities, she or he can and will exert substantial impact on nursing education and practice within the school/college/department and beyond. Undoubtedly, much joy and satisfaction can result from having such enormous impact on faculty, students, administration, the university, communities of interest, and the profession of nursing. The sheer variety of opportunities to initiate strategic, vision-driven actions and to witness their success offers nursing deans/directors the promise of great joy and satisfaction, as they experience growth and positive transformation of their organizations.

BOX 18.2

BUILDING JOY AS A NURSING DEAN/DIRECTOR: EXEMPLAR ACTIVITIES

- Leading innovative program and curriculum development
- Defining/refining the teaching/learning process
- Enhancing faculty development and engagement in scholarly activities and clinical practice
- Engaging interprofessional, administrative, and external communities of interest
- Promoting student success
- Building a safe, joyful, inspiring, and motivating culture for teaching/learning and related work

BEST PRACTICES FOR CULTIVATING JOY AND SATISFACTION

First and foremost, all nursing deans/directors are professional nurses. By virtue of their nursing knowledge and experience in education, clinical practice, and research/scholarship, they have integrated a strong nursing identity, philosophy, and vision that defines their work and propels it in a creative and meaningful manner. All success as a chief nursing administrator is dependent on this core condition. Fagin (2000) asserts that the power of being a nurse has been instrumental to her career progress, which included dean of the University of Pennsylvania School of Nursing and interim president of that university. She reminds professional nurses that we often fail to notice and acknowledge the "power of being a nurse," whether we choose to take on one of the numerous opportunities that nursing offers us or whether we move out of nursing and into some other field. She believes that all her career achievements "would not have come my way were I not a nurse" (Fagin, 2000, p. 28). We agree with Fagin: All other skills associated with leadership are secondary in importance to the dean/director's ability to articulate a clear philosophy of nursing and to create a workable vision of nursing education that actualizes that philosophy.

Chinn and Kramer (2018) define the term "philosophy" as "(a) form of disciplined inquiry for the purpose of discerning general traits of reality and principles of value" (p. 295). At the most basic level, the insight and creativity gained through a background of nursing knowledge and scholarship deeply inform the philosophy of a dean/director. That philosophy, in turn, confers the power to create a vision that, when actualized in educational initiatives, allows for transformational opportunities in nursing education for students, faculty, programs, the associated institution, and the nursing profession. Without doubt, having the ability to conceive and actualize strategic goals, seize transformational opportunities, and see them come to fruition provides a major source of joy and satisfaction that a dean/director can experience in her or his position.

Vision is defined as the ability to define and prioritize goals with a strategic future orientation. Vision flows directly from the dean/director's philosophy of nursing and provides a basis for managing, growing, and transforming a nursing unit in concert with the strategic goals and needs of the institution, communities of interest, and nursing profession. Leadership in nursing educational administration is primarily defined by one's ability to actualize one's vision. In semistructured interviews with 30 nursing deans, Wilkes, Cross, Jackson, and Daly (2015) found "having vision" to be the most frequently named leadership attribute that the nursing dean/director must possess. The dean/director's philosophy of nursing informs the vision. As a dean/director, having the opportunity and ability to put your beliefs into action and ultimately savor the success of your actions brings great joy and satisfaction.

Articulating and Activating a Philosophy and Vision for Nursing Education

The nursing metaparadigm posited by Fawcett (1984) illustrates how the philosophy and vision of a nursing dean/director can positively affect her or his leadership and yield workplace joy and satisfaction. Since the dean/director is fundamentally a professional nurse, she or he should relate philosophically to the four elements of Fawcett's metaparadigm, which include beliefs about persons, environment, health, and nursing. This philosophic foundation sets the stage for vision and strategic leadership.

Beliefs About Persons

Beliefs about persons will inform the dean/director's sense of the value and capabilities of others, usual leadership style, decision-making, and approach to students, faculty, university administrators, and members of the communities of interest. Since nursing deans/directors are professional nurses, beliefs about caring for others in a holistic manner will hopefully characterize their approach to leadership. The dean/director should embrace a belief in the dignity and value of all human beings, which necessitates respect and fairness. This belief should prompt the dean/director to be inclusive of all, valuing equally the voice of the "team player," the "naysayer," and the devil's advocate. This kind of philosophy also enables the dean/director to implement a democratic vision of leadership and shared governance based on the recognition that (a) all should have a say in the operation of the school/college/department; (b) all opinions are valued; and (c) all faculty, staff, students, and constituents have the ability to contribute to various programs and projects initiated within the school/college/department. Inclusiveness and respect for others can create an ongoing joyful attitude for all that encourages all people connected to the nursing school/college/department to bring ideas forward confidently. Furthermore, the dean/director should ensure that student, staff, and faculty are treated with fairness and kindness while simultaneously considering policies and procedures of the profession, nursing unit, and institution.

Beliefs About Environment

Philosophic beliefs of the dean/director concerning the educational environment are critical to her or his vision for optimal teaching/learning conditions, student success, and faculty and staff job satisfaction. Importantly, this element of the dean/director's philosophy will also contribute to her or his vision of strategic goals for the school/college/department relative to teaching strategies, curriculum, scholarship, service to the university, and advancement of the profession. Successful nursing deans/directors should adhere to a philosophy that supports establishing and maintaining a teaching/learning environment of joy, fulfillment, and success stemming from meaningful faculty and staff work experiences. Such an environment is based on developing the full potential of all individuals and teams (Sikka et al., 2015). Having a philosophy that emphasizes the potential of others to affect positive outcomes is critical to the ongoing ability of the dean/director to inspire joy and job satisfaction in self and others.

The dean/director is in the unique position of being able to inspire and mentor faculty, students, and university administration with her or his vision and to observe how this affects her or his thinking and practice. Furthermore, she or he can promote and support teamwork through effective communication and delegation, which can motivate and empower faculty, staff, and students to take ideas to the next level. There are constant opportunities for the dean/director to create a joyful, collaborative, cohesive, and inclusive spirit of inquiry that embraces the opinions of all team members and produces a supportive and empowered team. This can be facilitated through the "telling of stories" and personal reflections by the dean/director, faculty, staff, and students. A healthy workplace is one where a joyful and visionary dean/director encourages everyone to have the confidence to generate and communicate their ideas.

Celebration of successes in the nursing school/college/department can help cultivate an environment where joy will flourish. The dean/director can celebrate successes of faculty, staff, and students through announcements and postings that can range from bulletin boards to newsletters to press releases. Collaboration by deans/directors with multidisciplinary and interprofessional units on- and off-campus can spark research partnerships that will enhance the prestige of the school/college/department and contribute to the growth of the nursing knowledge.

The Institute for Healthcare Improvement (IHI) White Paper on promoting joy in the workplace (Perlo et al., 2017) provides a framework for thwarting the alarming rise in burnout and turnover among nurses. Several steps are described for improving joy in work, including roundtable discussions involving all members of the organization to identify what matters in their work; identifying barriers to achieving what matters; and working together to remove those barriers utilizing current best practices. By identifying factors that diminish workplace joy, the dean/director can nurture the faculty and staff workforce and address issues that sap joy. Perlo et al. (2017) maintain that staff who feel joyful, productive, and engaged also feel physically and psychologically safe, which enables them to better appreciate meaning and purpose in their work, improve camaraderie, and perceive equity and fairness in their work environment. The IHI recommends integrating mindfulness-based stress reduction methods into nursing curricula and healthcare work environments as a way of increasing connectedness, joy, and job satisfaction in the workplace, as well as reducing burnout (Perlo et al., 2017). This is a positive initiative that deans/directors can utilize to benefit the workplace environment.

Beliefs About Health and Nursing

The dean/director's philosophy about health and nursing will inform a vision that suggests goals for curricular innovation, program development, pedagogical methods, and interdisciplinary and community partnerships that are necessary to actualize these goals. The dean/director's vision should be based not only on educating students to meet nursing licensure and certification requirements but also on current population health and healthcare policy, health disparities, trends in the delivery of nursing and health services, and cutting-edge treatment methods. For example, the choice of how much clinical time students will spend in acute care, simulation, and community-based agencies is a function of the perspectives of the dean/director and the faculty concerning health and nursing, with the dean/director exercising a strong influence on faculty decisions about pedagogy. Additionally, deans/directors whose philosophy regarding health and nursing includes a belief in the essential confluence between education and practice will seek to strengthen collaboration between faculty and the various practice settings in which students engage in clinical experience. Joy in teaching/learning and a stronger knowledge base for both students and faculty can be fostered through ongoing mutual exchanges of expertise between the nursing school/college/department and their clinical practice affiliates.

CONCLUSION

As a nursing dean/director, great joy and satisfaction can be experienced as a result of two major investments: (a) building an academic culture of happiness and joy and (b) implementing your vision for nursing education. Nursing deans/directors are entrusted with educating the next generation of nurses. Attention should be continually focused on building competent, confident, caring nurses who remain resilient in the face of complex, chaotic, and rapidly changing environments. Deans/directors can bring joy to the academic process by operationalizing a clear vision of how to best educate nurses and by creating a teaching/learning environment and workplace in which faculty, staff, and students can thrive. For the nursing dean/director, it is deeply satisfying, joyful, and enriching to ensure the strength of the nurse who is developed through a sound vision.

For the nursing dean/director, joy and satisfaction also result from implementing one's vision of nursing education, research/scholarship, and clinical practice. Introducing and activating one's vision—the product of a personal philosophy of nursing—in the educational arena can elicit powerful feelings of joy. The vision of the dean/director spearheads the education of the next generation of students into competent, caring nursing generalists, specialists, educators, and scientists/scholars. The dean/director's example of leadership inspires the pursuit of leadership opportunities by students, faculty, and staff. Initiatives of the dean/director create a safe, joyful, and motivating academic environment that encourages innovation and engagement by all members of the organization. The dean/director's attention to scholarship encourages academic achievement that advances the discipline and profession of nursing.

RESOURCES

Bartol, T. (2017). Finding joy in the workplace: We all have a role to play. *Nurse Practitioner, 42*(11), 50–51. doi:10.1097/01.NPR.0000525236.53132.02

Galuska, L., Hahn, J., Polifroni, E. C., & Crow, G. (2018). A narrative analysis of nurses' experiences with meaning and joy in nursing practice. *Nursing Administration Quarterly, 42*(2), 154–163. doi:10.1097/NAQ.0000000000000280

Institute for Healthcare Improvement. (2016, February). *Creating a joyful workforce: A recommended reading list*. Retrieved from http://www.ihi.org/Topics/Joy-In-Work/Documents/IHIJoyInWorkBibliography.pdf

The Johnson Foundation at Wingspread. (2017, February). *A gold bond to restore joy to nursing: A collaborative exchange of ideas to address burnout*. Retrieved from https://www.nursesonboardscoalition.org/wp-content/uploads/NursesReport_Burnout_Final.pdf

Kerfoot, K. M. (2015). On leadership, the pursuit of happiness, science, and effective staffing: The leader's challenge. *Pediatric Nursing, 41*(2), 93–95.

Kern, L., Hawkins, R., Al-Hindi, K. F., & Moss, P. (2014). A collective biography of joy in academic practice. *Social & Cultural Geography, 15*(7), 834–851. doi:10.1080/14649365.2014.929729

Kester, K., & Wei, H. (2018). Building nurse resilience. *Nursing Management, 49*(6), 42–45. doi:10.1097/01.NUMA.0000533768.28005.36

Manion, J. (2004). Joy at work!: Creating a positive workplace. *The Journal of Nursing Administration, 33,* 652–659.

Middaugh, D. J. (2014). Can there really be joy at work? *Medsurg Nursing, 23*(2), 131–132.

Morath, J., Filipp, R., & Cull, M. (2014). Strategies for enhancing perioperative safety: Promoting joy and meaning in the workforce. *AORN Journal, 100*(4), 376–389. doi:10.1016/j.aorn.2014.01.027

Pendse, M., & Ruikar, S. (2013). The relation between happiness, resilience and quality of work life and effectiveness of a web-based intervention at workplace. *Journal of Psychosocial Research, 8*(2), 189–197.

Roper, L. D., Porterfield, K. T., Whitt, E. J., & Carnaghi, J. E. (2016). Embracing core values: Finding joy in the challenges of our work. *New Directions for Student Services, 153,* 155–167. doi:10.1002/ss.20168

Sirota, D., & Klein, D. (2014). *The enthusiastic employee: How companies profit by giving workers what they want* (2nd ed.). Upper Saddle River, NJ: Pearson Education.

Swensen, S., & Davis, T. (2018). *Promoting resilience, camaraderie and joy in work—And EHR efficiency too.* Retrieved from the Intermountain Healthcare Blog Network website, https://intermountainhealthcare.org/blogs/topics/transforming-healthcare/2018/03/promoting-resilience-camaraderie-and-joy-in-work-and-ehr-efficiency-too/

Whitt, E. J., & Carnaghi, J. E. (2016). What excites you? What keeps you going? *New Directions for Student Services, 153,* 39–53. doi:10.1002/ss.20167

REFERENCES

Broome, M. E. (2013). Self-reported leadership styles of deans of baccalaureate and higher degree nursing programs in the United States. *Journal of Professional Nursing, 29*(6), 323–329. doi:10.1016/j.profnurs.2013.09.001

Chinn, P. L., & Kramer, M. K. (2018). *Knowledge development in nursing: Theory and process* (10th ed.). St. Louis, MO: Elsevier.

Fagin, C. M. (1996). Executive leadership: Improving nursing practice, education, and research. *Journal of Nursing Administration, 26*(3), 30–37.

Fagin, C. M. (2000). *Essays on nursing leadership.* New York, NY: Springer Publishing Company.

Fagin, C. M. (2002). The leadership role of a dean. *New Directions for Higher Education, 1997,* 95–99. doi:10.1002/he.9809

Fawcett, J. (1984). The metaparadigm of nursing: Present status and future refinements. *Journal of Nursing Scholarship, 16*(3), 84–87.

Oxford Living Dictionaries. (n.d.-a). *Joy*. Retrieved from https://en.oxforddictionaries.com/definition/joy

Oxford Living Dictionaries. (n.d.-b). *Satisfaction*. Retrieved from https://en.oxforddictionaries.com/definition/satisfaction

Perlo, J., Balik, B., Swensen, S., Kabcenell, A., Landsman, J., & Feeley, D. (2017). *IHI framework for improving joy in work*. IHI White Paper. Cambridge, MA: Institute for Healthcare Improvement. Retrieved from http://www.ihi.org/resources/Pages/IHIWhitePapers/Framework-Improving-Joy-in-Work.aspx

Sikka, R., Morath, J. M., & Leape, L. (2015). The quadruple aim: Care, health, cost and meaning in work. *British Medical Journal Quality/Safety, 24*, 608–610. doi:10.1136/bmjqs-2015-004160

U.S. Department of Health and Human Services. (2015). *Individual resilience: Public health and medical emergency support for a national prepared*. Retrieved from https://www.phe.gov/Preparedness/planning/abc/Pages/individual-resilience.aspx

Wilkes, L., Cross, W., Jackson, D., & Daly, J. (2015). A repertoire of leadership attributes: An International study of deans of nursing. *Journal of Nursing Management, 23*(3), 279–286.

WORK–LIFE INTEGRATION AND SELF-CARE MANAGEMENT

JANICE BREWINGTON

CASE: LEARN HOW TO SAY NO!

I remember vividly a situation that occurred in 1981, when I was an assistant professor in a school of nursing. I was "Ms. Involvement." I was involved in committees in the school of nursing, the university, my church, my children's school, community organizations, and the state nursing organization. At the time, I do not think I knew the word "no" or even how to spell it. However, I eventually emerged from the unconscious state I was apparently in. I realized there was a problem when I had two meetings for different organizations and I was chairing both. I called the vice chairperson for one organization and explained my dilemma, and she graciously agreed to chair the meeting.

This was definitely a wake-up call, and I immediately put a plan in place. I wrote a big "SAY NO" sign and placed it on my telephone. There was an initial test when someone called to ask me to do something and I graciously declined but said I would offer to find someone else for the job. I soon realized I was making more work for myself and so I got better. When anyone called to ask me to do something, I finally learned to respond with no and a gracious thank-you.

Guilt will raise its powerful head many times in your personal and professional lives. When appropriate, my advice is to wrap the guilt in a box with a beautiful ribbon and mail it without a return address so it will not come back to you. The lesson I learned is that you cannot be all things to all people, and you must have boundaries to protect yourself and your time!

INTRODUCTION

Deans and directors in their new positions are challenged with demands such as strategic planning, budgeting, goal setting, decision-making, hiring and firing, and accreditation, all while building relationships with supervisors, colleagues, and faculty. Sometimes leaders are promoted from a faculty role into an administrative role and have not had formal leadership training—they may have been the "last man/woman standing." Without a crystal ball to forecast all expectations, or the lived experience of being in a similar demanding position, they may have difficulty managing the multifaceted and layered responsibilities required by their new position.

Because of the desire to do an excellent job, these leaders become immersed in their work and fail to think about how to incorporate work–life integration. They become so stressed that they become ineffective as leaders or even burn out. They forget to network with colleagues and use their knowledge and experience to help them navigate through the system and their new position. Thus, self-care management is important for survival.

WORK–LIFE INTEGRATION VERSUS WORK–LIFE BALANCE

Many studies have been conducted on work–life balance in corporate America (Matos & Galinsky, 2011), but there has been limited research in academia, especially among administrators, who play an important role in effectively managing the work of the academy. Although work–life balance refers to the desire on the part of both employees and employers to achieve balance between workplace and personal responsibilities, the responsibilities of employers are not the focus of this chapter. Rather, the focus here is on deans and directors who must become self-authorized to assume responsibility for their own work–life balance (integration). Work–life balance can be difficult to define and achieve, and leaders must take control over their own lives and determine what work–life balance means to them. They must make a commitment to have a healthy work life (Mattock, 2015).

Among demographic factors affecting work–life balance, nothing has been more important than gender. Most studies indicate that women have more issues with work–life balance than men and share more of family responsibilities. However, the tide is changing as some men assume more nontraditional roles, like "stay-at-home dads," or work from home to take care of the children. Sometimes the load of family responsibilities for women makes it difficult for them to balance work and family (Bird, 2006; Khan & Frazili, 2016). From another perspective, some researchers have seen that the impact of family on work is not confounded by gender, indicating that both genders have similar work–life balance issues (Hill, Hawkins, Frazili, & Weitzman, 2001; Khan & Frazili, 2016).

In recent years, work–life integration seems to be the new norm rather than work–life balance. This term is used commonly now because work–life balance creates a "binary position" between work and life, implying that there is competition between these two components (Haas School of Business, 2018). Work–life integration is "an approach that creates more synergies between all areas that define 'life': work, home/family, community, personal well-being, and health" (Haas School of Business, 2018). As work–life balance can be considered a myth, the better term to use is work–life integration to help us achieve a more realistic approach to our well-being (Mariama-Arthur, 2018).

Because of the demands of internal and external environments in today's society, there is more pressure to get the job done in less time. Technological innovations, which enable us to stay "plugged in" around the clock, also make it more difficult to balance the challenges of our work and personal lives. Always being connected by technology can decrease performance because of the mental overload of the technology (Groysberg & Abrahams, 2014). New deans and directors are not immune to this phenomenon, and exposure to these challenges is not gender specific. This is why self-care management is so important to help to manage stressors and prevent ineffectiveness and burnout. It is about intentionality and not happenstance. Thus, as leaders, you have to make a conscious effort and plan to be engaged in self-care strategies.

CULPRITS AND PITFALLS OF WORK–LIFE INTEGRATION IMBALANCES

Leaders are prey to an array of pitfalls—some right there and bold and some very subtle. But even with pitfalls right before us, we often behave as if we have cataracts and cannot see. Bold or subtle, pitfalls are with us every day. Over time, these culprits can become stressors.

Role Confusion

Sometimes there may be a lack of clarity about the responsibilities of new deans and directors. In essence, there may be incongruity between one's job description and the supervisor's expectations. Those new in their positions may not be assertive enough to find their voice and seek clarification. However, it is important for new deans and directors to meet with their supervisors and ask questions to ensure they know what is expected in their roles. If not, they may become frustrated and stressed.

Technology

Although innovations in technology have created more efficiency and productivity for employees, there is a negative perspective. New technologies blur the boundaries between work and personal life, making it difficult to differentiate between work time and personal time. Connected to their smartphones, employees perceive that it is the expectation of their employers that they must always be tuned in.

Wilk (2016) found that technology affected the lives of administrators in two ways. First, the existence and availability of technology pressured administrators to work beyond regular business hours or while they were away from the office. Second, one-fourth of the administrators in the Wilk study used technology as a strategy to avoid being bombarded by emails after a day or weekend off. In both situations, there was a price to pay for work–life integration as employees worked continuously, whether at home or at the office. According to Khan and Frazili (2016), "technology has generated a sense of feeling by employees of never being off from work due to increased expectations. Many studies have shown that stress, anxiety, and psychological well-being have been greatly affected by mobile technologies" (p. 23).

Boundaries

Boundaries are lines of demarcation or limits. They can allow people in or keep them out. Townsend and Cloud (2014) describe a boundary "as a property line that makes those things for which we are responsible." Boundaries define us and show where we begin and end. For example, we own our time, and we can make choices and decisions about how we use our time, when to give up some of our time, and to whom we give time. Although we have control over our time, sometimes we forget to use it.

Your roles have boundaries in which you function as a dean/director. When you fail to protect your boundaries, it is problematic, especially if you are new in the role; it can affect your time or even your authority. By allowing your office to become a revolving door, others will be able to usurp your authority. By being unable to say no, you may become overextended, which can lead to stress and unhealthy behaviors. The key is to learn how to say no.

Time Management

The failure to incorporate effective time management skills into our daily work is an important issue that should be addressed early on. Poor time management can lead to disorganization, the inability to complete tasks effectively, and missing critical deadlines. Various factors lead to poor time management, including procrastination and the unwillingness to set priorities and delegate tasks.

Administrators often wonder why subordinates seem to have more time than they do. Time management is related to how you manage your time in relationship to your boss, peers, and subordinates. Oncken and Wass (1974; Oncken, Wass, & Covey, 1999) describe five types of management time:

- Boss-imposed time is used to carry out those tasks that the boss requires and the manager cannot disregard. Not completing these activities may have consequences.
- System-imposed time is used to meet the requests of peers for support, which, if not met, may lead to overt and covert consequences.
- Self-imposed time is used to complete those activities that the manager initiates or agrees to do.
- Subordinate-imposed time is the time subordinates share from the manager's self-imposed time.

Discretionary time is the remaining part of the manager's time.

It is important to protect discretionary time and to get more. Sometimes managers lose control of their discretionary time and become consumed with subordinate-imposed time, a phenomenon that Oncken and Wass (1974; Oncken et al., 1999) refer to as "the monkey on your back." In other words, the manager is not managing his or her time even when tasks are delegated to subordinates because the subordinates have "seduced" the manager to complete the tasks. So, there goes the manager's time, and of course, with the manager unable to meet the boss-imposed time or the system-imposed time, stress builds up. For the manager who has not delegated effectively, there are many monkeys on the back. Self-care management becomes nonexistent, and deleterious effects of stress are imminent.

Covey supports the perspective of Oncken and Wass (Oncken et al., 1999) but offers an expanded approach. His notion is that, in some instances, where subordinates do not have the skills to complete the task, managers should invest time in developing them. Empowering subordinates takes more time, but in the long run, it is a good investment that will allow the managers to have more time in the future.

SELF-CARE MANAGEMENT: AN INVESTMENT IN YOU

Self-care management has been defined as "intentional actions aimed at taking care of oneself physically, mentally, emotionally, and spiritually" (Cardinal & Thomas, 2016, p. 5). It is a holistic perspective, beginning with you as the leader. You serve as a role model for faculty, staff, and students as well as your families.

Sometimes it can be difficult to know where to start because as leaders, we tend to become immersed in our work. And sometimes we can be so far into the work that we cannot see or so far out that we are not attuned to what is happening around us. Since this impacts our well-being as leaders, fully embracing self-care must be considered a leadership skill (Athitakis, 2018), as high on the ladder as other critical leadership competencies.

Self-care management should be viewed from a holistic perspective, along with the many factors that can lead to stress and drain us emotionally—for example, financial concerns, our physical health, and often our relationships. The early identification of these factors is essential. Reynolds (2017) presents a "Self-Care Checklist" (Exhibit 19.1) that all new deans and directors should complete. It will help you begin to strategically institute a self-care management plan.

In her self-care research and work with nurse leaders, Sherman (2012, p. 1–2) identifies five lessons learned about self-care. Focusing on these lessons will give you a framework for integrating self-care in your everyday life.

- Rest is an investment in yourself, your team, and your future.
- Recharging your battery will make you a better leader.
- Find an activity outside of work that brings you self-renewal.
- Make time to reflect on how you use your time and energy at work.
- Leaders set the example for self-care on their teams. (Sherman, 2012)

Johnston-Gingrich (2018) offers three beliefs or affirmations that serve as a foundation for how leaders integrate self-care into their lives. First, embrace that self-care shows up in your professional life—your life should not be one-sided. Second, you must decide that self-care is not selfish. You must give yourself permission to take charge of your life and be in control. Treat yourself well and do not play the guilt-ridden martyrdom game—you have to decide that you matter. Third, you have to embrace that you must teach people how

EXHIBIT 19.1

SELF-CARE CHECKLIST

ENVIRONMENT

- ☐ Is your office organized so you can find things easily?
- ☐ Are there more than two piles of papers, magazines, and books in your workspaces?
- ☐ Does your home provide you comfort and a peaceful place where you can think?
- ☐ Are your appliances in working order?
- ☐ Do you have backup systems in case of electric failure, including a backup energy source for your computers?
- ☐ Do you maintain your car regularly so everything works properly?
- ☐ Does your home have a smoke detector, fire extinguisher, and easy contact to the police?
- ☐ Do you keep enough home and office supplies so you do not run out?
- ☐ Do you find the colors and decor in your home and office pleasing?
- ☐ Is the temperature in your home and office comfortable?

PHYSICAL HEALTH

- ☐ Do you sleep 6 to 8 hours every day?
- ☐ Is your bed comfortable?
- ☐ Does your back feel fine after sitting in your chair at work?
- ☐ Do you eat fresh, healthful food almost every day?
- ☐ Do you exercise at least three times a week?
- ☐ Is your cholesterol count within the normal range?
- ☐ Do you drink at least five glasses of filtered water each day?
- ☐ Do you drink zero to two caffeinated drinks a day?
- ☐ Do you keep your sugar intake to a minimum?
- ☐ Do you get a medical physical annually?

MENTAL HEALTH

- ☐ Do you wake up looking forward to your day?
- ☐ Do you take the time to acknowledge what you are grateful for each night?
- ☐ Do you take at least two vacations a year that refresh and energize you?
- ☐ Do you have someone in your life who hugs you regularly?

(continued next page)

- ☐ Do you arrive at least 5 minutes early for your appointments?
- ☐ Do you take your time when driving?
- ☐ Do you promise only what you can deliver?
- ☐ Do you regularly explore new ways of perceiving the world?
- ☐ Do you have a good belly laugh at least once a day?
- ☐ Do you have at least two friends outside your immediate family who you feel free to talk with about anything?

MONEY
- ☐ Do you have little or no debt?
- ☐ Do you save at least 10% of your income?
- ☐ Do you carry enough cash with you to cover emergencies?
- ☐ Are you compensated adequately for your work?
- ☐ Do you recover from financial disappointments quickly, knowing things will improve?
- ☐ Do you have savings to cover home, car, and health emergencies?
- ☐ Are you amply insured for your home, car, and health?
- ☐ Do you invest in your own career development so you can earn more in the future? Or are you saving enough for your retirement?
- ☐ Do you have a special knowledge or skill that gives you job security?
- ☐ Do you have a reputable and knowledgeable financial advisor?

RELATIONSHIPS
- ☐ Do your family/friends/colleagues encourage your dreams?
- ☐ Do your family/friends/colleagues support your efforts to relieve your stress?
- ☐ Do you avoid no one?
- ☐ Have you said you were sorry to those who you've harmed in some way?
- ☐ Have you forgiven everyone who has hurt you?
- ☐ Do you tell those you love how much you care about them?
- ☐ Are you free of the need to fix other people?
- ☐ Are you free of people who repeatedly disappoint, frustrate, drain, or disrespect you?
- ☐ Do you feel significant with everyone you meet?
- ☐ Do you have relationship with nature, your God, or a force outside of yourself that recharges your faith?

TOTAL BOXES CHECKED ON (date)

(continued next page)

INSTRUCTIONS:
- ☐ Tally up the boxes you checked.
- ☐ Set goals to achieve the boxes left blank, one box at a time. Start with the category you scored the highest on so you begin on your strongest foot.
- ☐ Work on this checklist until your score reaches at least 45. As your score increases, notice how much your energy increases as well.

SOURCE: Reynolds, M. (2017). *Outsmart your brain: How to master your mind when emotions take the wheel.* Phoenix, AZ: Covisioning.

to treat you—how we treat ourselves sends a message to others. Essentially, to enhance your effectiveness, it is important to be strategic about self-care management. Deans and directors should incorporate a holistic approach such as including physical, mental/emotional, spiritual, and organizational components in their self-care strategies. Table 19.1 presents some useful self-care strategies.

BEST PRACTICES FOR SUCCESSFUL LEADERS: COACHING AND MENTORSHIP

Coaching is a process where a trained individual, a coach, facilitates a person's learning and performance. The coach addresses issues encountered by the coachee, or client, in the here and now. For example, a coach could work with a coachee on issues that interfere with the individual's job performance; for example, time management, setting boundaries, and delegation. Career development is also an option. Coaching is short term and task oriented. The coach can be hired contractually by the employer or by an individual.

Mentoring is an older concept, known throughout history. The word comes from Homer's *Odyssey*. When Odysseus left home to fight in the Trojan War, he entrusted his son Telemachus to the care of his friend Mentor (Reh, 2019). Mentoring is engagement in a usually long-term relationship where the mentor provides guidance, support, and wisdom around areas such as career development, personal development, or work–life integration. It focuses on development.

These two options can assist leaders to be more effective in their roles. Be proactive in choosing a mentor and use coaches as needed. In fact, you can have a coach and a mentor, and if you are fortunate, you can have more than one mentor.

TABLE 19.1 Self-Care Management Strategies

PHYSICAL	MENTAL/EMOTIONAL	SPIRITUAL	ORGANIZATIONAL
Aerobic exercise classes/sessions	Social networks/social support systems	Meditation	Setting priorities
Sports (e.g., golf, basketball, soccer, tennis)	Hobbies	Yoga	Time management
Walking	Mindfulness exercises: ■ Body scan: Led or self-guided meditation focused on recognizing body sensations and natural reactions with unbiased concentration (Andrews & Wang, 2009) ■ Loving-kindness meditation: Focused attention on feelings for loved ones followed by redirection mantras of those feelings toward self and larger circles of others (Good et al., 2016) ■ Walking meditation: Relaxed, leisurely, and quiet with direct focus on the experience and feeling associated with the movement (Andrews & Wang, 2009) ■ Mindful movement: Disciplined, relaxing movement coupled with attention centered on the physical experience and emotional response to the actions rather than focus on the activity itself (Andrew & Wang, 2009)	Prayer	Delegating
Running	Relaxation techniques	Mantras	Goal setting
Personal trainer	Massage therapy		Setting boundaries
	Cognitive behavioral therapy		

CONCLUSION

As a new dean/director, consider yourself a self-care investment broker. An investment broker arranges transactions between a buyer and a seller. Thus, as buyer and seller for work–life integration, you must intentionally decide how much time you are willing to sell and how much time you are willing to buy in order to have a healthy, well-balanced life. Then, celebrate the return on investment. As a leader, remember to *pause*, *exhale*, and *focus* when pressure mounts. Become self-authorized to take charge of your life and lead with courage.

RESOURCES

Dresdale, R. (2016, December 18). *Work-life balance vs. work-life integration, Is there really a difference?* Retrieved from Forbes website, https://www.forbes.com/sites/rachelritlop/2016/12/18/work-life-balance-vs-work-life-integration-is-there-really-a-difference/#2e2389163727

Fannin, K. (2018, January 29). *Why work-life integration is the new work-life balance and how to do it.* Retrieved from INTELIVATE website, https://www.intelivate.com/team-strategy/work-life-integration-work-life-balance/

Harvard Health Publishing. (2015, January). *Best ways to manage stress.* Retrieved from Harvard Health Publishing website, https://www.health.harvard.edu/mind-andmood/best-ways-to-manage-stress

Scott, E. (2018, August 31). *The top 10 self-care strategies for stress reduction.* Retrieved from very well mind website, https://www.verywellmind.com/self-care-strategies-overall-stress-reduction-3144729

Slatyer, S., Craigie, M., Rees, C., Davis, S., Dolan, T., & Hegney, D. (2017). Nurse experience of participation in a mindfulness-based self-care and resiliency intervention. *Mindfulness, 9*(3), 610–612. doi:10.1007/s12671-0802-2

REFERENCES

Andrews, D. R., & Wang, T. T. H. (2009). The importance of mental health to the experience of job strain: An evidence-guided approach to improve retention. *Journal of Nursing Management, 17*(3), 340–351. doi:10.1111/j.1365-2934.2008.00852.x

Athitakis, M. (2018). *Self-care as a leadership skill. Associations Now.* Retrieved from https://associationsnow.com/2018/04/self-care-leadership-skill/

Bird, J. (2006). Work-life balance: Doing it right and avoiding the pitfalls. *Employment Relations Today, 3*(3), 21–30. doi:10.1002/ert.20114

Cardinal, B. J., & Thomas, J. T. (2016). Self-care strategies for maximizing human potential. *Journal of Physical Education, Recreation and Dance, 87*(9), 5–7, Proquest. doi:10.1080/07303084.2016.1227198

Good, D. J., Lyddy, C. J., Glomb, T. M., Bono, J. E., Brown, K. W., Duffy, M. K., … Lazar, S. W. (2016). Contemplating mindfulness at work: An integrative review. *Journal of Management, 42*(1), 114–142. doi:10.1177/01492063156117003

Groysberg, B., & Abrahams, R. (2014). Manage your work, manage your life. *Harvard Business Review, 3*. Retrieved from http://hbr.org/2014/03/manage-your-work-manage-your-life

Haas School of Business. (2018). *Work/life integration*. Retrieved from https://haas.berkeley.edu/human-resources/work-life-integration/

Hill, E. J., Hawkins, A. J., Ferris, M., & Weitzman, M. (2001). Finding an extra day a week: The positive influence of perceived job flexibility on work and family life balance. *Family Relations, 50*(1), 49–65.

Johnston-Gingrich, R. (2018). Self-care strategies are part of professional success. *Journal of Business, 33*(12), A2.

Khan, O. F., & Frazili, A. I. (2016). Work-life balance: A conceptual review. *Journal of Strategic Resource Management, 5*(2), 20–25.

Mariama-Arthur, K. (2018, February 9). Why leaders need to make time for self-care. *Success*. Retrieved from https://www.success.com/why-leaders-need-to-make-time-for-self-care/

Matos, K., & Gilinsky, F. (2011). Workplace flexibility in the United States: A status report. *Families and Work Institute*. Retrieved from http://familiesandwork.org/site/research/reports/www_us_workflex.pdf

Mattock, S. L. (2015). Leadership and work-life balance. *Journal of Trauma Nursing, 22*(6), 306–307. doi:10.1097/JTN.0000000000000163

Oncken, Jr., J., & Wass, D. L. (1974). Management time: Who's got the monkey? *Harvard Business Review, 52*(6), 75–80.

Oncken, Jr., J., Wass, D. L., & Covey, S. (1999). Management time: Who's got the monkey? *Harvard Business Review*. Retrieved from https://hbr.org/1999/11/management-time-whos-got-the-monkey

Reh, F. J. (2019). *A guide to understanding the role of a mentor*. Retrieved from https://www.thebalancecareers.com/a-guide-to-understanding-the-role-of-a-mentor-2275318

Reynolds, M. (2017). *Outsmart your brain: How to master your mind when emotions take the wheel*. Phoenix, AZ: Covisioning.

Sherman, R. O. (2012). *Self-care for nurse leaders—5 lessons learned*. Retrieved from https://www.emergingrnleader.com/self-carefornurseleaders/

Townsend, J., & Cloud, H. (2014, March 12). *Boundaries: When to say yes, how to say no.* Retrieved from https://www.faithgateway.com/boundaries-when-to-say-yes-say-no/#.XIWcYa2ZOVw

Wilk, K. E. (2016). Work-life balance and ideal worker expectations for administrators. *New Directions for Higher Education* (Published online in Wiley Online Library), 2016, 37–51. doi:10.1002/he.20208

INDEX

AACN. *See* American Association of Colleges of Nursing
academic culture, and financial management, 139–142, 143
Academic Partnerships, 35
academic policies. *See* policies, academic
academic programs. *See* programs, academic
academic success coaches, 87–88
accreditation, 17–18
  agencies, and interim deans, 49
  and faculty, 18, 30
  and program quality, 108–109
  standards, 35
Accreditation Commission for Education in Nursing (ACEN), 48–49, 103, 108–109
ACEN. *See* Accreditation Commission for Education in Nursing
ACT. *See* American College Testing tests
acting deans. *See* interim deans
activity-based budgeting, 146
admissions. *See also* enrollment; enrollment management
  denials, 75–76
  freshman *vs.* junior, 77
  holistic admissions strategy, 80
  online learning, 107
  and student success, 83–84
advanced practice registered nurses (APRNs), 177
advancement offices, 114

advisers, appointments of students with, 86–87
Agency for Healthcare Research and Quality (AHRQ), 188
AHRQ. *See* Agency for Healthcare Research and Quality
alumni
  alumni officers, 119
  and fundraising, 30, 51, 119
  groups, 14
American Academy of Nursing, 183
American Association of Colleges of Nursing (AACN), 47, 48, 50, 75, 91, 152
  Executive Leadership Program, 199
  Leadership Network for Nursing Advancement Professionals, 119
American College Testing (ACT) tests, 84
American Nurses Credentialing Center (ANCC), 110
American Organization of Nurse Executives (AONE), 195, 196
ANCC. *See* American Nurses Credentialing Center
AONE. *See* American Organization of Nurse Executives
APRNs. *See* advanced practice registered nurses
Arizona State University, 35
Assessment Technology Institute (ATI)®, 89
assistant deans, 27, 30, 31, 45

associate deans. *See* assistant deans
ATI. *See* Assessment Technology Institute
Atlassian (software), 173
AVANCE Head Start, 190
awards, for faculty/staff, 31

Balanced Scorecard (software), 173
BCG. *See* Boston Consulting Group's business model
benefit finding. *See* posttraumatic growth
benefit packages, 152
Black Nurses Association, 99
block course scheduling system, 78
Bloom's taxonomy, 79, 80
bonus, in for-profit schools, 37
boss-imposed time, 229
Boston Consulting Group's (BCG) business model, 149
boundaries, and work–life integration, 228
Brazelton Touchpoints Framework, 182
budget, 18–19, 135, 143–144, 145
   activity-based budgeting, 146
   guides and resources, 154
   hearing, 156–157
   incentive-based budgeting, 146
   incremental budgeting system, 144, 146
   initiative-based budgeting, 146
   models, 75, 146
   performance-based budgeting, 146
   and recruitment of faculty/staff, 95
   Responsibility Center Management (RCM) budget model, 75, 145, 146
   zero-based budgeting, 146
budget officers, 18, 26, 28, 75
business manager, 18

calendar, 24–25, 49–50
California Children's Services (CCS) High-Risk Infant Follow-up Clinic, 178
career centers, 90

CASE. *See* Council for Advancement and Support of Education
cataclysmic professional role transitions, 58–60, 63–67
   career, rebooting/rebuilding, 66–67
   emotional trajectory, 64
   exit message, 65
   financial advisor, meeting with, 66
   interviews, 67
   legal consultation, 65
   log of transition process, 65
   negotiations, 65
   norms, consultation about, 65
   perks, 65
   professional voice, reclaiming, 64
   self-care, 63, 66
   support, seeking/accepting, 66
CBME. *See* competency-based medical education
CCNE. *See* Commission on Collegiate Nursing Education
CCS. *See* California Children's Services High-Risk Infant Follow-up Clinic
Centers for Medicare and Medicaid Services (CMS), Delivery System Reform Incentive Payment (DSRIP), 187, 190
certification, 110
challenges, deaning/directing, 205
   accreditation, 17–18
   administrative change, 209
   competing priorities, 208–209
   finances, 18–19
   fundraising, 116–117
   higher education, trends in, 205–207
   novice deans, 208
   nursing, trends in, 207–208
   personnel, 16–17
   turnover among college administrators, 209
charts, 173
chief academic nurse administrator, 49
chief nursing administrator, 48

Chronicle of Higher Education, 48, 152, 205
class notes, 84
classroom scheduler, 78
clinical instruction, innovation of, 149–150
CMS. *See* Centers for Medicare and Medicaid Services, Delivery System Reform Incentive Payment (DSRIP)
CNEA. *See* National League for Nursing (NLN), Commission for Nursing Education Accreditation
coaching, 233
COI. *See* community of inquiry model
collaborative strategic planning, 163, 171. *See also* strategic planning
Commission on Collegiate Nursing Education (CCNE), 48, 89, 103, 108, 109
communication, 136
   during crisis situations, 21
   email, 26–27
   and fundraising, 118, 121
   gaslighting, 155
   and interim deans, 49
   strategic planning, 169, 172
   of vision, 133–134
community, 49, 163
   community health partners, shared service agreement with, 99
   cultural proficiency, 182–183
   engagement, 133, 186, 190
   expectations, managing, 20
   service learning, 182
community advisory boards, 187
community nursing, 129
community of inquiry (COI) model, 79–80
compensation
   faculty, 152, 186
   in for-profit schools, 37–38
   for interim deans, 47

competencies of deans/directors, 56, 159, 196, 213–214
competency-based education, 108, 205–206
competency-based medical education (CBME), 108
competitors, and enrollment, 75, 76
comprehensive examinations, 110
consultants
   accreditation, 17, 18
   strategic planning, 166–167
Corinthian College, 34
corporate philanthropy, 114
cost of attendance, 76
Council for Advancement and Support of Education (CASE), 119, 120
counseling services, for students, 29
courage, 56
course scheduling, 77–78
cover letter, 5–6
credibility, and fundraising, 118
credit hours, 84
crisis management, 21, 128–129
cultural competence, 182
cultural proficiency, 182

day-to-day activities of deans/directors
   budget officer, checking in with, 26
   calendar, 24–25
   changing priorities, 25
   delegation, 30–31
   email, 26–27
   firing faculty and staff, 28–29
   hiring new faculty, 27–28
   organization, 23–24
   recognition and awards, 31
   student services, 29–30
   teaching, 27
debt, and for-profit schools, 34
delegation, 30–31
Department of Health and Human Services/Health Resources and Services Administration (DHHS/HRSA), 188, 189

Department of Justice, 188
development-focused boards, 121–122
development office, 114, 186, 187
development officers, 14, 30, 51, 114, 115, 118, 119, 121
DHHS/HRSA. *See* Department of Health and Human Services/ Health Resources and Services Administration
disability services, for students, 29
discretionary funds, 19, 26
discretionary time, 229
disruptive innovation, 165
diversity officers, 29–30
Dock, Lavinia, 177
documentation, strategic planning, 172
DSRIP. *See* Centers for Medicare and Medicaid Services (CMS), Delivery System Reform Incentive Payment

electronic health records, 185
elevator speeches, 133–134, 135
email, 26–27
emergency telephone tree, 21
employment, following graduation, 34, 89–90
English as a second language (ESL) students, 89
enrollment
   in for-profit schools, 33, 34, 36, 38
   open enrollment, 36
   Safe Harbor Act, 38
   and student success, 83–84
enrollment management, 73–74
   admission denials, 75–76
   best practices, 79–80
   capacity to increase enrollment, 76–79
   class sizes, 79
   cost of nursing education, 74–76
   course scheduling, 77–78
   diversity, 80
educational frameworks, 79
external competitors, 76
faculty qualifications, 78
faculty to student ratio, 78
freshman *vs.* junior admission, 77
holistic admissions strategy, 80
physical space, 78
plan, 73, 76
quality outcomes of program, 76–77
and resources, 77–78
strategic enrollment management, 74, 79, 80
strategy exercise, 74
environment
   educational, 76, 80, 144, 218–220
   scans, 169–170
   work, 100, 155, 219–220
Envisio, 173
ESL. *See* English as a second language students
evolutionary change, 58
executive leadership, 142, 195–196, 199
   competencies, 196
   exemplar, 196–199
   team approach, 196
   traits, 195
external stakeholder engagement, 125. *See also* stakeholder engagement
   NYU Rory Meyers College of Nursing, 126–129
   UC Davis Betty Irene Moore School of Nursing, 129–132

faculty, 7, 13, 15–16, 126
   and accreditation, 18, 30
   as advisers, 87
   awards, 31
   benefit packages, 152
   and budget, 19
   clinical instruction, 149–150
   of color, 99
   deans returning to, 44

Index

and enrollment management, 76
faculty to student ratio, 78
firing, 28–29
governance, 126–128, 131
nursing, value of, 150–151
partnership of interim dean with, 50
policies, 103
qualifications of, 78
recruitment of. *See* recruitment of faculty
retention of, 99–100
salary, 152–153
shortages, 152, 207
tenured, 29
track, 95
vacancies, 91
visiting, 96
X, Y, Z Faculty Practice Plan, 185–186
federal funding, 34, 39, 188
Federally Qualified Health Center (FQHC), 187, 189
fee-for-service house calls, 186
financial management, 18–19, 135, 139
   academic culture, 139–142, 143
   budget hearing, 156–157
   facilities, quality of, 153
   financial advisor, 66
   guides and resources, 154
   leadership, 153, 155–156
      humor, 155–156
      risk management, 155
      stewardship, 153, 155
   policy and processes, 142–153
      clinical instruction, 149–150
      efficiency, 148
      innovation, 148, 149–150
      nursing faculty, value of, 150–151
      productivity, 148
      resource allocation, parity in, 150–153
      sufficiency of resources, 143–147
   questions, for deans, 147

and recruitment of faculty/staff, 95
salaries, faculty/staff, 152–153
source/uses of financial and other resources, 144
firing of faculty/staff, 28–29
flipped classroom, 86
for-profit sector, 33–34
   business models, 34
   challenges for, 34
   deaning in
      compensation, understanding, 37–38
      compliance and scrutiny, 39–40
      growth and scaling, 36–37
      management, 38–39
      reporting to nonacademic business leader, 39
      successful, traits for, 36
   enrollment in, 33, 34, 36
   measures of success, 38
   and non-profit/public schools, similarities, 35–36
   online education, 34
FQHC. *See* Federally Qualified Health Center
freshman, *vs.* junior admissions, 77
fundraising, 30, 113, 186, 187
   approaches, 116
   best practices, 117–122
   and communication, 118, 121
   contextual challenges, 116
   development-focused boards, 121–122
   development priorities for academic leaders, 119
   donor-centric challenges, 116–117
   friend-raising, 121
   gifts, types of, 115
   giving continuum, 115
   in higher education, 114–116
   and interim deans, 51
   personal challenges, 116
   philanthropy, 113–114, 120, 121

fundraising (*cont.*)
    relationships, 117, 121
    resources for training/professional development in, 120
    setting the stage, 118–120
    time-tested principles of, 117–118

gap analysis, 171
gender, and work–life balance, 226–227
George Mason University, Health Policy Institute, 199
Georgia Center for Nonprofits, 120
gifts, 51, 115, 118
giving continuum, 115
Giving USA, 120
goal statements, 170
Gordon and Betty Moore Foundation, 130
graduate nursing programs, 74–75, 109
Grand Canyon University, 35
grant writing, 31, 186, 188–190
grants, 188–190

Harvard Business School, 184
Harvard Kennedy School, *Women and Power* program, 199
headhunters, 4, 6
Health Education Systems, Inc. (HESI)®, 89
healthcare agencies, collaboration with, 98
Healthcare Leadership Alliance, 196
HESI. *See* Health Education Systems, Inc.
HESI A2®, 89
Higher Learning Commission, 103
Hillman Innovations in Care, 190
hiring. *See* recruitment of faculty
holistic admissions strategy, 80, 84
human resources, 17, 28, 97
humor, 155–156
hybrid learning, 207

IHI. *See* Institute for Healthcare Improvement
Implementation Science, 184
incentive-based budgeting, 146
incentives, 96, 144–145
incremental budgeting system, 144, 146
Indiana University Purdue University of Indiana (IUPUI), Lilly Family School of Philanthropy, 120
initiative-based budgeting, 146
INMSI. *See* integrated nurse-led model for sustainability and innovation
innovation. *See also* integrated nurse-led model for sustainability and innovation (INMSI)
    of clinical instruction, 149–150
    disruptive innovation, 165
    program innovation, 107–108
    and strategic planning, 164–165, 166
    technological, 227, 228
Institute for Healthcare Improvement (IHI), 178, 219
institutional resources, for student success, 87–90
    academic success coaches, 87–88
    employment following graduation, 89–90
    NCLEX-RN®, readiness and preparation for, 89
    online platforms, 88–89
    tutors, 88
insurance, 187, 190
integrated nurse-led model for sustainability and innovation (INMSI), 177, 178–180
    benefits of, 190
    characteristics of, 180
    clinic implementation, expansion, and replication, 185–186
    clinic site selection, 185
    cultural humility and proficiency, 182–183

developing business and
reimbursement plan, 183–185
elements of, 178–179
funding mechanisms, 186–187
grants and grant writing, 188–190
health disparities, 186–187
Neonatal Intensive Care Unit
Follow-up Clinic, 178
risks and challenges, 190
setting the stage, 180, 182
sources of foundation funding with
nursing/healthcare goals, 189
training modules for, 181
interim deans, 5, 12, 43–45
vs. acting deans, 48
administrative direction, change in,
45–46
and career, 47–48
career balance, 52
compensation for, 47
decision making, 49–50
departure circumstances, 44–45, 46
emeritus faculty member, 47, 53
external candidates, 47, 53
first step, 48–51
internal candidates, 46, 53
leadership forums, 50
partnership, with faculty, 50
permanent deanships for, 46–47,
52, 53
philanthropy, 51
replacement of deans
with illness/family emergencies,
45
with planned retirement, 44, 46
returning to previous role, 52–53
succession planning, 45
transition plan for newly appointed
dean, 51, 52
unsuccessful, 47
internal stakeholder engagement, 125.
See also stakeholder engagement

NYU Rory Meyers College of Nursing,
126–129
UC Davis Betty Irene Moore School of
Nursing, 129–132
Internet, and disruptive innovation, 165
interviews
for dean/director position, 6–8
after cataclysmic professional role
transitions, 67
off-site, 6
on-campus, 7–8
on-site, 6–7
mock interviews, for students, 90
ITT Technical Institute, 34
IUPUI. *See* Indiana University Purdue
University of Indiana, Lilly Family
School of Philanthropy

job satisfaction. *See* joy/satisfaction, in
dean/directing
job search. *See* searching for dean/director
position
joy/satisfaction, in dean/directing, 211,
215
best practices for cultivation of, 217–220
deans/directors
personal qualities of, 214–216
qualifications of, 213–214
responsibilities of, 213, 214
demands of deaning/directing, 212
exemplar activities, 216
finding, 216
nursing knowledge and experience,
217
philosophy and vision, 217, 218–220
environment, beliefs about, 218–220
health and nursing, beliefs
about, 220
persons, beliefs about, 218

key performance indicators (KPIs), 195
KPIs. *See* key performance indicators

leadership, 11, 17
　core competencies, 56–57
　executive, 142, 195–200
　and financial management, 153, 155–156
　forums, 50
　hazards, in higher education, 57–58
　legislative, 142
　servant, 50
　steward, 50
　successful leaders, best practices for, 233
　team-based, 39
　toxic, hallmarks of, 57
　transformational, 213
　and vision, 217
learning management systems, 88, 89
legislative leadership, 142
letter of reference, 87
line allocations, faculty/staff, 91–92, 94–95, 96
LinkedIn, 4
Lippincott Pass Point®, 89

media training, 136
Medicaid, 187, 190
Medicare, 187
mentorship, 233
　programs, 99–100
Microsoft Project®, 173
mindfulness-based stress reduction, 220
mission
　guiding, 134–135
　statement, 128
　strategic planning, 170, 171
mock interviews, 90

NANAINA. *See* National Alaska Native American Indian Nurses Association
National Alaska Native American Indian Nurses Association (NANAINA), 99

National Association of Hispanic Nurses, 99
National Council Licensure Examination for Registered Nurses (NCLEX-RN®), 17, 86, 109, 110
　readiness and preparation for, 89
National Council of State Boards of Nursing (NCSBN), 109
National Institute of Nursing Research (NINR), 188
National Institutes of Health (NIH), 188
National League for Nursing (NLN), 48
　Center of Excellence in Nursing Education, 93
　Commission for Nursing Education Accreditation (CNEA), 49
NCLEX-RN®. *See* National Council Licensure Examination for Registered Nurses
NCSBN. *See* National Council of State Boards of Nursing
Neighborhood House Association, Head Start Health and Wellness Mobile Van, 178
neonatal nurse practitioner (NNP) track, 15, 97–98
net tuition revenue, 144
New York University (NYU) Rory Meyers College of Nursing, 125, 126–129
　Board of Advisors, 135
　Dean's Council, 135
　faculty governance, 126–128
　reputation, 126–128
　Superstorm Sandy, 128–129
Nightingale, Florence, 151–152, 177
NIH. *See* National Institutes of Health
NINR. *See* National Institute of Nursing Research
NLN. *See* National League for Nursing
NNP. *See* neonatal nurse practitioner track

nonprofit schools
  business models of, 34–35
  and for-profit schools, similarities, 35–36
normative professional role transitions, 58, 59
  decision to step up, 60–61
    organizational readiness for change, assessment of, 60–61
    personal reflection, 60
    strategic communication, 61
  exiting, 62
  new dean
    naming of, 61
    searching for, 61
  professional voice, reclaiming, 62–63
  retooling, 63
NPs. See nurse practitioners
nurse-led clinics. See integrated nurse-led model for sustainability and innovation (INMSI)
nurse practitioners (NPs), 96
nursing education, cost of, 74–76, 149
NYU. See New York University Rory Meyers College of Nursing

Obama, Barack, 34
objectivist–constructivist continuum, 79–80
off-campus programs, 98, 99
online advertisements, for recruitment of faculty/staff, 95
online education/learning, 34–35, 88–89, 107–108, 207
online newsletters, for recruitment of faculty/staff, 95
online program management (OPM) companies, 35
open-door policy, 25
open enrollment, 36
OPM. See online program management companies
Orbis Education, 35

organizational culture, 56, 140–141, 142
Oxford University, 199

patient revenues, 186
pay for performance contract, 187
Pediatric Nursing Certification Board (PNCB), 110
performance-based budgeting, 146
personal recruitment of faculty/staff, 93, 95
personnel, 16–17. See also faculty; staff
  costs, 19, 188
  firing of faculty/staff, 28–29
  hiring of faculty. See recruitment of faculty
PhD programs, 15, 16, 110
philanthropy, 51, 113–114, 120, 186. See also fundraising
philosophy of deans/directors
  environment, beliefs about, 218–220
  health and nursing, beliefs about, 220
  persons, beliefs about, 218
photocopying, and disruptive innovation, 165
PNCB. See Pediatric Nursing Certification Board
policies, academic, 103–104
  faculty policies, 103
  grade appeal policy, 104–105
  new program proposal, 105–107
  problem-solving, 104–105
  program innovation, 107–108
  program quality, 108–111
  school policies, 103–104
  student policies, 103
post-tenure reviews, 29
posttraumatic growth, 59
prelicensure nursing programs, 74–75
problem-solving, and academic policies, 104–105
programs, academic, 103–104
  Boston Consulting Group's (BCG) business model, 149

programs, academic (*cont.*)
  innovation, 107–108
    competency-based movement, 108
    online learning, 107–108
    stackable certificates, 108
  new program proposal, 105–107
  quality, 108–111
    accreditation, 108–109
    certification, 110
    completion rates, 110–111
    comprehensives, 110
    and enrollment, 76–77
    NCLEX-RN®, 109
    online teaching, 107
    rankings, 111
  rationale for offering nursing programs, 141
psychological services, for students, 29
public relations, 44, 46, 119, 136
public schools
  business models of, 34–35
  and for-profit schools, similarities, 35–36
Purdue University Global, 35

Quality Matters, 108

rankings, program, 111
RCM. *See* Responsibility Center Management budget model
RE-AIM (reach, effectiveness, adoption, implementation, maintenance) model, 184
readiness tests, 89
recruitment of faculty, 27–28, 91, 92–93
  convenience hire, 93
  finances, 95
  incentives, 96
  line allocation, 94–95
  maturity profile, 92
  mix of people, 94
  relationship building, 93
  revenue streams, 97–99

skillset, 92
temporary lines, 96
visa issues, 97
recruitment of staff, 91, 93–94
  finances, 95
  incentives, 96
  job requirements, 93
  line allocation, 94–95
  mix of people, 94
  revenue streams, 97–99
  teaching skills, 93
  visa issues, 97
reflective practice, 182
registered nurses (RNs), 25, 48, 88, 93, 104
registrar, 30, 78
reimbursement plan, 183
reputation management, 136
resilience, 215
resources, 141–142
  academic finance and budgeting, 154
  allocation, parity in, 150–153
  and enrollment, 77–78
  institutional, and student success, 87–90
  sources/uses of, 144
  strategic planning, 166, 172
  sufficiency of, 143–147
  for training/professional development in fundraising, 120
Responsibility Center Management (RCM) budget model, 75, 145, 146
restricted stock units (RSUs), 37–38
retention
  of faculty, 99–100
  of staff, 100
retirement, 62, 63
revenue margin, 144
revenue streams, 97–99, 186, 188
revolutionary change, 58
risk identification, 171
risk management, 155

RNs. *See* registered nurses
role confusion, and work–life integration, 227–228
RSU. *See* restricted stock units

sabbatical, 46, 48, 63, 64
Safe Harbor Act, 38
salary, faculty/staff, 152–153
Sametz Blackstone Associates, 120
SAT. *See* Scholastic Assessment Test
schedule changes, 25
Scholastic Assessment Test (SAT), 84
school policies, 103–104
searching for dean/director position, 3–4
    colleagues, 4
    headhunters, 4, 6
    interim deans, 5
    interviewing, 6–8
    needs and wants factors, 4–5
    negotiations, 8
    online sites, 3–4
    preparation of application, 5–6
    reasons for becoming dean/director, 3
seed grants, 96
self-care management, 21–22, 63, 66, 215, 227, 230–233
    checklist, 231–233
    definition of, 230
    strategies, 234
self-imposed time, 229
servant leadership, 50
service learning, 182
shared governance, 50, 92
shared service agreement, 99
sharing economy, 117
simulation labs, 75, 76, 78, 93, 207
Smith, Adam, 151
SOAR framework, 171–172
social determinants of health, 186–187
social ecology model, 127–128, 130
social media, 132, 134
Southern New Hampshire University, 35
specialty tracks, 97–98

Sperling, John, 33
SPOL (Strategic Planning OnLine), 173
spreadsheets, 23, 173
stackable certificates, 108, 205
staff, 7, 13, 14
    awards, 31
    and budget, 19
    and enrollment management, 76
    firing, 28–29
    recruitment of. *See* recruitment of staff
    retention of, 100
    salary, 152–153
    and student success, 87–88
    work environment of, 219–220
stakeholder engagement, 132–133
    cyclical nature of, 133
    feedback from stakeholders, 133
    NYU Rory Meyers College of Nursing, 126–129
    reputation management, 136
    setting strategy and guiding mission, 134–135
    sustainability, 135–136
    UC Davis Betty Irene Moore School of Nursing, 129–132
    vision, creation/communication of, 133–134
start-up funds, 96
state funding, 94, 131, 132, 188
stepping into dean/director position, 11–12
    arrival phase, 12–13, 18
    challenges and opportunities, 16–19
        accreditation, 17–18
        finances, 18–19
        personnel, 16–17
    crisis management, 21
    expectations, managing, 19–20
    hallway conversations/chance meetings, 12
    honeymoon phase, 13–14, 18
    informal meetings, 11–12
    launch phase, 14–16

stepping into dean/director (*cont.*)
  self-care, 21–22
  success factors, 56–57
  work–life balance, 20–21
stepping up from deaning/
    directing, 55
  cataclysmic professional role
    transitions, 58–59
    best practices, 59–60, 63–67
  normative professional role transitions,
    58, 59
    best practices, 59, 60–63
  retirement, 62, 63
  uniqueness of dean/director role,
    55–56
steward leadership, 50
stewardship, 153, 155
stock options, in for-profit schools,
    37–38
strategic direction, 164
strategic enrollment management,
    74, 79, 80. *See also* enrollment
    management
strategic planning, 159–160, 161–163,
    195
  approach to, 161
  benefits of, 161
  collaborative strategic planning, 163
  cycles, 162
  definition of, 161
  disruption, 164–165
  disruptive innovation, 165
  futuring, 165–166
  innovation, 164–165, 166
  internal and external consultants,
    166–167
  new plan, starting, 161–162
  phases of, 167–173
    documentation and communication,
      172
    groundwork, 168–169
    identification and prioritization of
      strategies, 172
    identification of resources, 172
    implementation and management,
      172–173
    internal/external environmental
      scans and data analysis, 169–170
    SWOT and risk identification,
      171–172
    vision, mission, values, and goals,
      170–171
  planning committee, 163, 168
  purposes of, 160
  resources, 166
  scope of plan, 162
  shared strategic directions and
    integration, 164
  and stakeholders, 162
  timeline, 163, 169
strategic thinking, 159, 160, 162, 163,
    164, 171, 173
student policies, 103
student satisfaction, in for-profit
    schools, 38
student services, 29–30
student success, 83
  admission and enrollment, 83–84
  advisers, appointments with, 86–87
  impact of psychological factors
    on, 87
  institutional resources, 87–90
    academic success coaches, 87–88
    employment following graduation,
      89–90
    NCLEX-RN®, readiness and
      preparation for, 89
    online platforms, 88–89
    tutors, 88
  test-taking strategies, 85–86
  time management, 84–85
study habits, 84
subordinate-imposed time, 229
substantive change, 49
succession planning, 45
support services, for students, 29

sustainability. *See* integrated nurse-led model for sustainability and innovation (INMSI)
SWOT analysis, 171
system-imposed time, 229

task/to-do list, 23
teaching
 clinical instruction, 149–150
 and interim deans, 48
 online, 107
 role of deans/directors in, 27
 skills, staff with, 93
 strategies, 86
team-based leadership, 39
team sport, fundraising as, 117–118
technology
 and communication, 116
 information technology, 185
 and work–life integration, 227, 228
test banks, 86
test-taking strategies, 85–86
third-tier tuition, 98–99
time management
 and student success, 84–85
 and work–life integration, 229
transformational leadership, 213
tutors, 88

Uber, and disruptive innovation, 165
undeaning, 58
 cataclysmic, 58–60, 63–67
 integrated identity, 62
 normative, 58, 59, 60–63
unfolding case studies, 86, 207
University of California Davis, Betty Irene Moore School of Nursing, 125–126, 129–132
 faculty governance, 131
 founding grant, 130

National Advisory Council (NAC), 131, 134, 135
 stakeholder engagement and plan development, 130–132
University of Pennsylvania, Wharton School of Business, 199
U.S. Department of Education, 103, 107
U.S. News & World Report, 111

value-based healthcare delivery, 184
values statements, 170–171
vision, 217
 creation and communication of, 133–134
 for nursing education, 218–220
 statement, 128, 170, 171
 strategic planning, 170, 171
visiting faculty, 96

Wald, Lillian, 177
Western Governors University, 35
women, and work–life balance, 226–227
work–life balance, 20–21, 226–227
work–life integration, 226, 227. *See also* self-care management
 definition of, 227
 imbalances, 227–229
  boundaries, 228
  role confusion, 227–228
  technology, 228
  time management, 229
workplace, promotion of joy/satisfaction in, 219–220
World Future Society, 165
Wrike (software), 173
writing centers, 88

X, Y, Z Faculty Practice Plan, 185–186

zero-based budgeting, 146